HEART OF A QUEEN

Also by Theo Aronson

THE GOLDEN BEES
The Story of the Bonapartes

ROYAL VENDETTA
The Crown of Spain (1829–1965)

THE COBURGS OF BELGIUM

THE FALL OF THE THIRD NAPOLEON

THE KAISERS

QUEEN VICTORIA AND THE BONAPARTES

GRANDMAMA OF EUROPE
The Crowned Descendants of Queen Victoria

A FAMILY OF KINGS
The Descendants of Christian IX of Denmark

ROYAL AMBASSADORS
British Royalties in Southern Africa 1860–1947

VICTORIA AND DISRAELI
The Making of a Romantic Partnership

KINGS OVER THE WATER
The Saga of the Stuart Pretenders

MR RHODES AND THE PRINCESS: a play

PRINCESS ALICE
Countess of Athlone

ROYAL FAMILY
Years of Transition

CROWNS IN CONFLICT
The Triumph and the Tragedy of
European Monarchy 1910–1918

THE KING IN LOVE
Edward VII's Mistresses

NAPOLEON AND JOSEPHINE
A Love Story

HEART OF A QUEEN

Queen Victoria's Romantic Attachments

THEO ARONSON

JOHN MURRAY

© Theo Aronson 1991

First published in 1991
by John Murray (Publishers) Ltd
50 Albemarle Street, London W1X 4BD

The moral right of the author has been asserted

British Library Cataloguing-in-Publication Data

Aronson, Theo
   Heart of a queen: Queen Victoria's romantic attachments.
   I. Title
   941.081092
   ISBN 0–7195–4822–5

Printed and set in Great Britain by
Butler & Tanner Ltd, Frome and London

For
Gunnar Andreas Dahl

Contents

Illustrations

(The pictures from the Royal Archives and the Royal Collection are
reproduced by gracious permission of Her Majesty The Queen)

Author's Note

QUEEN VICTORIA, on her own admission, had 'very violent feelings of affection'. It is with these feelings – and with the various men who inspired them – that this book is concerned. It is a study of Queen Victoria in relation to the six most romantically significant men in her life; and of them in relation to her. With the Queen in her various other roles – political, imperial, constitutional, matriarchal and domestic – I have not concerned myself. There is no shortage of books on these aspects of her life. Nor have I dealt with the lives, public or private, of these six men, other than as these affect their association with the Queen.

Never, not even in old age, was Queen Victoria the dour, censorious puritan of popular imagination: through her complex character ran a bright thread of romanticism. Within that dumpy, uncompromising-looking figure beat a very susceptible heart. She was, and again the words are her own, 'naturally very passionate'. That these passions were romantic rather than carnal makes them no less intense.

Queen Victoria's most intimate relationships were always with men. She had no really close woman friend. The theory that her status as a queen precluded any such feminine friendship should, by rights, be equally valid when applied to men. Yet it is not. Nor were the Queen's male friendships confined to men of equal, or even comparable, status. Even the Emperor Napoleon III, as the only fellow monarch to whom she was strongly attracted, was very much a parvenu. And men like John Brown and the Munshi were simply servants.

At first glance it is difficult to find any common characteristics between the various men to whom Queen Victoria was drawn – between the urbane Lord Melbourne and the semi-literate Munshi, between the upright Prince Albert and the Machiavellian Napoleon III, between the brusque John Brown and the silver-tongued Disraeli. But these apparently disparate characters did have some things in common. They were all men of distinctive personality. There was nothing ordinary or banal about any of them. Even with personalities like Prince Albert and John Brown, there was something exceptional, something *outré*. And they all – and this was probably their greatest appeal in the eyes of Queen Victoria – treated her as a woman first, a queen second.

For if the heart of Queen Elizabeth I was, as she once boasted, that of a man, then Queen Victoria's heart was indubitably that of a woman.

'My nature is too passionate, my emotions too fervent, and I am a person who has to cling to someone in order to find peace and comfort.'
Queen Victoria

THE GIRL-QUEEN

'A Girl Amid an Assemblage of Men'

SHE ENTERED her sitting-room in Kensington Palace, wrote the eighteen-year-old Queen Victoria of the morning that she succeeded to the throne, 'alone'. By alone she meant that she had not allowed her possessive mother, the widowed Duchess of Kent, to accompany her into the room. Waiting for her as she entered, still in her cotton dressing gown and with her hair streaming down her back, were the Archbishop of Canterbury and the Lord Chamberlain. Falling to his knees, the Lord Chamberlain told her that her uncle, King William IV, had died four hours before, at twelve minutes past two on that morning of 20 June 1837, and that she was now Queen.

For the young Queen Victoria it was the start of a day that was to plunge her, for the first time in her strictly chaperoned life, into the company of what Disraeli afterwards described as 'an assemblage of men'. Until that day, she had almost never been left alone with any man other than a relation or a member of her mother's household: 'no Boy after 7 years old was allowed to see the Child',[1] reported one of her aunts. When, for instance, the handsome young Lord Elphinstone – enchanted by the sight of Princess Victoria in a grey satin coat trimmed with roses – made a surreptitious sketch of her as she sat in church, the Duchess of Kent lost no time in having him banished to India. Until the day she ascended the throne, the Princess slept in her mother's room. And now suddenly the new Queen found herself, much to her satisfaction, not only free of her mother's oppressive presence but 'alone', as she repeatedly emphasizes in her Journal, among a varied host of men.

During breakfast the Queen had a long talk with that Coburg family factotum, Baron Stockmar. After breakfast she received the Prime Minister, Lord Melbourne, and then saw him again at eleven. Half an hour later she held her first Privy Council in the Red Saloon at Kensington Palace. Dressed in mourning for the late King, she entered the room unaccompanied and was conducted to her throne by her royal uncles, the Dukes of Cumberland and Sussex. On being faced by this august, intimidating and sizeable body of men (there was a record attendance that day) she blushed, but soon regained her composure. Having read her Declaration in the clear and silvery voice that was to remain one of her chief attractions, the Queen presided over the swearing-in ceremony. One after another these great figures of her realm – prelates, statesmen, politicians, officers of state – knelt to kiss her hand.

'I was not at all nervous,' she afterwards wrote, 'and had the satisfaction of hearing that people were satisfied with what I had done and how I had done it.'

The Council over, she saw her Prime Minister, Lord Melbourne, again and then granted audiences to the Home Secretary, the Master of the Horse, the Archbishop of Canterbury, Baron Stockmar and Dr James Clark whom she appointed as her personal physician. She saw Stockmar twice more that day and had a final meeting, lasting well over an hour, with Lord Melbourne.

In short, in the course of one day, Queen Victoria had been exposed, 'quite *alone*', to a greater variety of male company than she had during the first eighteen years of her life.

How did the new young Queen strike this great company of male dignitaries, many of whom were seeing her for the first time?

'There was never anything like the first impression she produced, or the chorus of praise and admiration which is raised about her manner and behaviour, and certainly not without justice,' raved Charles Greville, at Kensington Palace in his capacity as Clerk of the Privy Council. 'It was very extraordinary, and something far beyond what was looked for'. She went through the whole ceremony, he said, 'with perfect calmness and self-possession, but at the same time with a graceful modesty and propriety particularly interesting and ingratiating . . .'.[2]

All this was rendered more remarkable by the fact that the Queen was not particularly impressive to look at. For one thing, she was very small, not much over five foot. Nor was she a beauty; her chin was too weak, her mouth too rabbity, her hair too mousy. On the other hand, she was not without certain attractions. She had large blue eyes, a fresh complexion and that beautiful speaking voice. To these were added all the sparkle and enthusiasm of youth. Although dignified, her self-possession never became stiffness, and her composure was tempered by the most winning of blushes. The Queen might be conscientious and full of common sense but she was also an effusive, artless and affectionate girl. She was, reported one of the men attending the Privy Council, 'as interesting and handsome as any young lady I ever saw.'[3]

Lord Holland was even more enthusiastic. 'I am come back quite a courtier and a bit of a lover,' he claimed after a private audience with her, 'for really her manner and demeanour deserve all that is said of them, announce taste, a feeling of good breeding, and her looks, in my judgement, far exceed the most favourable account I heard. Though not a beauty and not a good figure, she is really in person, in face, and especially in eyes and complexion, a very nice girl and quite such as might tempt.'

'Like the rest of the world,' he wrote on a later occasion, 'I am captivated and surprised.'[4]

The Queen was no less captivated and surprised; the position in which she now suddenly found herself was full of excitements. To be consulted, deferred to, listened to, agreed with, involved in all sorts of political and domestic business, afforded her immense pleasure. 'With all her prudence and discretion,' claims Greville, 'she has great animal spirits, and enters into the magnificent novelties of her position with the zest and curiosity of a child.'[5]

That the young Queen Victoria should be revelling, not only in the interests and enjoyments of her new status but in the deferential attentions of so many important men, is understandable. Her girlhood had been singularly lacking in the presence of any reassuring and sympathetic masculine figure.

Her father, the Duke of Kent – fourth son of King George III – had died when she was only eight months old, in January 1820. His brothers were hardly of the stuff of which father-substitutes are made. Dissolute, rackety, prodigal, Princess Victoria's pack of 'wicked uncles' could certainly not be looked to for the giving of sound advice or the setting of suitable examples. In any case, Princess Victoria's mother, the widowed Duchess of Kent, was on such bad terms with her royal brothers-in-law that she kept her precious daughter well away from them. Contact with the court – first of the fat, florid, increasingly eccentric King George IV and then of his brother, the simpler-minded but excitable King William IV – was kept to a minimum. Her daughter's reign, the Duchess of Kent had long ago decided, must in no way resemble the ones preceding it.

Until she turned twelve Princess Victoria did have one uncle on hand on whom she could rely for support. This was her mother's brother, Prince Leopold of Saxe-Coburg. The handsome Prince Leopold had arrived in England in 1816 to marry Princess Charlotte, only child of the future King George IV and thus heiress-apparent to the British throne. The marriage was short-lived. Within eighteen months Princess Charlotte had died in childbirth.

Robbed of his chance of being the husband of a queen, the ambitious Prince Leopold was none the less able to console himself with the thought that he might one day be the uncle of one: in the year after Princess Charlotte's death, Prince Leopold's sister married the Duke of Kent. Less than a year after that, on 24 May 1819, Princess Victoria was born.

And so, for the first twelve years of the Princess's life, her Uncle Leopold paid weekly visits to Kensington Palace. But, knowing that both King George IV and his successor, King William IV, liked him no better than they liked his sister, Prince Leopold had to behave with a certain amount of circumspection. He must not be seen to be playing too influential a part in his niece's life.

In 1831, not long after Princess Victoria's twelfth birthday – at the very time that she stood poised on the threshold of the years during which his guidance would have proved most valuable – Prince Leopold accepted the offer of the throne of newly-independent Belgium. He never lived in England again. Indeed, over four years were to pass before uncle and niece even saw one another.

This did not mean, though, that Princess Victoria was denied the benefit of King Leopold's invariably sound and always copious advice. Year after year his letters, heavily larded with instructions, encouragement and protestations of affection, crossed the Channel to Kensington Palace. To his palace of Laeken in Brussels went Victoria's answers – appreciative, questioning, and no less affectionate. No letter from dear Uncle Leopold, no matter how heavily pedantic or tediously instructive, was received with anything less than unfeigned gratitude; no teacher could have hoped for a more receptive pupil.

But for all the value of Princess Victoria's contacts with her Uncle Leopold, it was not the same as having some supportive masculine figure permanently on hand. And the one man who was on hand and who would have been only too happy to fill the gap left by King

Leopold – Sir John Conroy, the Duchess of Kent's comptroller – was heartily loathed by Princess Victoria.

Handsome, ambitious, overbearing and unscrupulous, Sir John Conroy was the dominant figure at Kensington Palace. The Duchess of Kent had complete faith in him. Indeed, so thick was the still young and attractive Duchess with her comptroller that it was assumed they were lovers. Conroy certainly behaved as though he were master of the household.

Determined to secure a powerful position for himself in the years ahead, Conroy kept a tight grip on the future Queen. By the introduction of the so-called 'Kensington System', he kept her isolated from outside influences and entirely subservient to her mother. To the annoyance of the reigning King William IV, he packed her off on a series of semi-royal progresses through the country; he planned, by coercion if necessary, to get himself appointed as her future private secretary. If the young Princess Victoria did indeed feel the lack of a strong masculine hand at Kensington Palace, it was not through any want of trying on the part of Sir John Conroy.

But his efforts counted for nothing. Princess Victoria hated Conroy. He was the last person in the world in whom she would ever confide; to whom she would ever turn for advice or guidance. Some imagined that her abhorrence sprang from the fact that she had once caught him in the act of making love to her mother, but she always denied this. She certainly resented his familiarity towards the Duchess of Kent but she resented, far more, his arrogant attitude towards herself. And the more Conroy tried to force his will, the more she resisted him. The result was that relations between the Princess, on the one hand, and her mother and Conroy on the other, became increasingly strained.

By nature lively, warm-hearted and frank, the young Princess was forced to cultivate a cool, somewhat withdrawn manner. To the Duchess, Conroy and their circle, she appeared stubborn, wilful and far too independent for her own good. To the general public, she seemed unusually self-possessed. Only to her beloved governess, Baroness Lehzen, could the unhappy Princess reveal her true and very engaging self.

Yet it was by no means all gloom at Kensington Palace. And, significantly, it was in the company of young men that the Princess let slip the mask of imperturbability to reveal her pleasure-loving nature. Part of this delight in male company was due to her very natural yearning for the companionship of other young people, for what she calls the 'mirth' and 'merriment' of their times together; but another part was attributable to her Hanoverian blood, to the tastes and appetites of the royal house to which she belonged.

Such young men as Princess Victoria was allowed to meet or, at least, to spend any time with, were invariably relations. And although her late father's family – the British royal family – was conspicuously lacking in legitimate male heirs (of illegitimate ones there was no shortage), her mother's family – the Coburgs – suffered no such lack. In later years Bismarck always referred to Coburg as 'the stud farm of Europe'. This marrying-off of the stable of handsome Coburg princelings into various leading royal houses, be they Catholic or Protestant, had begun with Prince Leopold's marriage to Princess Charlotte; before long these young men were being paraded in half the courts of Europe, not least the British. Princess Victoria was exposed to no fewer than eight visiting male cousins between her thirteenth and eighteenth birthdays.

The Mensdorff-Pouilly princes, Hugo and Alfonso, sons of the Duchess of Kent's sister Sophie, came in 1832. The following summer brought a more exciting pair still: Alexander and Ernst Württemberg, the sons of the Duchess's sister Antoinette. The fourteen-year-old Princess Victoria found herself bowled over by their masculinity: they were tall, so handsome, so 'extremely amiable'.

They were as nothing, though, compared to the next set – the Coburg princes, Ferdinand and Augustus, sons of the Duchess's brother Ferdinand, who spent several weeks at Kensington Palace in the early spring of 1836. The Princess's Journal positively sparkles with descriptions of their good looks: of their 'beautiful dark brown eyes', their 'pretty noses', their 'very sweet' mouths. She was particularly taken with the nineteen-year-old Prince Ferdinand, despite the fact that he had just been married, by proxy, to the young Queen of Portugal and was now on his way to meet his bride for the first time. 'Oh! I love him *so* much, he is *so* excellent,' enthused Princess Victoria. When they left she was desolate; not only because she missed them personally but because their going meant the end of all those balls and parties that had been arranged for their entertainment, and in which she took such delight.

Within two months they had been superseded in her febrile affections by two more cousins – Ernest and Albert, sons of the reigning Duke of Saxe-Coburg and Gotha. This was as well, for it was the younger of the two princes, the sixteen-year-old Albert, whom Princess Victoria's dynastically ambitious uncle King Leopold had marked down as her future husband. He had chosen wisely. One look at the tall, well-built, blue-eyed and brown-haired Prince Albert, and the passionate young Princess Victoria melted. She could not praise him highly enough. His nose was beautiful, his mouth was sweet, his teeth were fine, his expression was delightful: 'full of goodness and sweetness, and very clever and intelligent'. And not only was he 'extremely handsome' but he was accomplished, clever, reflective.

In one regard only did Prince Albert disappoint. He could not match her zest for living. He hated late nights and rich food; he tended to fall asleep in company; he took no pleasure in dances, parties and entertainments. On one occasion he had to leave the ballroom early, 'pale as ashes'; on another a bilious attack obliged him to spend the day in bed. Princess Victoria, on the other hand, revelled in all this gaiety. Nothing laid her low; she could go on dancing until dawn. 'I can assure you,' she reported to her Uncle Leopold, 'all this dissipation does me a great deal of good.'

But that Prince Albert would one day make a suitable husband she had no doubt. 'I must thank you . . .', she wrote to a gratified King Leopold, 'for the prospect of *great* happiness you have contributed to give me, in the person of dear Albert. Allow me then, my dearest Uncle, to tell you how delighted I am with him, and how much I like him in every way. He possesses every quality that would be desired to render me perfectly happy.'

She was not, though, in love with him. That would come later.

King Leopold's satisfaction with this gradual evolution of his dynastic ambitions would have been given a severe jolt had he been able to read his niece's Journal for the following spring. In it, the seventeen-year-old girl dwelt at considerable length on the attractions of an altogether different sort of young man. This was her second cousin, Charles, Duke of Brunswick.

With his long dark hair and moustachios, Duke Charles was a Byronic-looking figure – swashbuckling, romantic, wicked. Adding to his air of bravado was the fact that he had been expelled from his country and its regency entrusted to a more conventional brother. The young Princess Victoria, who saw Duke Charles on several occasions that spring, was clearly fascinated. She could hardly take her eyes off him as he lounged in his box at the opera, his great fur coat slung over the back of his chair and his long hair parted in the middle and 'hanging wildly' to well below his ears: a style that might not suit ugly people, she decided, but which certainly suited 'these handsome ones'.

In the park she saw him at even closer quarters. He was so handsome, so elegantly dressed, so 'ferocious-looking', so 'very wild and odd'. In short, there was something about this desperado, with his bold stare and his shady reputation, that set the Princess's pulses pounding. She had noticed him looking at her; what if he were to speak to her?

Fortunately, she was never put to the test. But that her imagination was set aflame by this unconventional, rakish and sensual-looking gallant there is no doubt. It is the first indication of Queen Victoria's lifelong penchant for theatrical and mysterious-seeming men, which ran side by side with her appreciation of the sturdier masculine virtues.

And when she did first fall in love – albeit without fully realizing it – it was with a man in whom were combined both the father-figure for whom she was always searching and the romantic to whom she would always respond.

Part One

LORD MELBOURNE

2

'My Kind Good Friend'

THE MAN with whom Queen Victoria was now required to spend the greater part of her time was her Prime Minister, Lord Melbourne. Such time, as far as both the Queen and Lord Melbourne were concerned, could hardly have been better spent. Melbourne, who had become Whig Prime Minister for a second term in 1835, had appointed himself as the Queen's chief adviser and unofficial private secretary. Within a very short time their working relationship had developed into something more: it became a classic example of the first love of an unsophisticated young girl for an urbane older man. It was no less an illustration of the Queen's taste for the unorthodox.

At the time of Queen Victoria's accession William Lamb, Viscount Melbourne, was fifty-eight years old. Having been an exceptionally handsome young man, he was still a very attractive one: his blue-grey eyes were fringed with dark lashes and topped by heavy brows, his nose was boldly arched, his iron-grey hair luxuriantly curly. His figure still retained something of the elegance and virility of youth. To these striking looks Lord Melbourne added a great charm of manner. His air was sophisticated, insouciant, seductive; his conversation was witty and entertaining, shot through with cynicism. He had the sort of amused detachment most women found irresistible.

He was equally drawn to them. Although thoroughly at ease in masculine company and as ready as any of his fellows to 'talk broad', Lord Melbourne preferred the society of women. He was very susceptible to feminine influence. Only in the company of a good-looking woman could he be sure of the intimate and concentrated sympathy which his personality needed. The relationship did not need to be overtly sexual; a platonic but flirtatious friendship was what he liked best. In short, and in common with another man with whom Queen

Victoria was one day to establish an *amitié amoureuse* – Benjamin Disraeli – Lord Melbourne was, in an emotional rather than a carnal sense, a great lover of women.

They had certainly played a significant part in his life. His mother, born Elizabeth Milbanke, had been a remarkable person: assertive, ambitious, far more masterful than her husband. Indeed this husband – the first Viscount Melbourne – seems to have contributed even less to his family's advancement than might be supposed: no one, he least of all, could be absolutely certain that he had fathered all six of his wife's children. In her determination to make her way in the world (as her husband had only recently been ennobled, there was still a fair way to make) the beautiful Lady Melbourne never hesitated to take influential lovers. Her second son William, later Lord Melbourne, and her third son Frederick, are said to have been fathered by Lord Egremont; her fourth son George by the Prince of Wales – the future King George IV. (Although Lady Melbourne's sojourn in the Prince of Wales's bedchamber was short-lived, it at least allowed her time to have her cuckolded husband created a Lord of the Bedchamber.) Who Lady Melbourne's two daughters had been fathered by was apparently anyone's guess.

It was very largely due to the social manœuvrings and sympathetic encouragement of this strong–minded mother that William Lamb, born on 15 March 1779, made such good progress. At school at Eton, at university in Cambridge and Glasgow and for the short time that he practised law in London, the young Lamb was spurred on by Lady Melbourne. She early appreciated that he was more intelligent and sensitive, if no less lively, than his brothers and sisters. His youth was not entirely given over to the roistering and whoremongering that characterized the life of so many well-born young men of the period. He was more interested in things of the mind: in literature, in history and in serious conversation.

If the influence of William Lamb's mother was almost entirely beneficial, that of his wife proved wholly disastrous. In the summer of 1805 the twenty-six-year-old William Lamb married the nineteen-year-old Caroline Ponsonby, only daughter of the third Earl of Bessborough. She was an extraordinary creature – small, fey, unpredictable and, as far as the young bridegroom was concerned, utterly enchanting. He was deeply in love with her. So virile and practical himself, Lamb was attracted to Caroline's vulnerability and whimsicality. Always something of a teacher, he started their married life by treating Caroline like the artless and wilful child she was.

The marriage very soon began to deteriorate. 'You see,' as Melbourne afterwards explained to Queen Victoria, 'a gentleman hardly knows a girl till he has proposed, and then when he has an unrestrained intercourse with her, he sees something and says, "This I don't quite like".'[1] Before long, there were a great many things about his wife that the young husband did not quite like.

With each passing year Caroline Lamb became increasingly eccentric: more imprudent, more uncontrollable, more of an *enfant terrible*. He, always one for avoiding trouble, simply did not know how to handle her; she, finding him too unresponsive to her flights of fancy, sought excitement elsewhere.

She found it in, of all people, Lord Byron. (It was the infatuated Caroline Lamb who first described Byron, in her diary, as 'mad, bad and dangerous to know'.) These two flamboyant egoists – Byron and Caroline Lamb – embarked on a turbulent love affair, a great deal of which was conducted in public. When Byron's assumed ardour began to cool, Caroline grew frantic. Her behaviour became so outlandish that she was regarded as having lost her mind. But still the long-suffering William Lamb refused to yield to his family's insistence that he break with her. Long after the Byron affair was over, and Caroline had embarked on a series of no less tempestuous adventures, her husband remained loyal. It was not until 1825, after twenty years of an exhausting marriage, that he could bring himself to part from her. Caroline died three years later. The couple's only surviving son, who was born abnormal, died in his twenties.

This searing experience of marriage did not, however, diminish William Lamb's interest in women. After Caroline's death he was involved in several other relationships. Some, like his friendship with Emily Eden, were tranquil affairs. Others, like his romances with the headstrong Lady Branden and the equally temperamental Caroline Norton, were far stormier. He was cited by the husbands of both these women as co-respondent in divorce cases; the last case was heard in the year before Queen Victoria's accession, when Melbourne was already Prime Minister.

Is it any wonder, then, that there clung about Lord Melbourne's handsome head an aura of high romance? Greatly enhancing his physical and social attractions were the melancholy of his domestic tragedies and the piquancy of his sexual adventures. When one considers in addition the potency of his political power, one can appreciate his appeal, particularly to someone as unworldly as the eighteen-year-old Queen Victoria.

★

William Lamb gave up law to enter politics in 1805, when he was twenty-six. This was when the untimely death of his elder brother had ensured that he would one day succeed his father, as the second Viscount Melbourne. It was in the same year that he married Caroline Ponsonby. Early in 1806 he was elected to Parliament. William Lamb was a Whig: a supporter of that party of rich, land-owning, theoretical liberals; a party 'strong', as one historian has put it, 'on principles but weak in practice'.[2] Lamb, in fact, was not even very strong on principles, for the good reason that he never really felt very strongly about anything. This lack of any firmly-held political convictions enabled him to accept with equanimity a long period when he was out of Parliament; and even, at one stage, to hold office under the Duke of Wellington's Tory administration.

On his father's death in 1828 (the year in which his wife also died) he succeeded to the title. Within a couple of years Melbourne had been appointed Home Secretary in the new Whig government. In 1834 he became Prime Minister. His administration was short-lived. By the end of that same year he had been dismissed by King William IV. In less than six months, on the collapse of the Tory government, he was once again summoned by the King, and in April 1835 Lord Melbourne embarked on his second term as Prime Minister.

The generally accepted picture of Lord Melbourne is that of a somewhat apolitical figure, a nonchalant amateur who happened to find himself, against his own inclinations, cornered into positions of political importance. This picture is very largely his own creation. He liked to give the impression of being a dilettante, of not taking himself too seriously, of not quite following the matter under discussion. In fact, Lord Melbourne was a shrewd, ambitious and able politician, far more industrious than he is usually given credit for.

On the other hand – and with Melbourne it is always a question of the other hand – his want of any strongly held political beliefs tended to make him casual, cynical, indifferent to injustice or social ills. He was the most conservative of liberals; he agreed to reforms only when he considered them inevitable. Worldly-wise, he tended to see each question from too many sides; naturally pessimistic, he doubted that any problem could ever be satisfactorily solved; disliking direct action, he imagined that things were always better left as they were. When in doubt about what should be done, he once advised, do nothing. And on another occasion he startled an earnest archbishop not only by his passive attitude towards slavery, but also by reflecting that it was only by avoiding any active do-gooding that one could hope to keep out of trouble.

'I like what is tranquil and stable'[3] is the closest Lord Melbourne seems ever to have come to summarizing his own political creed.

In the same way that his political beliefs lacked definition, so did his character seem diffuse, many-faceted, contradictory. 'His whole personality was a paradox,' writes Lord David Cecil. 'Racy and refined, sensible and eccentric, cynical and full of sentiment, direct and secretive, each successive impression he made seemed to contradict the last.'[4]

At times Lord Melbourne seemed the very picture of patrician indolence as he lounged about in his beautifully cut but untidily worn clothes, eating hearty meals, making flippant comments and passing outrageous opinions. He had a strongly sensual, almost earthy streak, but he could be very sentimental. His tongue might have been caustic and his attitudes world-weary, but his heart was warm. He was capable of tears; his emotions could be easily stirred; he was very forgiving. He was also, of course, a clever man: well-read, sharp-witted, reflective. As a conversationalist, he could hardly be matched.

All in all, Lord Melbourne was an original: a genuinely independent and highly unconventional character.

Such was the man who, in his late fifties, found himself in the position of mentor to the young Queen Victoria. Few positions could have suited him better. All his chivalry, all his paternalism, all his conversational and tutorial skills could now be brought into play. And so, too, could the powerful romanticism which lay just below that sophisticated and sardonic surface.

From the time of their first meeting after her accession, Queen Victoria was very taken with Lord Melbourne. To her, Lord M, as she called him, was perfection. One can understand her attitude. She had passed – quite literally overnight – from the unsympathetic and intimidating authority of her mother's comptroller and ally, Sir John Conroy, into the bland and deferential care of this highly civilized statesman.

What impressed her most forcibly, apparently, was her Prime Minister's 'goodness' – his honesty, his straightforwardness, his kindheartedness. These were not, perhaps, the qualities that would have been most apparent to some of Melbourne's political colleagues; but to Queen Victoria, after years of Conroy's duplicity, Melbourne's openness came as a wonderful change. 'I have, alas!', she wrote to her Uncle Leopold, 'seen so much of bad hearts and dishonest and *double* minds, that I know how to value and appreciate *real worth*.'

No other minister, she claimed in her emphatic fashion, 'has that kindness, mildness and open frankness, and *agreeability* which I find in my friend Lord Melbourne; he *alone* inspires me with that feeling of great confidence and I may say *security*, for I feel *so safe* when he speaks to me and is with me.'

She found their times together a delight. Both at Buckingham Palace and at Windsor Castle, into which she had moved from Kensington Palace, Lord Melbourne was in almost constant attendance. Their meetings were not confined to what she calls her 'Closet for Political Affairs'; they rode out together every day, they sat beside each other at meals; they played artless board games or leafed through albums in the evenings. Greville estimated that the Queen and her Prime Minister spent at least six hours together every day: 'more hours than any two people, in any relation in life, perhaps ever do pass together.'[5] And when they were separated – when affairs of state kept Lord Melbourne in London – they exchanged letters, sometimes as often as three times a day.

She had never heard a man talk like this. Nothing in her past life – not the strictures of Sir John Conroy, the sermonizing of Uncle Leopold, the raillery of her young Coburg cousins – had prepared her for his brilliant flow. It was all so amusing, so epigrammatic, so irreverent, so *outré*. There was no subject on which Lord M did not have some pungent comment to make. Every opinion seemed to challenge the orthodox view.

The Queen was deeply impressed by his 'stores' of knowledge; his 'sayings' became gospel to her. Into her Journal, in her candid, detailed, inimitable style, she conscientiously copied all his remarks and aphorisms; even if, as often happened, she failed to understand them or to appreciate that they were not meant to be taken seriously.

People who spoke about railroads and bridges, she inscribed gravely, were generally Liberals. People with small features and 'squeeny' noses never achieved anything. French books were concise, English books prosy and German books obscure. Men wrote the best books and women the best letters. Women were very rarely kind to one another. Wife-beating was almost worthwhile when one considered how much sympathy the woman could arouse. Far too much fuss was made about education: none of the Paget family could read or write and they managed very well. One should never waste too much time in trying to understand complicated theological questions, such as the Trinity or the true nature of Christ: they were beyond comprehension. It mattered very little to what church one belonged; the Church of England, as the 'least meddling', was probably the best.

When the Queen one day observed that there were not many good preachers (on what evidence one does not know), Lord M agreed. But there was not *many very good anything*, he added. This was *'very true'* noted the Queen solemnly. She was quite sure, though, that *he* was one of the *very* good.

There were times when even she realized that he was being funny. In fact, one of his many attractions was that he made her laugh so much. No Derby, he said, could be considered perfect unless someone had been killed during the race. When the Duke of Richmond grumbled about the fact that people often came out of prison worse than they went in, Lord Melbourne said that there were many places out of which one came worse than one went in: one often came out of a ballroom worse than one went in. At this the Queen shrieked with laughter, showing her little white teeth and pink gums.

But there were tears, too, chiefly in Lord Melbourne's eyes. The Queen was touched to find that this apparently cool and rational man could be highly emotional, particularly where she was concerned. Time and again she notes that her Prime Minister has cried while speaking to her. The truth was that, with his strong sense of history, Melbourne was profoundly moved by the concept of this young and unspoilt girl occupying the ancient throne. He was moved, too, by her many admirable qualities: her diligence, her enthusiasm, her eagerness to learn. The ambitious Sir John Conroy, in his determination to become a power behind the new Queen's throne, had put about that she was immature, backward, not up to her monumental task. Half an hour in Queen Victoria's company had put paid, as far as Lord Melbourne was concerned, to that canard. He had never met a young woman with more natural command or greater strength of character. Far from having to deal with some nonentity, 'it became his province', as the ubiquitous Greville puts it, 'to educate, instruct and form the most interesting mind and character in the world.'[6]

And this is what, with great expertise, Lord Melbourne set out to do. Behind all his entertaining talk was invariably a piece of valuable information or sage advice. He taught her royal history by discussing the various monarchs (Henry VIII's wives 'bothered' the poor King so); he initiated her into the workings of the political system by way of anecdotes and character sketches; he guided her through the intricacies of social behaviour by happy reminiscence; he defined her role as the guardian of national morals by advising her not to appear so censorious as to get herself disliked, nor yet to sanction anything that might compromise the dignity of the crown.

He gave more intimate advice as well. When she confided in him about her shyness in speaking to strangers, he explained that the more one thought about it, the worse it became. Better to say something commonplace than nothing at all. In any case, her shyness was simply a sign of a 'sensitive and susceptible' temperament. When she lamented the fact that she was so short and that 'everyone grows but me', he merely laughed and said, 'I think you are grown.' Not, he added that her lack of inches was any misfortune. Nor was it. Throughout her long life, Queen Victoria's diminutive stature never detracted from her natural aura of majesty.

He lectured her on the duties, both public and private, of a constitutional monarch. He explained the day-to-day business of kingship, and how to handle politicians. Even if she disliked someone, she must always try to understand their point of view. Her ceremonial duties were very important and must never be shirked. Once, when the Queen announced that she would not open Parliament because the date had been brought forward, he insisted that she must. When still she demurred, he said, gently but firmly, 'Oh, you will do it.' And she did.

Gradually, in his expert hands, the young Queen became more confident, more sophisticated, more determined to do her best. He taught her, in short, how to be a queen. Although there is no doubt that, given her innate sense of duty and force of personality, Queen Victoria would herself have mastered the art of being a sovereign, Lord Melbourne was able to make the learning process so much more fun.

But there was a great deal more to the relationship than that of pupil and teacher, girl-queen and elder statesman. The couple were strongly attracted to each other.

What, exactly, was the secret of this attraction? For Lord Melbourne, in this autumn of his life, the young Queen had precisely the qualities that were needed to set his own temperate being aflame: a combination of passion and naïvety. She was about the same age as his wife Caroline had been at the time of their marriage, which gave him another opportunity for what he so much enjoyed: the fashioning of a young mind. With the Queen his task was infinitely more rewarding; unlike the young Caroline, she was neither eccentric nor complex. She had a straightforwardness and a simplicity that greatly appealed to him.

No less appealing were those qualities which had drawn him to all the women in his life, including Caroline: vitality, enthusiasm, positiveness. So scoffing, so without illusions himself, Lord Melbourne found the Queen's artlessness wonderfully invigorating. Added to all this was the fact that she was a nubile and attractive young woman; one, as Lord Holland said, 'as might tempt'.

Queen Victoria came into Lord Melbourne's life at exactly the right moment. His turbulent association with that other Caroline – Caroline Norton – had just ended, and he was someone to whom the love and companionship of a woman was essential. The Prime Minister was a man, says Greville, 'with a capacity for loving without anything to love.'[7]

Queen Victoria's feelings were no less passionate, but rather more unconscious. Her Journal might dwell on Lord Melbourne's honesty and nobility, but these virtues would not have made anything like the same impression had he not been so handsome and seductively mannered a man. There were times, though, when she did make mention of his physical attractions: of how striking he looked in his dark blue 'Windsor uniform' with its red facings, of how appealingly his silver curls were ruffled by the breeze, of the fact that he was wearing a new olive-green velvet waistcoat. How handsome he must have looked, she commented when he told her that, as a schoolboy at Eton, he had worn his hair very long.

His every change of mood, his comical grimaces, his odd expressions of approval, his hearty appetite (three chops and a grouse for breakfast), the appearance of his rooms, his way of saying 'goold' for gold and 'Room' for Rome, all these she jotted down in her Journal.

Tirelessly she questioned him about his family: his parents, his brothers and sisters, the family homes. She was especially interested in his late wife, but as she could hardly question him about her directly, she relied on the Duchess of Sutherland for information. The Queen was shocked and saddened by what she heard of Caroline's behaviour, and of the tragic life of the couple's abnormal son. All these domestic dramas merely added to the aureole of romantic melancholy that seemed to encircle her hero's head.

The better she came to know him, the more enraptured she became. Their time together was not confined to Buckingham Palace and Windsor Castle: they would go riding in Richmond Park, they attended the Eton festival of Montem, he stood near her at the Opening of Parliament, they even wandered together through the exotic rooms of King George IV's Pavilion at Brighton. Eventually she could hardly bear to have him out her sight. It was noticed that her eyes followed him wherever he moved; when he left the room, she would give a slight, involuntary sigh. If he were ill for a day, she would announce herself *'quite annoyed* and *put out'*. If she thought that one of her ladies was monopolizing him at the dinner-table, she would become extremely jealous. When she considered that he was spending too much time with the famous Whig hostess, Lady Holland, she accused him of finding the ageing Lady Holland more attractive than herself.

'Lord Melbourne dines with Lady Holland tonight,' she complained to her Journal. 'I wish he dined with me!'

Inevitably there was speculation about the true nature of the association between this ageing man of the world and his starry-eyed pupil. Among cynics it seemed inconceivable that the close friendship should not have a physical basis. 'I hope you are amused', wrote Lady Grey to Thomas Creevy, 'at the report of Lord Melbourne being likely to marry the Queen.'[8] But not everyone was so ready to be amused. On one occasion, disapproving cries of 'Mrs Melbourne' greeted the Queen as she appeared on a balcony beside her Prime Minister. In the same way, forty years later, at the height of the John Brown scandal, would she be greeted with cries of 'Mrs Brown'.

Melbourne, testified Charles Greville, was everything to her. Her feelings, 'which are *sexual* though She does not know it . . . are probably not very well defined to herself.'[9]

Greville was probably right in claiming that her feelings were sexual but unconscious. Queen Victoria was, on her own admission, 'naturally very passionate', but she was passionate in an emotional rather than in a physical sense. She had a fiery temper, she was given to fierce loyalties, she was capable of an all-consuming love. There is no doubt that she was physically attracted to Lord Melbourne, but this did not mean any slackening of her own high moral code. Her undoubted affection for Lord M was a frank, unknowing and innocent emotion. She loved him, certainly, but she thought of him as a 'dear friend'. If, as Greville said, Lord Melbourne was 'passionately fond of her as he might be of his daughter if he had one',[10] then she loved him as she might have loved her father.

Of course, in the final analysis, there was rather more to this famous partnership than that. No relationship between a father and a daughter could have been as exciting, as explorative, as unclouded and as rich in sexual undertones as the one between Lord M and Queen Victoria. 'At once his sovereign, his daughter and the last love of his life,' writes Lord David Cecil, 'Queen Victoria inspired Melbourne with a sentiment tenderer if not more vehement than he had ever felt before.'[11]

For the two of them, Lord Melbourne in the sunset of his career and Queen Victoria at the dawn of hers, it was an idyllic time.

3

'Mrs Melbourne'

ONE OF THE first problems to be tackled by Lord Melbourne on behalf of the delectable little Queen was that of her mother's comptroller and personal adviser, Sir John Conroy. Realizing that his hopes of becoming the *éminence grise* of the new reign had come to nothing, Conroy let Melbourne know, through Baron Stockmar, the terms on which he was prepared to withdraw from the scene. They were exorbitant. Conroy was demanding, among other things, a peerage, the Grand Cross of the Bath, and a large annual pension.

Melbourne was astonished: a baronetcy and the pension were all that he was prepared to grant. But Conroy insisted on a peerage and on the advice of Stockmar, who considered the getting rid of Conroy to be worth any price, Melbourne promised Conroy the first available Irish peerage. Conroy accepted the promise. But not until it had been fulfilled, he 'sneeringly' told Stockmar, would he resign his position in the Duchess's household. Melbourne's customary inability to act firmly allowed the mischief-making Conroy to remain on the scene.

The Prime Minister should have been firmer, too, about persuading Queen Victoria to soften her intransigent attitude towards her mother. The daughter's suddenly enhanced status allowed her to treat her mother more openly with the contempt and coolness she had felt for her during the last few years at Kensington Palace. She would dearly have liked, of course, to leave her mother at Kensington Palace, but Melbourne advised against this: it would not do for an unmarried young woman to live without another woman of her own rank.

Once installed in Buckingham Palace, however, the Queen might just as well have been living without her maternal chaperone. She saw to it that the Duchess's apartments were well away from her own, while at the same time arranging for a communicating door to be cut between her own rooms and those of her beloved governess, Lehzen. She instructed her mother never to visit her apartments without written permission to do so; and her reply, whenever presented with one of the Duchess's applications, was invariably that she was too busy to see her. She preferred the two of them to meet in public only, at dinner or in the drawing-room, yet whenever the Queen attended a public function outside the palace, she made a point of leaving her mother at home. And she resolutely refused, in spite of all the Duchess's pleadings, to have anything to do with Sir John Conroy.

It was no wonder that the Duchess of Kent, ostrich feathers all a-tremble in her elaborate coiffure, could complain to a dinner-guest that she now counted for *'nothing'*.[1]

Melbourne, instead of encouraging the Queen to make allowances for her admittedly difficult mother, simply backed her up in her criticisms. He had never seen so foolish a woman, said Melbourne on one occasion; 'which', noted the Queen gleefully, 'is very true, and we both laughed.' He suggested that the Queen allow him to answer her mother's persistent and pestering notes with a formal reply. 'My appeal was to *you* as my Child,' answered the outraged Duchess on receiving one of Lord Melbourne's stiff replies, 'not to the Queen.'[2] And when the Queen protested that she sometimes had to remind her mother *'who I was'*, Lord Melbourne was all approval. Such reminders, he said, were disagreeable but necessary.

The Prime Minister should have realized – indeed he did realize – that an open breach between mother and daughter would do the Queen considerable harm. But so prone was he to taking the line of least resistance and so anxious to placate the young Queen that he let the unfortunate situation continue. In this, he was encouraging Queen Victoria in two of her most regrettable character traits: her stubbornness and her partisanship.

The one aspect of the Duchess of Kent's affairs in which the Prime Minister was obliged to take action was her financial situation. With debts amounting to about £60,000 the Duchess, egged on by Conroy, asked the Queen to settle half of them out of her Privy Purse; she would settle the remainder herself, provided her own income was suitably increased by the government. Melbourne would not hear of it. It was 'impossible and entirely out of the question', he declared, to expect the Queen to pay anything towards the settling of her mother's debts.

Instead, Melbourne suggested that Parliament be asked to grant the Duchess an additional £8000, thus bringing her annual income from the state to £30,000. The Duchess was obliged to agree. The Queen duly asked Parliament for this increase in her mother's allowance and, not without some dissention, her request was granted. A relieved Lord Melbourne assured the Queen that her mother's annuity had been granted only out of affection and respect for herself; he told her this, she notes, 'with tears in his eyes'.

There were tears again in plenty in Lord Melbourne's eyes when he played his part in that most triumphant and emotional of ceremonies – Queen Victoria's coronation on 28 June 1838. The concept of this young and pretty girl being crowned in long-established ritual among the historic splendours of Westminster Abbey was one to touch his sentimental heart.

Yet in the weeks leading up to the ceremony he took great care to keep the Queen from dwelling too much on the momentousness of the great day. He was not one for explaining either the solemnity or the significance of the occasion. 'Oh, you'll like it when you are there,' he said airily when she admitted her nervousness. He kept her diverted with amusing asides and snippets of gossip. With one hundred and sixty more peers planning to attend this coronation than the last, it might be as well to dispense with the peers' customary kissing of the newly crowned sovereign: this would surely, he thought, be more than flesh and blood could stand. Would he be missed, one peer asked the Prime Minister, if he stayed away? The Queen would certainly miss him, answered Melbourne gravely, and would ask why he had not attended. 'Oh! then I'll go,' promised the worried man. The only peers who knew how to put on their robes properly, claimed Melbourne, were two who had taken part in amateur theatricals.

He considered the dresses chosen for the Queen's train-bearers – white and silver and trimmed with roses – to be quite beautiful: they would make the Queen look as though she were floating on a silvery cloud. He also insisted that the special cream horses be brought over from Hanover to draw the cumbersome coronation coach; any other horses would look like rats or mice.

On the great day itself the Prime Minister had almost as much cause for worry as did the Queen. Throughout the previous day he had suffered violent diarrhoea and, in an effort to check it and get through the five-hour-long ceremony, had taken generous doses of laudanum and brandy. In the procession up the nave he walked immediately ahead of the Queen, carrying the Sword of State. 'Melbourne looked very awkward and uncouth', noted Disraeli, in the Abbey as a member of the House of Commons, 'with his coronet cocked over his nose, his robes under his feet, and holding the great Sword of State like a butcher.'[3] To the Queen, who would never have agreed with Disraeli's carping description, Lord Melbourne did afterwards admit that the sword was 'excessively heavy'.

At the supreme moment of the ceremony – when the Archbishop of Canterbury placed the jewelled Crown of State on the Queen's head, the peers and peeresses put on their coronets and the silver trumpets blared out – Lord Melbourne was, in the Queen's words, '*completely* overcome' by his emotions.

During the Homage, at which the bishops, the royal dukes and then all the peers knelt in turn before her, the Prime Minister was again completely overcome. 'When my good Lord Melbourne knelt down and kissed my hand, he pressed my hand and I grasped his with all my heart, at which he looked up with his eyes filled with tears and seemed much touched.'

In St Edward's Chapel ('which, as Lord Melbourne said, was more *unlike* a Chapel than anything he had ever seen: for what was *called* an *Altar* was covered with sandwiches, bottles of wine, etc., etc.') the overwrought Prime Minister drank a glass of wine. He then took up his position in the final procession in which the Queen, '*loaded*', as she puts it, with the crown on her head, the sceptre in one hand and the orb in the other, and an ermine-lined purple velvet mantle about her shoulders, passed down the nave and out of the Abbey. 'I shall ever remember this day as the *Proudest* of my life,' she afterwards wrote.

But the day was not yet over, and Lord Melbourne still had some more crying to do. That night he sat beside the newly crowned little Queen at dinner. 'My kind Lord Melbourne was much affected in speaking of the whole ceremony,' she noted. '"And you did it all so well – excellent!" said he, with tears in his eyes.' There were more tears when, after dinner, he sat beside her on the sofa and spoke of the 'unprecedented' number of peers attending the ceremony. 'You must be very tired,' he remarked. 'And you did it beautifully – every part of it, with so much taste; it's a thing that you can't give a person advice upon; it must be left to a person.'

It was well after eleven when the two of them finally parted: the exhilarated Queen to go out onto the balcony to watch the dazzle of fireworks in Green Park, and the exhausted Lord Melbourne home to dose himself with calomel and take a week off.

Not quite everything in the garden in which Queen Victoria and Lord

Melbourne were so happily wandering was as lovely as it seemed. Their mutual obsession was bringing certain disadvantages. It meant, not only that the Queen unquestioningly believed everything that her Prime Minister told her, but that she was disinclined to listen to anyone else. He became her only confidant and mentor. Even King Leopold, hitherto Queen Victoria's chief adviser, discovered that his influence was beginning to weaken. The tone of her letters to him became more imperious. When he wrote to his niece on political maters, it was as the Queen of England that she now answered.

One regrettable result of all this was that the Queen came to identify herself completely with Lord Melbourne and his Whig government. 'As for the confidence of the Crown,' she exclaimed, 'God knows, no *Minister*, no *friend* EVER possessed it so entirely as this truly excellent Lord Melbourne possesses mine!' Try as Melbourne might – and he did try – to make her appreciate that her constitutional position raised her above party, she refused to hear any good of dear Lord M's political opponents. To her all Tories were enemies; this was something, she once told an amused minister, that she simply could not get Lord Melbourne to understand.

It was to take several years, and a man with even more influence over her, to make Queen Victoria behave in the proper constitutional manner.

A distinctly more regrettable result was that the impressionable young Queen came to see the question of social reform entirely through Melbourne's eyes. His droll turns of phrase, which she so dutifully noted down, reflected a certain heartlessness in the Prime Minister's nature. The Queen came to accept that his lackadaisical, unenlightened, unconcerned attitude towards the social evils of the day was the only sensible one. All discontent, he assured her, was the work of a handful of agitators. Child labour, flogging, poverty, overcrowding and rebellious Irishmen were the natural order of things, and not to be tampered with. When on one occasion the Queen asked Lord Melbourne what happened to the 'poor Irish' who were evicted by their landlords, he drawlingly replied that they were '*absorbed* somehow or other'. This made them both laugh heartily.

The scant concern which Queen Victoria always paid to the conditions in which the majority of her subjects lived can be partly attributed to the early influence of Lord Melbourne.

Nor was his tutelage of her entirely disinterested. 'Take care', the Queen's disgruntled mother once warned her, 'that Lord Melbourne is not King.'[4] There was no fear of that; not even in the sense that the

Duchess meant it. But although Melbourne was scrupulous about not
using his special relationship with the Queen to influence her politically,
it did give him an enormous advantage. The throne was still a powerful
institution, and Melbourne, who was a more ambitious man than his
flippant manner would suggest, clearly relished his privileged position.
He might not have used it for personal gain, but he certainly used it
for personal satisfaction.

Inevitably, there was grumbling about the extraordinary amount of
time and attention that the Prime Minister was devoting to the Queen.
He was accused of being too fawning and courtly, of neglecting his
more serious political and administrative duties. In the House of Lords,
Lord Brougham referred to the Prime Minister's 'glozing and flattery'
and Lord Holland complained that 'constant intercourse' with the girl-
Queen had 'warped his judgement'.[5] Melbourne was always quick to
deny any such allegations.

Not that all the time spent in the Queen's company was unalloyed
pleasure. For this worldly man, with his delight in the company of
beautiful women, his taste for spicy gossip and his quirky sexual tastes
(Melbourne's private letters reveal that he had a marked interest in
whipping) to adjust himself to the nursery-like atmosphere of the
young Queen's court was not easy. He was obliged, for instance,
to temper his free-and-easy attitude towards sexual morality. Lord
Melbourne was so 'truly excellent and moral', enthused the Queen; he
had such strong feelings against 'immorality and wickedness'. Instead
of the racy table-talk at famous Whig meeting places like Holland
House there were now long evenings given over to games of draughts,
shilling whist and the early version of jigsaw puzzles known as dissected
pictures.

Something of the stultifying atmosphere of these evenings at court
is re-created by Charles Greville in his celebrated report of a conversation with the Queen. She had stopped, in her slow circling of the
guests, to speak to him.

Q. Have you been riding today, Mr Greville?
G. No, Madam, I have not.
Q. It was a fine day.
G. Yes, Ma'am, a very fine day.
Q. It was rather cold though.
G. [like Polonius] It *was* rather cold, Madam.
Q. Your sister, Lady Frances Egerton, rides I think, does not she?
G. She does ride sometimes, Madam.
   [A pause, when I took the lead, though adhering to the same topic]

G. Has Your Majesty been riding today?
Q. [with animation] Oh yes, a very long ride.
G. Has Your Majesty got a nice horse?
Q. Oh, a very nice horse.[6]
This far from scintillating exchange over, the Queen smiled, nodded her head and passed on to the next guest.

Can one wonder that Lord Melbourne sometimes made excuses to stay away?

Yet it was at his peril that he did so. The Queen's devotion to him was making her increasingly exacting in her demands on his time and attention. She insisted that he join her five minutes after she had left the dinner-table instead of remaining to drink port and swap stories with the other gentlemen; she scolded him if he were late for one of their appointments; she was seriously annoyed if the press of public affairs kept him away altogether. Once she openly admitted that she was jealous of his visits to Holland House; her affection for him, she said frankly, was greater than Lady Holland's.

Not many men are told this by girls a third of their age; particularly when that girl is also their sovereign. 'He smiled kindly,' noted the Queen, 'and bowed assent.'

By now there was almost no area of Queen Victoria's life in which Lord Melbourne did not have a say. She turned to him for everything.

In the months following the coronation, it was noticed that the Queen was beginning to lose her fresh prettiness. Her complexion was becoming muddier, her fair hair darker, her figure decidedly fuller. She was 'horrified' to find, by the end of the year 1838, that she weighed almost nine stone.

Inevitably, she consulted Lord M about the problem of her appearance. He, just as inevitably, was reassuring. The best figure for a woman, he maintained, was 'fine and full with a fine bust'. In any case, as she had obviously inherited the Hanoverian tendency towards plumpness, she 'stood a good chance of getting very fat'. He had heard, from Lady Holland who was visiting Paris, that the Queen was ordering her dresses a size larger. She admitted that this was true but the reason, she said, was that she could not bear to wear anything tight. And when she was criticized for patronizing French dressmakers in the first place, Lord Melbourne was quick to defend her. It was impossible to look good in English clothes, he declared: English women were all badly dressed; their clothes simply did not fit.

(Many years later when the by then notoriously badly dressed Queen

Victoria was paying a state visit to the Emperor Napoleon III, she one day appeared in a dress upon which the Emperor finally felt able to compliment her. Had it been made, he asked politely, in London? No, she answered in her engagingly frank fashion, it was the only one of her many new dresses to have been made in Paris.)

Lord Melbourne did, though, encourage the Queen to eat more sparingly, if only for the sake of her health. Over-eating, he warned her, was a Hanoverian family failing. Indeed, the Queen's appetite was enormous. She particularly liked drinking beer. One should eat only when one was hungry, said Melbourne; in that case, answered the Queen, she would be eating all day, since she was always hungry. He advised her to take more exercise; she should walk more. When she complained that walking made her feet swell and that she got stones in her shoes, he refused to listen; she would lose the use of her legs if she did not walk, he teased. He was disturbed to hear that she was becoming lazy about dressing; that she was taking her bath last thing at night instead of before dinner so as to cut down on the number of times she must change her clothes. Nothing was so bad for a woman, he lectured, as not dressing when she was at home. Dressing, he said, 'brushes women up'.

He was obliged to protect her interests in more controversial matters as well. One night at Windsor Castle the ebullient Lord Palmerston, then a member of Melbourne's administration, blundered into the bedroom of one of Queen Victoria's ladies-in-waiting. Having got that far, Palmerston decided to make the most of things by forcing himself on the understandably startled lady. She escaped and appealed to Stockmar, who in turn reported the matter to Melbourne. The Prime Minister's main concern (he himself had never, he declared, forced his attentions on any woman against her will) was for the reputation of the Queen. A scandal such as this could do her court incalculable harm.

Melbourne insisted that Palmerston write an apology to the lady-in-waiting; she, very obligingly, accepted it and the matter was hushed up. But, according to Greville, when the Queen came to hear of it she was furious. Only the reasoned arguments of Lord Melbourne prevented her from taking any action against Lord Palmerston.

In her relationship with her uncle, King Leopold of the Belgians, Lord Melbourne was able to play a similarly placatory role. With King Leopold's influence waning as Lord Melbourne's waxed, the Queen found herself becoming increasingly irritated by what she considered her Uncle Leopold's political importuning. When in 1838 he asked her to use her influence with Lord Melbourne on behalf of Belgium in its dispute with the Dutch over the Treaty of 1831 (whereby Belgium won its independence of Holland and King Leopold his crown) she refused to do any such thing. Instead, she very properly handed King Leopold's letter over to the Prime Minister. He drafted a soothing but non-committal reply which she signed in her usual 'devoted and most affectionate' manner.

When this failed to stop her uncle's badgering, she answered more crisply: she would not, the Queen wrote firmly, wish 'to change our present delightful and familiar correspondence into a formal and stiff discussion upon political matters'. King Leopold's influence, as the Queen assured the gratified Lord Melbourne, was now '*very small*'.

But Queen Victoria's chief family irritant remained her mother, the Duchess of Kent. Both she and Lord Melbourne were shocked to discover that, far from having cleared her debts as promised, the Duchess owed over £70,000. Although Coutts' bank had come to her rescue, the Duchess could still not live within her allowance; the Queen and Lord Melbourne suspected that Sir John Conroy was helping himself to some of it.

What annoyed them even more was that Conroy claimed the Duchess's parlous financial state was due to the fact that she was being obliged to pay off the debts of her late husband, the Duke of Kent. As Queen Victoria, unknown to her mother was busily paying off her father's debts herself, Conroy's claim was particularly galling. Only much later, and then by accident, did the Duchess of Kent come to hear of her daughter's generosity. When the astonished Melbourne asked the Queen why she had not told her mother what she was doing, her answer was curiously touching.

'I don't like to praise myself,' answered the Queen.

One day in coronation year the Duchess, in an attempt at reconciliation, went to see Lord Melbourne. Admitting that she might, inadvertently, have made mistakes in the past, she now proposed that Sir John Conroy be sent abroad. Melbourne, always suspicious of the Duchess's motives and mistrusting what he assumed to be her mask of humility, refused her request. He had no intention of buying Sir John off with some well-paid foreign posting. If the Duchess wanted to be rid of Sir John Conroy, she must dismiss him herself. Nor did he think much of her idea of making it up with her long-standing rival for her daughter's affections – the Queen's adored Lehzen – by writing her an appeasing letter. The Duchess's new air of contrition, Melbourne told

the Queen, was put on; between them they agreed that the Duchess
was a foolish woman, not to be trusted.

The Prime Minister would have done better to send Conroy away
and accept the Duchess's offer of friendship. In that way, the Queen
might have avoided the full force of the domestic storm which was
about to break over her head.

4

'I Thought my Heart Would Break'

THE EXTRAORDINARY Lady Flora Hastings affair, which erupted during the opening months of 1839, is notable chiefly for the light it throws on the relationship between Queen Victoria and Lord Melbourne.

Lady Flora Hastings was one of the Duchess of Kent's ladies-in-waiting. Thirty-two and unmarried, Lady Flora was a reserved and pious young woman, with a somewhat chilling manner. This, combined with the fact that she was very attached to the Duchess, disliked the Queen's confidante Baroness Lehzen intensely, and was a member of an aggressively Tory family, would have been enough to prejudice the Queen; what set the Queen against her even more firmly was that Lady Flora was very friendly with Sir John Conroy. In fact, so convinced was Queen Victoria that Lady Flora was Conroy's spy that she warned Lord Melbourne to be careful of what he said in her presence.

During the second week of January 1839 the Queen and Lehzen noticed that Lady Flora's waist was looking suspiciously thick. They immediately jumped to the conclusion that she must be pregnant. Their conclusion was bolstered by the fact that Lord Melbourne had, with a 'knowing' look, remarked that the Duchess of Kent was jealous of Lady Flora's intimacy with Sir John Conroy. This was exactly what Queen Victoria wanted to hear. Already her ladies were gossiping about Lady Flora and Conroy having recently travelled down from Scotland in the same carriage. The Queen had no doubt that it was that 'Monster and Demon Incarnate', Sir John Conroy, who was responsible for Lady Flora's condition.

With the Queen and her ladies in a highly excited state about Lady Flora's supposed pregnancy, the senior lady of the bedchamber, Lady Tavistock, went to see Lord Melbourne about it. She should, of course, have gone to the Duchess, but with the Queen and her mother barely on speaking terms, and the Queen and her Prime Minister so close, Lady Tavistock considered it more politic to go to Melbourne. The Prime Minister, in turn, called in the Queen's physician, Sir James Clark.

Clark, whom Lady Flora had already consulted about the puzzling protuberance of her stomach, simply did not know whether she was pregnant or not. On learning this, Melbourne determined on a characteristic course of action: they must do nothing. His advice could hardly have been worse. He should have insisted that the Queen discuss the matter with her mother and that, if necessary, Lady Flora submit to a proper medical examination so that the charge could be proved one way or the other.

As things stood, the gossip simply spread. Lady Flora continued to consult Sir James Clark who (because the patient prudishly refused to be examined without her clothes) became more and more convinced that she was indeed pregnant. Only after several weeks and much manœuvring by all concerned did Lady Flora agree to a proper examination. The result was a complete vindication. Lady Flora Hastings was a virgin.

'The Court is plunged in shame and mortification . . .' wrote Charles Greville. 'The Palace is full of bickerings and heart-burnings, while the whole proceeding is looked upon by society at large as to the last degree disgusting and disgraceful. It is inconceivable how Melbourne can have permitted this disgraceful and mischievous scandal, which cannot fail to lower the Court in the eyes of the world, and from a participation in which discredit the Queen's youth and inexperience can alone exempt her. There may be objections to Melbourne's extraordinary domicilation in the Palace; but the compensation ought to be found in his good sense and experience preventing the possibility of such transactions and *tracasseries* as these.'[1]

Most mortified of all was Queen Victoria. On hearing the news of Lady Flora's innocence she immediately sent for her but as the lady-in-waiting was feeling too ill, almost a week passed before they met. Without actually apologizing – or even admitting that she might have been in any way responsible for the unfortunate incident – the Queen extended the hand of friendship to Lady Flora. It was, apparently, gratefully received.

And there the matter should have ended. But Sir James Clark, it seems, still had his doubts. Together with the other doctor who had examined Lady Flora, he communicated these doubts to Melbourne.

It was possible, the doctor told the Prime Minister, in spite of everything, that Lady Flora was indeed pregnant. Melbourne, only too ready to believe the worst, passed the information on to the Queen. She seemed equally ready to believe it.

By this stage, the story of Lady Flora's persecution had reached the ears of her family. They, understandably, were furious. They demanded of Lord Melbourne that the scandal be traced to its source and the instigator exposed. If it had been Clark, why was he still in the Queen's service? The Duchess of Kent had lost no time in dismissing him from hers. If it had been one or more of the Queen's ladies, why had they not been dismissed? Had the Queen's confidante, Baroness Lehzen, been the culprit?

In the centre of this whirlwind of angry demands, Lord Melbourne remained inactive. He dare not instigate an enquiry in case the Queen's part in promoting or even originating the slander become known.

Unsatisfied, the Hastings family published Lady Flora's full and astonishingly frank account of the business in *The Examiner*. This led to an outbreak of vicious attacks on Melbourne and the 'Palace party' in the press. The Queen's popularity plummeted. When she and Lord Melbourne rode out together in Hyde Park, they were hissed. But instead of being chastened by this public hostility, Queen Victoria was enraged. The two fashionable women who had hissed her and her Prime Minister as they drove down the course at Ascot should be 'flogged'; the editor of Lord Melbourne's most virulent critic – the Tory *Morning Post* – should be hanged; so, indeed, should the entire Hastings family. The atmosphere between the Queen's and the Duchess of Kent's households became more poisonous still. The Queen even took to cutting 'that *nasty* woman', Lady Flora, in public.

One thing only could bring this shameful situation to an end. On 5 July 1839 Lady Flora Hastings died. A *post mortem* examination revealed that she had been suffering from a tumour of the liver.

Lady Flora's death left the Queen in a highly emotional state. Yet, with almost childish obstinacy, she assured Lord Melbourne that she 'felt *no* remorse, I felt *I* had done nothing to kill her.' Despite fears that it might be stoned, she sent a carriage to represent her to the funeral.

The whole unfortunate episode revealed the Queen and Lord Melbourne at their worst; she at her most headstrong, he at his most indecisive. The root of the trouble lay in the Queen's dislike of her mother, Conroy, and their circle; but as a man of the world, Melbourne should have seen to it that this antipathy did not lead the Queen into a compromising position. And the imbroglio was an illustration of Queen Victoria at her most partisan: as strong in her dislikes as she was in her likes. The facts had to be made to fit her preconceived notions. She was not dishonest, she could never tell a lie or simulate a feeling, but once she believed something to be true, or right, it took a great deal to change her mind.

The Flora Hastings affair had still not run its course before Queen Victoria and Lord Melbourne were plunged into an even more serious crisis. For some time now Melbourne's Whig administration, with its small and shifting majority in the House of Commons, had been shaky. Then, on 6 May 1839, a combination of Tories and some Radicals, voting against the government on an issue concerned with the enforcement of certain plantation workers' rights in Jamaica, reduced its majority to unworkable proportions. On the following day, after a specially convened cabinet meeting, Lord Melbourne let the Queen know that his government had no option but to resign.

She was appalled. 'The state of agony, grief and despair into which this placed me may be easier imagined than described!' she wailed. '*All, all* my happiness gone! That happy peaceful life destroyed, that dearest kind Lord Melbourne no more my minister ... I sobbed and cried much; could only put on my dressing gown.'

Lord Melbourne arrived to see her soon after midday. It was some minutes before she could muster up enough courage to go in and face him. 'When I did,' she writes, 'I really thought my heart would break; he was standing near the window; I took that kind, dear hand of his, and sobbed and grasped his hand in both mine and looked at him and sobbed out, "You will not forsake me"; I held his hand for a little while, unable to leave go; and he gave me such a look of kindness, pity and affection, and could hardly utter for tears, "Oh! no," in such a touching voice ...'.

But he had no choice. The Queen would be obliged to accept a new, Tory, prime minister. Three times during that afternoon she wrote to Melbourne, begging him to dine or, at least, to call on her again. He refused to dine; it would not be proper while the negotiations for forming a new government were in progress. Could they not perhaps meet, suggested the Queen, as though by chance, in the park? In the end he did call on her, bringing with him written instructions for the course she would now have to follow.

'You don't know what a dreadful thing this is for me,' she said, and when he again told her that he had better not see her until the new government had been formed, she broke down. 'I sobbed much, again held his hand in both mine, and kept holding his hand for some time fast in one of mine, as if I felt that in doing so he could not leave me . . .'.

But eventually he did, and on the following morning the Queen was forced to send for Sir Robert Peel. In the course of a twenty-minute audience she asked him to form a new government. She hated doing so. Throughout the audience she remained, she claimed proudly, 'very much collected, civil and high.' Not only could she not bear the thought of losing Lord M, but she disliked Peel intensely. Melbourne had warned her to make allowances for Sir Robert Peel's 'close, stiff' manner, but she was incapable of doing any such thing. She found Peel chilly, gauche, unattractive. To her, he seemed to have the mincing precision of a dancing-master; his smile was said to resemble the silver plate on a coffin. A 'cold, unfeeling, disagreeable man', is how the Queen described him; 'how different, how dreadfully different, to that frank, open, natural and most kind, warm manner of Lord Melbourne,' she wrote.

In fact, in many ways Peel was a more admirable man than Melbourne. The Queen's description of Lord M as 'a most truly honest, straightforward and noble-minded man' would have suited Sir Robert Peel much better. Not only in integrity, but in intelligence and ability, Peel outranked Melbourne. But, lacking Melbourne's charm, good looks and slightly raffish air, Peel could not hope to please the Queen.

For exactly the same reasons, forty years later, did Queen Victoria prefer the seductive Disraeli to the more upright Gladstone.

She did not have to put up with Peel for long. Melbourne's parting advice that the Queen should express to Peel the hope that she would be allowed to keep her ladies-in-waiting put an idea into her head. She dried her tears and prepared to do battle. Peel, in the course of his first interview with her, had suggested that a few of the more important posts in the Queen's household be changed. His request was perfectly reasonable. He, as the Tory Prime Minister, could hardly be expected to countenance a situation in which all the ladies surrounding the sovereign were the wives of his political opponents. He had no intention of removing all the Queen's ladies; only of changing those holding the more important posts.

But the Queen would have none of it. During her second interview with Peel, she announced that she had no intention of giving up her ladies. When the disconcerted Peel asked if she meant to retain them all, her reply was unequivocal. 'All', she snapped. Unless she surrendered *some* of them, countered Peel, he could not accept the premiership.

This was exactly what she wanted. In a foam of excitement, she scribbled a note to summon Lord Melbourne. 'It was a true and real and unexpected happiness to see him again after so much anxiety,' she enthused. 'I took and pressed his hand warmly.'

At a hastily convened meeting of Whig ministers, Melbourne read out a summary of his letters from the Queen on the subject of her ladies. At the sound of their defiant phrases, almost worthy of Queen Elizabeth I addressing her troops on the eve of the Armada ('they wished to treat me like a girl, but I will show them that I am Queen of England', Victoria had written[2]), the ministers were overwhelmed. How could they possibly desert such a woman and such a monarch? A letter was drafted to the effect that the Queen was not prepared to give up her ladies. This she was only too ready to sign. On 10 May, the fourth day of the crisis, Peel declined office.

The following day, Lord Melbourne was somewhat disconcerted to find that the Queen had been less than honest with him. She had all along given the impression Peel had insisted that she change *all* her ladies; now, on seeing the most recent letter from Peel to the Queen, Melbourne realized he had asked for only *some* changes. '*Some* or *all*', declared the Queen, 'was the same.'

This was when Melbourne should have acted with more firmness; when he should have convinced his colleagues that it would be both unwise and dishonest to pretend that Peel had insisted on the dismissal of all the ladies. But he allowed himself to be swept along by those who were determined to champion the Queen. Stifling his own misgivings, Melbourne resumed office as Prime Minister. He was resuming office, he declared in a ringing speech to the House, 'solely because I will not abandon my sovereign in a situation of difficulty and distress.'[3]

That night he dined with the Queen. 'He was very excited the whole evening,' she wrote, 'talking to himself and pulling his hair about, which always makes him look so much handsomer.'

Excited Melbourne may have been, but he was not nearly as excited as the Queen. The success of the so-called Bedchamber Plot had been almost entirely due to her. In it, the Prime Minister had played a curiously passive role. The theory that he had cynically instructed her to provoke a clash with Peel for his own political ends is as mistaken as the theory that he had allowed his devotion to the Queen to overcome his better judgement. Melbourne, as Philip Ziegler has put it, 'was neither Machiavelli nor Galahad'; 'if anyone did the manipulating it was the Queen.'[4]

Queen Victoria knew perfectly well that Peel had not threatened to change all her ladies. She did, though, suspect that *some* might eventually lead to *all*; that in time Peel would sweep away all her friends and supporters, including Baroness Lehzen. The Bedchamber Plot had erupted in the middle of the Flora Hastings affair, with the Tories championing the Queen's adversaries – her mother, Conroy and the Hastings family. Might not a bevy of hostile Tory ladies-in-waiting gang up against her; might they not reveal that it was she and Lehzen who had first voiced suspicions that Lady Flora might be pregnant? How, in fact, could the Queen hope to face the continuing and acrimonious Flora Hastings affair without the support of Lord Melbourne?

Sixty years later, Queen Victoria admitted that she had behaved improperly. 'Yes, I was very hot about it and so were my ladies,' she said to her private secretary, Sir Arthur Bigge, 'as I had been so brought up under Lord Melbourne; but I was *very* young, only twenty, and never should have acted so again – Yes! it was a mistake.'[5]

What the Queen did not admit to Bigge, however, was the strength of her feelings for Lord Melbourne at the time. It was in connection with the Bedchamber Plot that Charles Greville made his penetrating comment on the nature of these feelings. His comment can bear repeating in full. 'The simple truth in this case is that the Queen could not endure the thought of parting with Melbourne, who is everything to her,' he wrote. 'Her feelings which are *sexual* though She does not know it, and are probably not very well defined to herself, are of a strength sufficient to bear down on all prudential considerations . . .'.[6]

As so often with Queen Victoria, passion had overcome prudence; her heart had run away with her head.

And so the idyll could be resumed. The four-day crisis was over. Although Melbourne did not realize it at the time, he was to remain at the Queen's side for almost two more years. Once again the two of them could sit together in the intimacy of the Queen's Blue Closet, or go out riding under the great trees in Windsor Park, or page through albums in the lamplight after dinner. All, writes Lord David Cecil lyrically, seems as before: 'the mingling, shimmering, enchanted flow of entertaining instruction and ironical wisdom and delicate sentiment and carefree fanciful fun.'[7] Melbourne could continue to startle her with his heterodox opinions or amuse her with his wryly expressed asides.

And he could still touch her by his romantic gestures. Every week, for instance (and in spite of the fact that he always claimed that city flowers were much better than country ones and that gardens were 'dull things'), he had a bouquet send up to her from Brocket, his country house. And she would retaliate. 'The Queen sends the little *charm* which she hopes may keep him from *all* evil ...' she one day wrote from Windsor.

This period brought the Queen other satisfactions as well. In June 1839 Sir John Conroy suddenly resigned from the Duchess of Kent's household and left the country. Those who hoped that his going might lead to a reconciliation between the Queen and her mother were disappointed. The Duchess seemed willing enough, but not even Lord Melbourne could persuade the Queen to meet her mother half-way.

It was towards coaxing the Queen out of this sort of stubborn partisanship that Melbourne now began to direct his energies. Appreciating that, sooner or later, his still precariously balanced government would fall and that she would be forced to work with Sir Robert Peel, he tried to get her to think more kindly of the Tory politician. Peel, he said, always spoke very highly of her; his faults were of manner and inexperience; unlike Melbourne, Peel was not accustomed to 'talking with Kings'. The Tories were not as bad as she imagined; how could she hope to do business with them if she treated them as enemies? She should be polite to Tory ladies, even invite leading Tories to dinner now and then.

But the Queen would not hear of it. To her, personalities were always more important than politics. In her eyes the Tories meant Peel, whom she disliked; and the Whigs Melbourne, to whom she was devoted. Nothing that her Prime Minister could say could overcome her prejudices. Once, when Greville congratulated him on the way he handled the Queen, Melbourne exclaimed 'By God, I am at it morning, noon and night!'[8]

The two of them were beginning to have their differences about religion as well. The better the Queen came to know her Prime Minister, the more she wondered if he were quite as pious and moral as she had at first assumed. He certainly did not go to church very often and, when he did, he sighed and fidgeted. He did not like going to church, he explained in his wry fashion: he was a Quietist, which meant that he was so perfect that he was exempt from all external forms of worship.

'Nobody is gay now,' he one day sighed, 'they are so religious.' But that, replied the shocked Queen, was as it should be; how could anyone be *too* religious? The truth was that Lord Melbourne was a relic of the easy-going, rational eighteenth century, while Queen Victoria was representative of the more serious-minded age that was to bear her name.

Once, when the Queen spoke of her horror of the hard-drinking days of the Regency and of the scandalous dissipations of her wicked uncles, Melbourne tried to soften the harshness of her strictures. 'But they were jolly fellows . . .' he said wistfully; 'times have changed, but I do not know if they have improved.'

He was beginning to feel his age. He was just over sixty, and a life of heavy eating and drinking was taking its toll. He often felt ill and tired; he suffered from lumbago and indigestion. The Queen noticed that he was becoming absent-minded; sometimes he would nod off to sleep as he sat chatting to her. When she urged him to seek medical advice, he argued that it would do no good. It was old age, he sighed, old age and constant worry.

Sympathetic she may have been, but the Queen resented it whenever ill-health or the pressure of work kept him from her. As possessive as ever, she accused him of neglecting her. Why did he now spend only two days a week at Windsor when he used to spend five? Why did he take his leave of her so early in the evenings? How dare he say that he was unable to dine with her? Was it that he preferred dining at Holland House?

'The Queen has received both Lord Melbourne's notes', she once wrote imperiously from Buckingham Palace; 'she was a good deal vexed at his not coming, as she had begged him herself to do so, and as he wrote to say he would, and also as she thinks it right and of importance that Lord Melbourne should be here at large dinners; the Queen *insists* on his coming to dinner tomorrow, and also begs him to do so on Wednesday, her two last nights in town, and as she will probably not see him at all for two days when she goes on Friday . . .'.

Although Queen Victoria did not realize it, her peevishness and possessiveness were symptomatic of a deeper dissatisfaction. She was after all, a young, high-spirited and warm-blooded girl with all a normal girl's yearnings for the company of her male contemporaries. Delightful as Lord Melbourne undoubtedly was, he could not provide for all her needs. Gradually, she was passing out of her hero-worshipping stage; she was beginning – quite consciously – to feel the need of a more emotionally and sexually fulfilling relationship.

The Queen could not have been insensible of the fact that one of her gentlemen, the dashing Lord Alfred Paget, was very taken with her. Not only did this 'handsome young Calmuck-looking fellow'[9] always wear her portrait; he did not hide his admiration as in black velvet riding habit, top hat and floating veil the Queen went riding at the head of one of her great cavalcades through Windsor Park.

What she thought of Lord Alfred Paget one does not know but – to her Journal at least – the Queen made her feelings about the young Tsarevich, Grand Duke Alexander, who visited her in May 1839, only too clear. His tall, magnificently uniformed figure, his dazzling smile, his warm handshake and, above all, his masterful dancing, made a considerable impression. Under the blaze of candles in the Red Drawing-room at Windsor, the Grand Duke (who was 'so strong') wheeled her round in mazurkas and valses and guided her through the new German country dance, the *Grossvater*, which entailed much jumping over and crawling under a large handkerchief. At one stage, as they bent their heads together, he caught his hair in her wreath of flowers. 'I never enjoyed myself more. We were all so merry . . .' wrote the excited young Queen. 'I got to bed by a quarter to three and could not sleep till five.'

'I really am quite in love with the Grand Duke', she wrote a couple of days later; 'he is a dear, delightful young man.' When he took his leave at the end of his stay at Windsor, he pressed her hand and kissed her cheek 'in a very warm and affectionate manner.' She was, she repeated, 'quite in love' with him, hastily adding that she was only 'talking jokingly'.

The departure of the Russian Grand Duke left Queen Victoria feeling, she complained to Lord Melbourne, 'dull and flat'.

'A young person like me must *sometimes* have young people to laugh with,' she sighed. 'Nothing so natural,' replied the always sympathetic Prime Minister. But his eyes, she noticed, were wet with tears.

Yet the idea of marriage remained repugnant to the Queen. For most of the time she was quite content with the company of the urbane Lord M. One day, in the spring of 1839, the two of them had a talk on what she described, with her Germanic spelling, as a 'schocking' subject: her possible marriage. Mustering up her courage (the topic, she admitted in her Journal, 'terrified' her), the Queen told her Prime Minister that her Uncle Leopold and her Uncle Ernest (the Duke of Saxe-Coburg) were pressing her to marry her cousin, Prince Albert. She could, she explained to Lord M, decide nothing until she had seen

Albert again. This would not be until the autumn, when King Leopold was arranging for Cousin Albert to visit her.

The subject was hardly less 'schocking' to Lord Melbourne. Alive to both the Queen's reluctance and the fact that a husband would put an end to the intimacy between them, he raised several objections. 'How would it be with the Duchess?' he asked; in other words, might not Prince Albert, as the Duchess of Kent's nephew, side with her against the Queen? 'I assured him he need have no fear *whatever* on that score,' she replied.

Casting about for other objections, Melbourne claimed that the marrying of cousins was 'not a good thing'. Her Coburg cousins, particularly, were not a good thing: they were unpopular abroad and the Russians hated them. The Duchess, he pointed out, was a 'good specimen' of the Coburgs; at this the two of them laughed heartily.

They then ran through the names of other possible princes; not one of them was suitable. In any case, argued Melbourne, no foreigner would be popular. But nor would it do for her to marry an Englishman; it would bring her down to a dangerous equality with her subjects and create all sorts of difficulties and jealousies.

One Englishman whom the Queen could have married, and whose rank would have created no difficulties, was her first cousin, Prince George of Cambridge. A couple of months older than she, Prince George was the son of Adolphus, Duke of Cambridge, seventh son of King George III. The late King William IV had certainly been very anxious for Victoria to marry her cousin George, and there can be no doubt that the marriage would have been popular. Even as a young man Prince George was the sort of John Bull figure that the public appreciated. 'Upon returning to England', he once said, 'one feels that everything here is so superior to what one has seen [abroad] that one is doubly proud of being an Englishman and of belonging to a nation that has such a country to live in.'[10] This was exactly the kind of remark his countrymen loved to hear.

How different, one wonders, might Queen Victoria's life have been if she had married the Duke of Cambridge? His subsequent history hardly suggests that he would have made a suitable husband for the impressionable young Queen. At the age of twenty-eight he contracted a private marriage with an actress, Louise Fairbrother, who became known as Mrs FitzGeorge and who bore him three FitzGeorge sons. Bluff, philistine and increasingly reactionary (his thirty-nine-year spell as Commander-in-Chief of the British Army was chiefly remarkable for his opposition to any suggestion of modernization or reform),

George, Duke of Cambridge would never have been the sort of preceptor the Queen both craved and needed. She would have learned precious little from him. A loveless marriage – and that is what it would have been – for a woman who always needed to be loved and in love, might have been calamitous.

Looking in later years 'like a very old fat red-faced baby in his uniform', writes one observer, the Duke of Cambridge 'only cared for parades and the social side, and considered that a pretty wife was one of the best recommendations an officer could have for promotion.'[11] The middle-aged Queen Victoria always referred to him as 'poor George'.

Her adjectives, in these early days, were distinctly more robust. She considered her cousin George an 'odious boy' and once described him as '*very* ugly, his skin in a schocking state'. Not for one moment, it seems, did she ever seriously consider marrying him.

So Lord Melbourne's arguments against marriage merely backed up the Queen's own reservations. There was no need for her to worry at all for three or four years, she declared.

'I said I dreaded the thought of marrying', she noted in her Journal that evening; 'that I was so accustomed to have my own way that I thought it was ten to one that I shouldn't agree with anybody.'

'Oh,' answered Melbourne, who by now knew his headstrong young mistress very well, 'you will have it still.'

But she was not so sure. In any case, her 'present feeling' as she put it, 'was quite against ever marrying ....'.

And so, to the great gratification of both Queen and Prime Minister, the matter was shelved.

Uncle Leopold, though, was not to be so easily fobbed off. Knowing his niece, he felt sure that one glimpse of the handsome young Prince Albert was all that would be necessary to overcome her reservations. So he continued with his preparations for the autumn visit to England of Prince Albert and his elder brother, Prince Ernest. At this, Queen Victoria took fright. On 15 July 1839 she wrote King Leopold a long letter which she sent by special courier. In it, she asked him to cancel the proposed visit of her cousins.

Did Albert know, she asked, of his father's and his uncle's marriage plans? And did he know that there was '*no engagement*' between him and her? 'I can make *no final promise this year*, for, at the *very earliest*, any such event could not take place till *two or three years hence*.' She had a '*great* repugnance' to any change of her present position; nor was there any '*anxiety* evinced in *this country*' for her early marriage.

'Though all the reports of Albert are most favourable, and though I have little doubt that I shall like him, still one can never answer beforehand for *feelings*, and I may not have the *feeling* for him which is requisite to ensure happiness. I may like him as a friend, and as a *cousin*, and as a *brother*, but no *more*; and should this be the case ... I am very anxious that it should be understood that I am not guilty of any breach of promise, for I *never gave any* ...'.

The astute King Leopold knew better than to press the matter too strongly. As a man of the world, and a particularly well-informed one at that, he would have understood his niece's preoccupation with Lord Melbourne. The King agreed that she need not give Albert any immediate answer: all he asked was that the proposed visit of his nephews take place. To this Queen Victoria acquiesced. And Lord Melbourne, when she discussed the matter with him, was equally acquiescent. There would be no harm in the Queen just seeing her cousins. As for marriage, said Lord Melbourne emphatically, 'It is *not* NECESSARY.'

In the meantime, decided King Leopold, it might be as well to expose his niece to a little Coburg family *gemütlichkeit*; what better way of softening her up for the arrival of Prince Albert? So in the course of the autumn she was submerged in a positive flood of Coburg relations. Her uncle Duke Ferdinand of Saxe-Coburg brought three of his children – her cousins Augustus, Leopold and Victoire. With them was yet another cousin, Alexander Mensdorff-Pouilly, whose brothers she had met in her Kensington Palace days. The family party was then joined by King Leopold and his second wife, Queen Louise.

Throughout this gathering of the Coburg clan, Queen Victoria was in ecstasies. As warm-hearted, as sentimental, as effervescent as ever, she could hardly praise her relations highly enough. She revelled in their nicknames, their family jokes, their good-natured teasing. Gabbling away in German, she experienced the sort of sense of belonging that she had not felt for years. They were all '*so* intimate, *so* united, *so* happy'; she was half in love with the lot of them. Her particular favourite was the half-French Alexander Mensdorff-Pouilly and, as always with Queen Victoria, it was his appearance that attracted her. When Lord Melbourne teased her about her infatuation with Alexander's looks, she frankly admitted that she was 'not insensible to beauty'. Even Lord M had to agree that Alexander had beautiful hair; no German, he said in his bantering way, could ever have such hair.

The parting from this merry crowd, as they sailed away from Woolwich, left the Queen feeling, as all partings tended to, desolate.

Even dear Lord M seemed incapable of filling the gap in her life. In fact, she accused him of being glad that her cousins had gone. She found herself becoming increasingly jittery and short-tempered as the time for Prince Albert's arrival drew near. She even began to snap at Lord Melbourne.

On one occasion her temper flared up and she swept out of the room. On her return she was still angry with him and the Prime Minister, accustomed to seating himself without her invitation, suddenly felt that he dare not do so. She had to give him permission. 'I cannot think what possessed me,' she afterwards wrote, 'for I love this *dear excellent* man who is kindness and forbearance itself, *most dearly.*'

On the morning of 10 October 1839, as she and Lord Melbourne were walking on the Terrace at Windsor, one of her pages came dashing up with a letter for her. It was from King Leopold: it told her that her cousins would be arriving at Windsor that very evening.

At 7.30 p.m. the Queen was standing at the head of the great stone staircase to receive her cousins. She had been prepared for Albert to be good-looking, but at the sight of this tall, well-built, astonishingly handsome young man, she was overwhelmed. In a flash, she fell in love.

'It was with some emotion that I beheld Albert,' she afterwards wrote, 'who is *beautiful.*'

Part Two

PRINCE ALBERT

'Bliss Beyond Belief!'

AT FIRST GLANCE, Prince Albert would seem to fit very uneasily into that company of flamboyant, unorthodox men to whom Queen Victoria was usually drawn. He has gone down in history as a cold, dreary, pedantic figure, virtuous to a fault and high-minded to the point of tedium. This perception of the Prince Consort as a plodding and un-interesting worthy was to a large extent fostered by the widowed Queen herself. Determined to immortalize her late husband as Albert the Good, she merely succeeded in presenting him as Albert the Dull.

This sombre portrait, never an accurate one, was considerably less true of the Prince in his younger days, at the time when he first became engaged to Queen Victoria. Although at no stage raffish, or debonair, Prince Albert was a warm, sympathetic, deeply sensitive and highly romantic young man. His eyes filled with tears as easily as Lord Melbourne's, and his tastes and interests were far from those of the average philistine princeling. This nonconformity, combined with his dreamy good looks, cast the twenty-year-old Prince Albert of Saxe-Coburg and Gotha in very much the same mould as those other colourful personalities who set the Queen's pulses pounding so pleasurably.

Prince Albert's childhood in the Duchy of Coburg was relatively unconventional. As his father, Duke Ernest of Saxe-Coburg and Gotha, was persistently unfaithful, his vivacious mother – born Princess Louise of Saxe-Gotha-Altenburg – eventually felt driven to seek consolation elsewhere. When Prince Albert was five (he was born on 26 August 1819, almost exactly three months after his cousin, the future Queen Victoria) his parents separated. His mother left Coburg and, after her divorce from Duke Ernest, married her lover. Albert and his elder brother Ernest were raised by their father and never saw their mother again. But Albert did not forget her. Nor, apparently, did he ever blame her for deserting her profligate husband.

A rumour has persisted to this day that Prince Albert was illegitimate: that his father was Baron von Meyern, a 'cultivated' Jewish chamberlain at the little court at Coburg. It was apparently Lord Melbourne's chance remark to Queen Victoria – that marriage between first cousins was 'not a good thing' – which gave rise to the story. Melbourne's reservations about the proposed marriage between the Queen and her first cousin Albert were only overcome, it is claimed, on his being told the 'secret', by King Leopold and Baron Stockmar, that Victoria and Albert were not really cousins.

The allegation found its way into print in a virulently anti-Semitic book published in Berlin in 1921. Giving weight to the story was the fact that Prince Albert in no way resembled his father or brother; neither in looks, temperament nor morals. To some, he seemed to have a slightly Jewish cast of face and a definitely Jewish air of melancholy.

The story is highly unlikely. There is no evidence that Albert's mother was unfaithful in the early years of her marriage, during the time when her two sons were born. Indeed, far from being a frequently faithless wife, Princess Louise seems to have had only one extra-marital affair – with the man whom she eventually married. Nor would Lord Melbourne have forbidden a marriage between the Queen and her first cousin. Such marriages were commonplace among the royal families of Europe at the time, and it is extremely unlikely that King Leopold, Lord Melbourne and Baron Stockmar would have been party to a marriage between the Queen of England and a bastard.

The rumour is relevant only in that it was Prince Albert's type of beauty – romantic, *triste*, un-English – which made a particular appeal to Queen Victoria.

Unlike Lord Melbourne, in whose life women had played an influential role, the young Albert had been fashioned in a world of men. Even as a child he is said to have shown 'a great dislike to being in [the] charge of women.'[1] This dislike may have had its roots in the veneration in which he held his beautiful, betrayed and vanished mother. He was apparently determined that no one else should take her place; or perhaps he feared that contact with women always led to trouble.

Prince Albert grew up in the company of his strict but genial father, his extrovert brother and his adored tutor, Herr Florschütz. His education was completed in the all-male atmosphere of Bonn

University. The ubiquitous Baron Stockmar shepherded him on a tour of Italy. His father's younger brother, King Leopold, subjected him to a tireless course of grooming for his designated role as Queen Victoria's future husband.

This almost exclusively masculine society did not in any way coarsen him. Prince Albert matured into a sensitive and scholarly young man with a remarkable range of interests. His cultural enthusiasms – for music, literature and painting – were pronounced. In the Sistine Chapel, he once reported to his more pedestrian brother Ernest, he 'stood silent, just letting its splendours sweep over me in waves of ecstasy.'[2] For his native Coburg, and particularly for the family's country home the Rosenau ('the paradise of our childhood') he harboured feelings of almost feminine sentimentality.

Nor did he show any trace of the licentiousness of his father and brother; or, indeed, of so many of his male contemporaries. Prince Albert was not a prig, but sexual adventuring held no attractions for him. In fact, he remained largely impervious to feminine charm and beauty. His attitude towards women was always chivalrous, but remained unemotional. Never during these years of growing up, nor in later life, did any woman other than Queen Victoria play a significant part in Prince Albert's life.

Inevitably there have been innuendos, from Lytton Strachey and others, that Prince Albert's 'marked distaste for women' was attributable to 'his peculiar upbringing or to some more fundamental idiosyncracy';[3] in short, that he was homosexual. There is no more substance in this allegation than there is in the rumour that he was Jewish. Prince Albert was simply that rare nineteenth-century royal phenomenon: a chaste young man who, once married, became a loyal, loving and faithful husband.

But it must have been with some trepidation that this shy and serious-minded prince considered the question of his proposed marriage to Queen Victoria. He had not been nearly as taken with his cousin as she had been with him during their first meeting in the spring of 1836, when they were both sixteen. Since then his father had strengthened his reservations by reporting, after a visit to England, that she was a 'virago queen' whose household was in a state of turmoil. This description was backed up by King Leopold's well-meant warnings about the Queen's defects of character: her high-handedness, her moodiness, her partisanship. The peremptory tone of her letters and the conditions which she was laying down before she would even consider marriage further unnerved him.

As Prince Albert set out in October 1839 on the journey to Windsor
which was to decide his fate, he must have imagined that he was about
to meet, if not exactly a monster, then certainly a very difficult young
woman.

Although it was for his exceptional cerebral qualities that Queen
Victoria came to admire Prince Albert so passionately, it was for his
physical attractions, and those alone, that she fell so instantly in love
with him. She always responded – would always respond – to masculine good looks, and at the sight of this handsome young man all
hesitations about their proposed marriage were swept away. Within a
few hours of first seeing him, and without getting to know him any
better, she had made up her mind.

For the first four days of his stay (by the morning of the fourth she
had proposed to him) almost all her thoughts were of his beauty.
'Albert really is quite charming, and so excessively handsome,' she
gushed; 'such beautiful blue eyes, and exquisite nose, and such a pretty
mouth with delicate mustachios and slight but very slight whiskers; a
beautiful figure, broad in the shoulders and a fine waist; my heart is
quite *going* ...'. To see him dance was a delight: 'he does it so beautifully, holds himself so well with that beautiful figure of his.' A gratified
Uncle Leopold was treated to a paean on Albert's '*most striking*' looks,
and again and again in her Journal the enraptured Queen made note
of his manifold physical attractions: his bewitching eyes, the colour of
his 'dear lovely face', his muscular thighs in 'tight cazimere pantaloons
(nothing under them) and high boots'.

'Oh! when I look at those lovely, lovely blue eyes,' she sighed, 'I
feel they are those of an angel.'

On 15 October 1839 the Queen summoned Prince Albert to her
sitting-room and made her celebrated proposal of marriage. As Queen
of England, it was she who was obliged to do the proposing: he would
never have presumed, she naïvely claimed, 'to take the liberty' himself.
Once he had accepted, 'we embraced each other over and over again,
and he was *so* kind, *so* affectionate; Oh! to *feel* I was, and am, loved
by *such* an Angel as Albert was *too great a delight to describe*; he is
perfection; perfection in every way – in beauty – in everything!'

That dearest, dearest Albert should have been a trifle overcome by
the suddenness and intensity with which Queen Victoria fell in love
with him is understandable. 'The climax', as he admitted in a letter to
Baron Stockmar, 'has come upon us with surprise, before we could

have expected it.' But he was well enough satisfied. Before arriving at Windsor he had not known whether the marriage would take place at all; now he could only be pleased and flattered by the ardour of the Queen's feelings for him. 'The openness of manner in which she told me this quite enchanted me,' he reported to one of his grandmothers, 'and I was quite carried away by it.'[4]

It is often implied that an emotionally and sexually indifferent Prince Albert was stampeded into marriage by the irresistible force of Queen Victoria's passion and by the dynastic machinations of King Leopold. This is not true. Although he was not as besotted with her as she was with him, his feelings towards her were warm and loving. The Queen was, after all, an attractive and lively young woman, at her best in his company. With his natural reserve, Prince Albert was incapable of making a public show of his emotions. Indeed, he bemoaned the fact that even in private – in his letters to her – he appeared 'so cold and stiff'.

Those who knew him intimately claim that, out of the public eye, Prince Albert was quite different from the withdrawn, formal and circumspect figure of popular imagination. On the contrary, and particularly in these younger days, he was cheerful, amusing, amiable. Lord Melbourne's sister, Lady Cowper, describes him as 'a very charming young man, very well mannered and handsome and gay.'[5] In his red leather top-boots, and with his sleek greyhound Eos at his heels, Prince Albert could look positively dashing.

To his confidant Stockmar Prince Albert admitted that his engagement marked 'one of the happiest days of my life'. He even quoted Schiller: 'The eye sees Heaven open/The heart is bathed in blessedness.'

Had Prince Albert not returned Queen Victoria's feelings, he would have had to be an actor of consummate skill or a charlatan of considerable calculation to convince her, so completely, that he loved her. 'He was *so* affectionate, *so* kind, *so* dear,' she wrote; 'we kissed each other again and again and he called me "Darling little one, I love you *so* much" and that we should have a very fortunate life together. Oh! what *too* sweet delightful moments are these!! Oh! how *blessed*, how happy I am to think he is *really* mine; I can scarcely believe myself to be *so* blessed. I kissed his dear hand and do feel *so* grateful to him; he is such an Angel, such a *very* great Angel! We sit so nicely side by side on that little blue sofa; no two Lovers could ever be happier than we are!'

She was even prepared to delight in his somewhat backhanded compliment that he could hardly believe that her little hands *were* hands, as the only hands he had hitherto held were those of his brother Ernest.

Yet even now, when the Queen seemed to be taking all the initiative, Prince Albert was emerging as the tutor and she the pupil. Queen Victoria may have been stubborn, headstrong, determined to have her own way and deeply conscious of her position, but she was still in search of a father-figure. She still craved guidance.

And in Prince Albert, no less than in Lord Melbourne, she had an only too willing master. This, after his beauty, was what made him so attractive to her. She sensed that he was morally and intellectually her superior. He was more earnest, more conscientious, more controlled than she. 'I intend to train myself to be a good and useful man,' he had once written, and it was this moral strength in him that appealed to her. Before long she was promising to cure herself of bad habits, to try to control her temper, even to improve her handwriting. 'Dearest beloved Albert,' she wrote, 'I pray daily and nightly that I may be more worthy of you, dearest, dearest Albert.'

Having remained at Windsor for over a month, and with the wedding date set for three months hence, 10 February 1840, Prince Albert returned to his beloved Coburg. The Queen pressed her face against 'that dear soft cheek, fresh and pink like a rose,' and then watched him drive away. She 'cried much, felt wretched, yet happy to think we should meet so soon again!' she wrote that evening. 'Oh! how I love him, how intensely, how devotedly, how ardently!'

Only after Prince Albert had gone could the Queen once more give her full attention to Lord Melbourne. She apologized for being so tiresome and stupid these days. She could think, she explained, of only one thing.

That, said Lord Melbourne quietly, was 'very natural'.

Bowing to the inevitable, Lord Melbourne helped prepare the ground for the Queen's forthcoming marriage. While admitting that Prince Albert was 'certainly a very fine young man, very good looking,' he was not quite so sure about his other qualities. 'As to his character,' he reported to Lord John Russell, 'that we must always take our chance of.'[6]

Yet, for all his philosophic acceptance of the situation, the Prime Minister could not help regarding the Prince as something of a usurper – of his place in the Queen's heart, and of his position as her most trusted adviser.

Appreciating the feelings of a great many of his countrymen that in

Prince Albert they were simply having another penniless and unimportant German princeling foisted on them, Melbourne was aware that he had to move with great circumspection in making the arrangements. He was not, unfortunately, circumspect enough. In the three months between the Queen's engagement and her marriage, the Prime Minister was embroiled in several major arguments, not only in Parliament, but with the Queen and her prospective bridegroom.

One such argument concerned the Prince's future title. King Leopold was all for Prince Albert being made a peer: it would make him less foreign-sounding. With this suggestion none of the principals agreed: Albert because he wanted to retain his own name; Melbourne because it might lead to the accusation that the Prince, as a member of the House of Lords, was meddling in politics; and the Queen because it was not nearly good enough for her dearest Angel. She wanted him created King Consort. Melbourne would not hear of it.

'For God's sake, Ma'am,' he warned, 'let's have no more of that. If you get the English people into the way of making kings, you'll get them into the way of un-making them.'[7]

This question of his title led directly to that of his rank. The Queen was determined that, in order of precedence, her husband must rank immediately after herself. In this she came up against the opposition, both of her royal uncles and of the Tories in Parliament. Melbourne's mishandling of the matter in the House resulted in it being left in abeyance. Not until after her marriage did the Queen discover that she was empowered to declare her husband's precedence by royal prerogative.

In the meantime, the parliamentary opposition infuriated her. She was, she declared, 'perfectly frantic'. To Melbourne she raged against the 'abominable infamous Tories'. As long as she lived she would never forgive 'these infernal scoundrels', these 'vile, confounded, infernal Tories'.

'Don't be angry,' advised the Prime Minister. But he was blowing against a hurricane. 'Poor dear Albert,' she raged, 'how cruelly are they ill-using that dearest Angel! Monsters! You Tories will be punished. Revenge! Revenge!'

She was equally incensed by Parliament's refusal to grant Prince Albert the expected £50,000 annual income. Melbourne had assured her that it would be granted without question; in the event, the allowance was reduced to £30,000 a year. To calm her anger, Melbourne was obliged to draw her attention – for the first time in their association – to the various economic ills besetting the country. They, he explained, were the underlying reason for the cut in the Prince's allowance. He only half-convinced her. She was more inclined to blame the infernal, infamous Tories.

She blamed them, too, for the trumped-up outcry about Prince Albert's 'papistical leanings'. Lord Melbourne, in composing the Queen's Declaration of Marriage to the privy counsellors, had omitted any reference to Prince Albert's religion. The Prime Minister had wanted to avoid giving offence both to his Irish Catholic supporters and to those members of the Coburg family who had readily embraced the Catholic faith in order to make dynastically advantageous marriages. The Duke of Wellington outwitted Lord Melbourne – and put an end to the outcry – by successfully moving an amendment to the effect that the adjective 'Protestant' be added to the word 'Prince' in the Congratulatory Address in the House of Lords.

Where Queen Victoria and Lord Melbourne joined forces against Prince Albert was in the matter of the Prince's future household. Albert, very properly, wanted his staff to be composed of both Whigs and Tories, but the Queen and the Prime Minister insisted that they all be Whigs, or rather, 'non-party' Whigs. Indeed, Lord Melbourne's own private secretary, George Anson, was assigned to the Prince.

In vain did Prince Albert protest against these arrangements. In a series of condescending letters to the Prince, the Prime Minister spelt out the young man's obligations in the matter. Queen Victoria was no less emphatic. Her letters may have been more gracious, but they were equally resolute. Not for the last time did Prince Albert catch a glimpse of that steeliness which was at the core of the Queen's personality; 'a vein of iron', reported Lady Lyttleton, when in charge of the royal children, 'runs through her most extraordinary character.'[8] She who was so anxious to be led was no less anxious to be obeyed.

Prince Albert had no choice but to submit. 'I am glad to say,' reported the triumphant Queen to her Uncle Leopold, that Albert 'consents to my choosing his People.'

Yet there was no denying that gradually, as the wedding date drew near, the Queen and her Prime Minister often found themselves on opposing sides. In that struggle for the Queen's heart and soul, Prince Albert was winning hands down. This was particularly true in matters of sexual morality. Melbourne's easy-going, eighteenth-century attitudes were in stark contrast to the virtuousness of the young couple. When Prince Albert wrote to suggest that the Queen choose only bridesmaids whose mothers had led blameless lives (more, one imagines, for the sake of the Queen's reputation than from excessive prudery), Melbourne was astonished. While such conditions might apply to lowly-born people, he argued, they could not possibly be applied to people of rank. It was the Queen's turn to be astonished. How, she asked, could there be one moral standard for the low and another for the high?

Talking one day of the amorous adventures of a young Russian grand duke, the Queen swore that she could never marry a man who had loved another woman.

'Oh! one affair before marriage is nothing,' said Lord M airily. In any case, if she really loved the man, she would not mind his having had an affair.

'Yes, I should,' declared the Queen.

On another occasion she admitted to the Prime Minister that one of the things she liked most about Prince Albert was that he paid no attention to other women.

'No,' answered the cynical Lord Melbourne, 'that sort of thing is apt to come later.'

The Queen was shocked. 'I shan't forgive you that,' she snapped.[9]

On 8 February 1840 the sight of Albert's dear, dear face (even if still pale as wax from a frightful Channel crossing) put the Queen's mind at rest, she says, 'about everything'. In spite of the Duchess of Kent's outraged reaction to such impropriety, the Queen and her husband-to-be spent the two nights before the wedding under the same roof. As that roof covered the great sprawl of Buckingham Palace (still the elegant, honey-coloured Nash building with its open courtyard) there was really nó cause for alarm. The Queen dismissed such narrow-minded superstition as 'foolish nonsense'. On the morning of her wedding day – 10 February 1840 – she wrote that for the last time she had slept 'alone', and then, with her customary precision about time, noted that she had risen at a quarter to nine ('well, and having slept well') and breakfasted at half past nine. She then scribbled Prince Albert a reassuring little message.

The couple were married in the Chapel Royal, St James's Palace. Melbourne's warning that on this occasion the 'confusion' of the last public marriage of a reigning monarch – that of King George III in 1761 – must be avoided was blithely ignored; not least by Melbourne himself. Greville complained that because the Queen had been 'as wilful, obstinate and wrong-headed as usual',[10] only five Tories had been invited, and three of them were connected with her household. Only on Melbourne's insistence had she, reluctantly, invited the Duke of Wellington. Prince Albert, although looking magnificent in the skin-tight uniform of a British field-marshal, was clearly ill at ease. He had been given no instructions as to what he should do as he waited for the bride, and was further unnerved by the widowed Queen Adelaide giving him the order of procedure in a loud stage whisper.

A flourish of trumpets announced the arrival of the Queen. In a white satin dress trimmed with lace, a wreath of orange blossom in her light brown hair, she looked remarkably composed. Less composed were her twelve bridesmaids. Their mothers may have led blameless lives, but as they were all tall girls and the Queen's train was rather short, it was only by taking tiny, tottering steps that they could avoid bumping into each other.

Queen Victoria entered the church on the arm of her uncle the Duke of Sussex, who was not, even on this momentous occasion, prepared to dispense with his customary and comfortingly warm black skull-cap. Another of her ageing uncles, the Duke of Cambridge, made loud, good-natured comments throughout the ceremony. The Duke of Norfolk lost his spectacles and in his insistence, as Earl Marshal, on being the first to sign the register, kept everyone waiting until he found them.

Miss Agnes Strickland, in her suppressed biography *Victoria from Birth to Bridal*, gives a highly coloured account of the Queen's emotions during the ceremony. The bride, claims Miss Strickland, 'moulded her blanched and trembling lips into a faint smile, was agitated and with difficulty restrained her feelings.' Queen Victoria's comments, on reading these purple passages many years later, are characteristically robust. 'Not true,' she scrawled in the margin. The bride turned from the altar, continues the author doggedly, looking 'pale and thoughtful', acutely conscious of her new status as wife as well as sovereign. 'Not so,' commented the Queen. '*Only* felt *so* happy.'

The newly married couple returned together to Buckingham Palace. They sat, the Queen noted meticulously, alone from ten minutes to two until twenty minutes past two in her drawing-room and then joined the rest of the company for a gargantuan wedding breakfast. Soon after that they set off for Windsor and their two-day honeymoon. ('You forget, my dearest Love, that I am the Sovereign and that business can stop and wait for nothing,' the Queen had written crisply to Prince Albert when he dared to suggest a rather longer honeymoon.)

'They went off', grumbled Greville, 'in a very poor and shabby style. Instead of the new chariot in which most married people are accustomed to dash along, they were in one of the old travelling coaches, the postillions in undressed liveries, and with a small escort, three other coaches with post horses following.'[11]

No such carpings marred the Queen's account of that drive to Windsor. Their reception, all along the route, had been 'most enthusiastic and hearty and gratifying in every way.' But its satisfactions paled beside the joy of what was to come. It needed a rash of underlinings, double underlinings and capital letters for the Queen to do justice to the delights of that evening when, at long last, she and her new husband were left undisturbed.

Never, never had she spent such an evening; how *could* she ever be thankful enough to have a husband of such beauty, such sweetness, such tenderness; how could she have *hoped* for such feelings of heavenly love and happiness; it was all 'bliss beyond belief.'

'This Beloved Being'

THERE NOW began Queen Victoria's celebrated, twenty-two-year-long marriage to Prince Albert. In the course of it the Prince was transformed from an obscure German princeling into King in all but name. This was the result, not only of his exceptional qualities, but also of his wife's obsessive love: the Queen was determined that her husband must be her guide and master in all things.

But it was a gradual process. At first the Queen was not always able to abide by her 'great wish': 'to make this beloved Being happy and contented'. The long-suffering Prince had to battle against his wife's imperiousness, stubbornness and flaring temper. She remained very conscious of her status as sovereign. Prince Albert's complaint to a friend that he was 'only the husband, and not the master in the house'[1] was fully justified. Neither in her official life nor in the management of her household was he allowed to play any significant part. During her meetings with ministers the doors would be closed against him; decisions about the day-to-day running of their lives would be taken without reference to him. In vain did King Leopold bombard him with instructions to assert himself more forcefully. Without the Queen's encouragement, there was not much that he could do. And encouragement, in spite of her great love for him, she was incapable of giving.

There were frequent scenes between husband and wife. The worst of these concerned the Queen's one-time governess and now confidante, Baroness Lehzen. Grateful to Lehzen for her support and protection during those unhappy childhood days in Kensington Palace, Queen Victoria would not hear a word against her now. Lehzen was allowed every liberty; the Queen trusted her judgement implicitly.

But in Prince Albert's eyes Lehzen was a meddlesome, malicious and incompetent busybody: a thoroughly bad influence on his wife.

In her conviction that the Queen should never discuss any controversial – and certainly no political – subjects with Prince Albert lest it spoil their relationship, Lehzen was largely responsible for the Prince's unsatisfactory position. Love and politics, Lehzen assured the Queen, could never mix. Only after one particularly violent quarrel concerning Lehzen, following which husband and wife exchanged a series of impassioned letters, did the Queen agree that Lehzen must go. Her departure, more than two years after his wedding day, finally allowed Prince Albert to feel that he could command his wife's full confidence.

By then the Prince was free of another, albeit more benevolent, rival for Queen Victoria's confidence and affection. The fall of the Whigs in the summer of 1841 meant the departure of Lord Melbourne.

At her wedding ceremony Lord M had been, noted the Queen, 'very much affected'. He had every reason to be. Not only was he about to yield his own place in her life but, being so devoted to her, he was seriously concerned about her future happiness. Her ecstatic letter to him on the morning after her 'most gratifying and bewildering' wedding night could not really have consoled him on either score. 'She never thought she could be so loved as she is by *dearest, dear* Albert ...' she scribbled. Such rapture, the worldly Lord Melbourne must have thought, could never last; and as yet he doubted whether Prince Albert was worthy of it.

He soon changed his mind. The Prime Minister appreciated that the Prince's qualities of calm, conscientiousness and intelligence were exactly what the Queen needed in a husband. To Charles Greville he predicted that the Prince would one day 'acquire boundless influence'.[2] Melbourne began to discuss matters with the young husband and urged the initially reluctant Queen to involve him more in the day-to-day business of the monarchy. 'The Prince understands everything so well and has a clever, able head,' he told her.[3]

For his part, Prince Albert was equally appreciative of Lord Melbourne. He soon realized that the Prime Minister's nonchalant manner masked a shrewd mind. The relaxed, flippant way in which Melbourne talked to the Queen was designed to flatter her into imagining that she was cleverer than she was, whereas the Prince's more serious-minded conversation had the opposite effect. In exactly the same way, many years later, did the flowery Disraeli make the Queen feel clever while the austere Gladstone made her feel stupid.

Melbourne's parting advice, on leaving office in August 1841, was that she should put her trust in her husband. 'Lord Melbourne', he wrote, 'has formed the highest opinion of his Royal Highness's judgement, temper, and discretion, and he cannot but feel a great consolation and security in the reflection that he leaves your Majesty in a situation in which your Majesty has the inestimable advantage of such advice and assistance . . .'.[4]

The parting from Lord Melbourne took place without those cascades of tears which marked the previous occasion on which he had relinquished office. Even the prospect of Sir Robert Peel had been rendered less horrific by Prince Albert's tactful negotiations with the incoming Prime Minister on the vexed question of the Queen's ladies. They could not risk another Bedchamber Crisis. The Queen was now willing to compromise in the matter.

Melbourne's parting words to the Queen as they stood together 'in the starlight' on the Terrace at Windsor were very touching. 'For four years I have seen you daily,' he said, 'and liked it better every day.'

The Queen was profoundly affected. 'After seeing him for four years, with very few exceptions, *daily*,' she wrote to King Leopold, 'you may imagine that I *must* feel the change.'

Yet within a year the Queen was able to discuss her earlier obsession with Lord M quite dispassionately with her husband. What, she wondered, had caused her 'unbounded admiration and affection' for her Prime Minister? She could only put it down to her 'naturally warm feelings' and her need of someone to cling to. 'Albert thinks I worked myself up to what really became, at last, quite foolish,' she wrote frankly.

As Queen Victoria's naturally warm feelings and need of someone to cling to remained unaltered, it was Prince Albert who benefited most from the departure of Lehzen and Melbourne. Year by year he asserted greater authority. From being trusted to blot her signature on official documents, the Prince graduated to reading dispatches; from reading dispatches, to giving advice; and from giving advice to making decisions. Entrusted with the keys to the boxes of confidential state documents, he replaced Lord Melbourne as her unofficial private secretary. Never again, during Prince Albert's lifetime, did Queen Victoria come under the sway of a prime minister. At ministerial meetings Prince Albert was always by her side. There were few subjects on which he was not prepared to write a long, solemn but eminently sensible memorandum. From now on the Queen spoke as 'we', not as 'I'. In her absence (and her recurring pregnancies made them frequent) he held levees; and presentations to him were considered the equal of presentations to the Queen herself.

'We women', she would even go so far as to protest, 'are not *made* for governing.'

'He is become so identified with her that they are one person,' wrote Greville, 'and as he likes, and she dislikes, business, it is obvious that while she has the title, he is really discharging the functions of the Sovereign. He is King to all intents and purposes.'[5]

Prince Albert's influence spread to other spheres as well. He set about filling the many gaps in the Queen's education. Conscious of her intellectual and cultural shortcomings, she tended to avoid the company of clever people. Gradually the Prince encouraged her to take a more intelligent interest in things. He introduced her to the wonders of art and science; under his guidance, her reading became more serious. People were invited to court because of their accomplishments rather than because of their lineage; to a certain degree, the court became more democratic.

Although both the Queen and Prince Albert had a strict regard for the limits of constitutional monarchy, they felt that the powers and prestige of the Crown should be somehow enhanced. By the blamelessness of their private life and the high moral tone of their court, the monarchy came to command more respect than had been the case for many years. In addition to this, Prince Albert encouraged the Queen, not only to take a great interest in foreign – which at that time meant European – affairs, but to insist on her right to be consulted on them. Foreign affairs became her particular province just as, in the years ahead, imperial affairs were to hold a special interest for her. Domestic politics were never able to fire her imagination to the same extent.

Another of Prince Albert's achievements was to lift the Crown above party politics. At the time of his marriage to Queen Victoria she had been, of course, an ardent Whig; her predecessor, King William IV, had been an ardent Tory. Gradually Prince Albert convinced her that she must give allegiance to neither party; that the Crown must stand high above the political *mêlée*. It was one of his most significant contributions to British political life, and to the monarchy. By making the Crown more impartial, he made it more powerful: more authoritative, more revered, more sacred.

With the birth of each child Prince Albert's position was strengthened. Early on in their marriage a bill was passed by the terms of which, in the event of the Queen's death, the Prince would become Regent for their eldest son. ('Three months ago they would not have done it for him,' claimed Melbourne at the time. 'It is entirely his own character.') Yet the wretched question of his precedence had not been satisfactorily settled. The Queen's surviving uncles were still quite likely to elbow him out of the way on official occasions, and on the Continent he was expected to give precedence to mere archdukes.

All this infuriated the Queen. So passionately in love with him, so appreciative of his many talents, so convinced of his moral and intellectual superiority, she could not bear the thought of his taking second place to any man.

'Oh!' she once exclaimed, 'if only I could make him King.'

Their private life seems to have been very happy. Lady Palmerston, who as Lord Melbourne's sister knew them very well, claimed that 'it is quite impossible for any two people to be more happy';[6] and the Queen, remembering what she called her 'artificial and superficial' life with Lord Melbourne, wrote 'Thank God! I know now what *real* happiness means!'

Having spent the night in their double bed, the Prince – who slept in long white drawers that enclosed his feet – would rise at seven, as soon as a maid had opened the shutters. He would go immediately to his sitting room. Lighting his green-shaded 'student's' lamp, which he had brought from Germany, he would begin work. After an hour or so of reading and writing, he would wake his wife with the rousing German phrase '*Est ist Zeit, steh' auf!*' ('It is time, get up!'). The couple breakfasted at nine. The Queen talks of Prince Albert being 'always so merry' at the breakfast table, and one member of her family agrees that he often kept the company diverted by his hilarious mimicry, imitations of pompous court officials or politicians. The Prince was one of those men who when ill at ease or bored can seem intimidatingly distant, yet in congenial company can be cheerful and amusing.

After breakfast they would walk, in the gardens of Buckingham Palace if they were in London, or on the Terrace if they were at Windsor, with two or three dogs scampering about them. They would then start their day's work. At first they sat at tables placed romantically side by side, but as the burden increased they were obliged to work in separate rooms. Eventually, almost everything the Queen saw had passed through Prince Albert's hands first. He ensured that her papers were properly minuted, filed, commented on and answered in draft. He cut out articles for her to read; he wrote memoranda and résumés. At the end of the morning's tasks he would go to her room and they would discuss business, make plans or read to each other.

Luncheon was at two, taken with the household and guests. Fewer than a dozen at table merited a comment in the Queen's Journal. If there were no audiences to be granted in the afternoon, the couple might paint or sketch or play the piano. If the Prince went hunting, 'he never went out or came home without coming through my room or into my dressing room', writes the Queen. 'Dear, dear Angel with a smile on his dearest beautiful face ... and I treasured up everything I heard, kept every letter in a box to tell and show him, and was always so vexed and nervous if I had any foolish draft or despatch to show him, as I knew it would distress and irritate him and affect his poor dear stomach ...'.

There were regular visits to the Queen's mother, who soon after her daughter's marriage had moved out of the palace into nearby Ingestre House. The move, allied to the departure of Lehzen and the gentle persuasion of Prince Albert, had improved relations between mother and daughter. The Queen and the Duchess of Kent were now on much better terms.

Late afternoon brought a visit to the rapidly filling nursery. Charles Greville's jibe that the royal couple's short wedding night was 'not the way to provide us with a Prince of Wales' was wide of the mark.[7] Just over nine months after their wedding the Queen gave birth to her first child, a daughter who became the Princess Royal. The Prince of Wales was born a year later. And children continued to arrive regularly; there was scarcely a year in which the Queen was not pregnant. No fewer than five children were born during the first seven years of marriage; in all, there were nine.

Those who regarded Prince Albert as humourless and unbending would have been astonished to see him crawling about the nursery carpet as he played with his children. 'It was pretty to see him yesterday,' wrote Lady Lyttleton, who was in charge of the royal children, 'after Mrs Sly [one of the nurses] had vainly endeavoured to get on the Prince of Wales's glove (you know what a difficulty) and thrown it aside at last as too small, just coax the child on to his own knee, and put it on, without a moment's delay, by his great dexterity and gentle manner; the Princey, quite evidently glad to be so helped, looking up very softly at his father's beautiful face. It was a picture of a nursery scene. I could not help saying "It is not every Papa who would have the patience and kindness" and got such a look of flashing gratitude from the Queen!'[8]

Before dinner the Queen and the Prince might go out driving; both were passionately fond of being out of doors. Dinner was at eight and was always a large and formal occasion. Guizot, the French foreign minister, dining with the Queen in 1842, was greatly impressed by the congenial atmosphere: the bowls of flowers, the blazing fires, the lively conversation. The hostess was particularly animated.

The Queen disliked the custom of the men remaining at table after the ladies had left. The Prince, who liked it no better (after-dinner conviviality, as the port went round and the talk became broader, was anathema to him) would remain for a few minutes only and then rejoin the ladies. Not that he was any more comfortable in their presence; he was not one for flowery comments, attentive gestures or flirtatious remarks. Prince Albert was most comfortable with men like himself – scholarly, idealistic, practical. With Guizot, for instance, he could discuss his guest's study of the English Revolution of the seventeenth century. On some nights he would play cards or chess; on others he would sing duets with the Queen. Both were very fond of Italian opera and, with his more informed taste, the Prince greatly extended the Queen's interest in and knowledge of music.

Liking the English custom of sitting up talking until the early hours no better than that of remaining with the men at table, Prince Albert insisted that the party break up at eleven at the latest. The royal couple were usually in bed by midnight.

Their intimate marital life was apparently very successful. To Prince Albert, Queen Victoria was his 'own darling', his 'little wife', his *Fräuchen*. When they were apart, his letters were full of endearments. The Queen hated these rare periods of separation. When he had to go to Coburg for his father's funeral early in 1844 she was distraught. 'I have *never* been separated from him for even *one night*', she complained to her Uncle Leopold, 'and the *thought* of *such* separation is quite dreadful.'

A legend has taken root to the effect that Queen Victoria was a highly sexed woman, positively Hanoverian in her appetites; and that, by the fervour of her love, she wore poor Prince Albert out. There is no way of proving this. In any case, Prince Albert was never the chilly, prudish, asexual man he is often made out to be. As much as his wife does he write in terms of falling into her arms and lying in her arms. The couple never hesitated to buy and hang the sort of paintings of nudes that would never have been given house-room by the bourgeoisie whose tastes and morals the royal couple were supposed to epitomize. In Prince Albert's bathroom at Osborne House hung Anton von Gegenbaur's 'Hercules and Omphale' in which a muscular god embraces a naked young woman. For his wife's birthday the Prince gave her a neo-classical statue of a nude woman; for his she gave him a drawing of a nude man.

After Prince Albert's death the Queen spoke of being 'clasped and held tight in the sacred Hours at Night when the world seemed only to be ourselves.' The nights, above all the nights, she wailed, were now 'too sad and weary'.

As much as the Queen may have enjoyed these claspings in the night, she deeply resented their consequences. Each time she discovered she was pregnant, she was miserable. She loathed the whole business of child-bearing. When a delighted King Leopold wrote to congratulate her on the birth of the Princess Royal and to say that he hoped she would become the 'Mamma d'une *nombreuse* famille', he earned the sharp edge of her tongue. 'Men never think, at least seldom think,' she answered, 'what a hard task it is for us women to go through this *very often* . . .'.

Queen Victoria always referred to child-bearing as *die Schattenseite* – the shadowy, negative, less pleasant side – of the marital union. 'You men are far too selfish!' she later wrote to her son-in-law Prince Frederick Wilhelm of Prussia. 'You only have the advantages in such a case, whereas we poor women have to bear all the pain and suffering (of which you can have no conception).'

To her tirades, the long-suffering Prince Albert would answer with admirable patience. Trust in God, 'whose wisdom and goodness should lift you above the feeling of degradation, indignation etc. etc. which you describe,' he once wrote. 'That relationship is sacred, in spite of the pains and trials which women have to suffer. My love and sympathy are limitless and inexhaustible.'

He certainly demonstrated this during the times the Queen was laid up in childbirth. In stark contrast to the average husband of the period, he could hardly have been more attentive. 'The Prince's care and devotion', she wrote after his death, 'were quite beyond expression. He refused to go to the play, or anywhere else . . . He was content to sit by her [the Queen] in a darkened room, to read to her, or write for her. No one but himself ever lifted her from her bed or sofa into the next room. For this purpose he would come when sent for instantly from any part of the house.' His care of her, she claimed, 'was like that of a mother, nor could there be a kinder, wiser or more judicious nurse'.

The Queen's dread of child-bearing (only during the birth of her later children was she given chloroform) may partly explain her somewhat lukewarm attitude towards babies. She was not exactly indifferent to her children when they were very young, but she was certainly not ecstatic about them. Of the two, Prince Albert was the more affectionate parent. Queen Victoria was always a wife first, a mother second. She loved none of her children to the extent that she loved her husband. Nor was she ever as emotionally involved with her children as she was with men like Lord Melbourne, John Brown and Benjamin Disraeli.

Indeed, there were times when she seemed like a child herself; when she and Prince Albert were more like father and daughter than husband and wife. His letters to her always began 'Dear Child', and to her eldest daughter Vicky, the Queen once admitted 'Papa is my father, my protector, my guide and adviser in all and everything, my mother – as well as my husband.'[9]

What this devoted couple with their growing family lacked was a suitable setting for their domestic idyll: a home of their own. Although Prince Albert, during the first years of their married life, had turned his formidable talents to a thorough reorganization of the chaotic finances and no less chaotic running of Buckingham Palace, it remained a cheerless, inconvenient, official residence. By now Queen Victoria had identified herself almost completely with her husband's tastes and preferences: she had turned her back on the parties, dances and late nights of younger days and had come to hate the bustle and clamour of London. Their life there lacked the one thing they valued most – privacy.

There was not much more at Windsor. Although the Queen had to admit that the castle was beautiful and comfortable, it was still, she complained, 'a *palace*'. And as the Office of Woods and Forests held authority over it, Prince Albert was obliged to seek approval for every change and innovation. All his plans for building, gardening and farming were constantly being frustrated or delayed.

The couple had the use of Claremont House, which they liked, but it belonged to King Leopold and continued to do so until his death. Their other home, King George IV's extravagant Pavilion at Brighton, was not only too bizarre for their more restrained tastes, but highly unsuitable as a family home.

So in 1845 they bought, with their own money, Osborne House on the Isle of Wight. To Lord Melbourne the Queen reported that 'it is impossible to imagine a prettier spot – valleys and woods which would be beautiful anywhere; but all this near the sea (the woods grow into the sea) is quite perfection; we have a charming beach quite to ourselves. The sea was so blue and calm that the Prince said it was like Naples ...'.

To complement this Neapolitan setting, and as the existing house was far too modest, Prince Albert designed a new one. With its campaniles, its loggia, its formal terraced gardens, its fountains, urns and statuary, Osborne House was about as near – both aesthetically and geographically – to a Mediterranean villa as an English home could hope to be. Within, its scale was surprisingly intimate. The ceilings were relatively low and the rooms relatively small. The cheerful clutter of furniture, pictures, busts, *objets*, replicas in marble of the royal infants' hands and feet, made the rooms as 'cosy' as even the Queen could wish for. Throughout the house were the lovingly entwined initials, V and A.

'We are more and more delighted with this lovely spot,' reported the Queen one June day in 1845; 'the air so pure and fresh, and in spite of the hottest sun which oppresses one so dreadfully in London and even at Windsor ... really the combination of sea, trees, woods, flowers of all kinds, the purest air ... make it – to us – a perfect little Paradise.'

The summer days would pass like a dream. Breakfast in the summerhouse, sauntering along the terraces, reading, writing, sketching, walking with Prince Albert through the woods and listening to him as he whistled to the nightingales in 'their own peculiar long note which they invariably answer', picking strawberries with the children until eight at night, dinner alone with the Prince, then standing arm-in-arm on the balcony outside her sitting-room to watch the moonlight shimmering on the quiet sea.

'How happy we are here!' she sighed. 'And never do I enjoy myself more, or more peacefully than when I can be so much with my beloved Albert and follow him everywhere!'

But not even here, it seems, in this paradise, could she be alone with him as often as she would have liked. Osborne House, in spite of the frequently choppy waters of the Solent, was still too accessible; the couple were always having their privacy disturbed by visiting ministers and officials. What they needed was something even more remote, and with a rather more bracing climate.

They found it in the Scottish Highlands. Already, in the course of a couple of visits to Scotland, the couple had become enchanted by the country – by its rugged scenery, its clear air and its straightforward people – and in 1848 they took a lease on Balmoral Castle on Deeside. Within four years they were able to buy the estate and, once again, Prince Albert set about designing a new house.

Where Osborne House was Italianate in style, Balmoral Castle was a mixture of German *schloss* and Scottish baronial hall: pale granite walls, pepper-pot turrets, stepped gables, battlements. Inside it was a riot of tartan: tartan wallpaper, tartan curtains, tartan carpets, tartan upholstery. Whatever woodwork managed to evade this tartan tide was covered in dark, marmalade-coloured paint, and such antlers as did not adorn the walls were fashioned into chairs and settles.

Into tartan too, went the young royal family. The Queen would be in satin tartan, the Prince in the kilt, the children in 'Highland things' which they passed down one to another, irrespective of gender. Thus suitably kitted out, they flung themselves into the delights of Highland life: Scottish dancing, pony rides, deer-stalking, ptarmigan shooting, picnicking, rowing on the lochs, day-long excursions. 'It was wonderful not seeing a single human being, nor hearing a sound, excepting that of the wind, or the call of the blackcock or grouse,' enthused the Queen after one of their excursions.

Such human beings as they did see – the crofters, gillies and tenants – were all such admirable people: so natural without being uncouth, so respectful without being obsequious. With her eye for masculine good looks, Queen Victoria greatly admired the strong physique and proud bearing of the Highland men. Typical of these was the young gillie whom the couple met on their second Balmoral holiday, John Brown. The son of a local farmer, with an expert knowledge of the area, the good-looking Brown became a great favourite of both the Queen and the Prince. During the following dozen years, until the death of Prince Albert, Brown was a valuable member of their many Highland 'expeditions'.

For Queen Victoria these times spent with Prince Albert at Balmoral always held a special magic. Charles Greville, paying an official visit to Balmoral, grudgingly admitted that the royal couple were at their best in these relatively simple surroundings. The visit also opened his eyes to the Prince's many admirable qualities. Until now, Greville had regarded him as a typically pedantic and censorious German; now he came to appreciate, not only Prince Albert's intelligence and quick comprehension, but his informality and high spirits.

One of the reasons for Prince Albert's enjoyment of these holidays in the Highlands was that they were as close as he could get to the carefree days he had spent among the mountains of his native Thuringia. As for Queen Victoria, it was enough to know that her dearest Angel was happy. Their love, she maintained, was 'younger and stronger than ever'; no other queen 'has ever enjoyed what I am fortunate enough to enjoy'.

7

'An Angel of Light'

QUEEN VICTORIA'S first meeting with the man who was one day to fill so important a place in her heart – John Brown – took place within a year of the death of one who had once filled an equally important place – Lord Melbourne.

During the first year or so after Melbourne's fall from power there was a frequent exchange of letters between him and the Queen, with Melbourne happily, if injudiciously, giving her advice on both personal and political matters. (In just the same way did the Queen, under Gladstone's nose, continue to correspond with the fallen Prime Minister Disraeli.) It needed the intervention of the horrified Baron Stockmar, backed up by Prince Albert, to put an end to this constitutionally inadvisable practice.

Given Prince Albert's steadily growing ascendancy over the Queen the ex-Prime Minister's influence would have dwindled anyway, but Lord Melbourne could not help feeling his gradual distancing from the Queen very keenly. He continued to write, and every now and then brought out one of those famously cynical comments with which, in earlier days, the Queen's Journal had been so deliciously crammed. He was particularly dry about the Queen's new-found enthusiasm for the Highlands. The Scottish scenery, he agreed, was indeed beautiful: 'There is nothing to detract from it, except the very high opinion that the Scotch themselves entertain of it.'[1] And, yes, the clans were undoubtedly romantic and picturesque; what a good thing, considering their history of insurrection against the Hanoverian monarchy, that there were so few of them left.

The occasional glimpses the old man had of the young Queen were almost unbearably upsetting. Once, at a ball, he missed his chance of being presented to her. Afraid that she might think he had been deliberately uncivil, he wrote her an agitated letter of explanation: it had been a piece of 'blundering stupidity' on his part, he pleaded. On another occasion, as he was driving past Buckingham Palace in the spring twilight, he could see, through the open windows, all the familiar furniture and pictures in the sitting-room in which the two of them had so often sat chatting. Suddenly, the main door of the palace opened and the tiny, bejewelled figure came out and stepped into her waiting carriage.

Late in 1842 Lord Melbourne suffered a stroke. His recovery was gradual and from then on he began spending more time at his country home, Brocket, and less in London. From time to time the Queen made polite enquiries after his health, and occasionally they would meet. An evening at Chatsworth proved especially distressing to him. He had been almost childishly excited at the prospect of meeting the Queen, but she was able to chat to him for only a minute or two before dinner, and during the meal she soon turned her attention to the person sitting on her other side. The old man's disappointment was painfully apparent but, in fairness to the Queen, she had been flustered by the sad change in his appearance and was afraid of tiring him with too much talk.

He continued to write to her, but weeks might go by before she answered. Yet his advice often made very good sense. In their earnest, idealistic way, the Queen and Prince Albert were putting their minds to the question of the future education of their eldest son, the Prince of Wales. He must be fashioned, they had decided, into a moral and intellectual paragon, the 'perfect man'. Lord Melbourne struck a more realistic note. 'Be not over-solicitous about the education ...', he advised; 'it may mould and direct the character but it rarely alters it.'[2] The couple would have done well to follow his advice.

But often the old gentleman's letters struck a more poignant note. 'Lord Melbourne cannot say otherwise', he once wrote, 'but that he continually misses and regrets the time when he had daily confidential communication with Your Majesty.'[3]

Although the Queen was touched by such sentiments, she could no longer share them. Her association with Melbourne's Tory successor, Sir Robert Peel, had proved to be far less onerous than she had at one time feared. What Melbourne might consider to be Peel's short-comings – his dull, unemotional, middle-class worthiness – looked more like strengths to Prince Albert. Encouraged by the Prince, the Queen worked in almost complete harmony with Peel.

Moreover, Queen Victoria was too honest, and in a way too egocentric, to simulate a sentiment which she did not feel. For Lord Melbourne she now felt very little. Her overwhelming feelings for Prince Albert left no room for anyone else. Now and then she would scribble Lord Melbourne a line, or send him a present, or even pay him a brief visit. When he appealed to her – quite unnecessarily, as it turned out – for a loan of £10,000, she unhesitatingly advanced it. More typical was her letter to him at the end of July 1843.

'The Queen is extremely sorry to leave England without seeing Lord Melbourne,' she wrote on the eve of a visit to Scotland, 'and without having seen him all the season; but something or other always prevented us from seeing Lord Melbourne each time we hoped to do so.'[4]

It was a far cry from the days, a mere five years before, when she had resented his spending even one evening away from her dinner-table.

With the fall of Peel's Tory administration in the summer of 1846, and the assumption of office by the Whigs under the premiership of Lord John Russell, Melbourne scented a possible return to public life. Perhaps he might be offered a seat in the cabinet or even some honorific post? It was not to be. In a tactful letter Lord John Russell explained that he had not included Melbourne's name among those submitted to the Queen for the new ministry; he did not think that his lordship's health would be equal to the strains of office. The old statesman accepted the explanation with a good enough grace. Valiantly he assured the Queen that he would not, in any case, have accepted a post.

In the spring of 1848 Lord Melbourne suffered another stroke, and on 24 November 1848, at the age of sixty-nine, he died. 'Our poor friend Melbourne died on the 24th,' wrote the Queen to King Leopold. 'I sincerely regret him for he was truly attached to me, and although not a good or firm minister, he was a noble, kind-hearted, generous being.'[5]

Her Journal shows something of this same blend of faint praise and self-obsession. Although mourning him 'truly and sincerely', she dwelt chiefly on his kindness to, and affection for, herself. Except for Lehzen and Stockmar, she writes, he had been her only friend during the early years of her reign.

There were times when she was not prepared to give him full credit even for this. In the year before Lord Melbourne died, the Queen was one day remembering the turbulent period before her marriage. How unedifying it had all been – the rows with her mother, the superficiality of her life, the Lady Flora Hastings affair, the Bedchamber Crisis. She could not bear to think about it. Even Lord Melbourne, 'whom I clung to . . . did not, from being too good-natured' give her the advice and guidance which she had so desperately needed.

And then Albert, she gushed, 'had really come like an angel of light to save me and take me out of my difficulties . . .'.

Never, in Queen Victoria's eyes, had this angel of light shone more brightly than in the year of his most spectacular achievement so far: the Great Exhibition of 1851.

It is easy to forget that Prince Albert was still in his twenties when, in the summer of 1849, he first conceived the idea of the Great Exhibition; and that he was only thirty-one when it opened in May 1851. For one thing, he had the sagacity and *gravitas* of a more mature man; for another, he looked much older. Balding, paunchy, care-worn, the Prince was fast losing the good looks which had so impressed the young Queen a decade before. Not that she minded. By now she had come fully to appreciate her husband's more sterling qualities.

'I must always stand amazed at his wonderful mind,' she wrote to Baron Stockmar that year. 'Such large views of everything, and such extreme lucidity in working all these views out. He is very, very great.'[6]

Together, the couple had emerged unscathed from the revolutionary storms that raged through Europe during 1848. While so many Continental thrones had collapsed or been shaken (Louis Philippe, King of the French, had lost his), Queen Victoria's had remained secure. The reasons for this were complex, but not the least of them was articulated by the Queen when she reported — after some public ceremony — that the newspapers had been 'most kind and gratifying; they say *no* Sovereign *was more* loved than I am (I am bold enough to say) and *that*, from our *happy domestic home* – which gives such a good example.'

It was in the aftermath of this period of revolutionary upheaval that Prince Albert conceived his idea of an exhibition dedicated to the benefits of peace. The exhibition was to be, he insisted, an 'international' one: a showcase to promote the results of co-operation both between individuals and between nations. It would celebrate that 'honest toil' by which he set so much store; it would be a glorious coming together of art, agriculture and industry. 'I *do* feel proud', enthused the Queen, 'at the thought of what my beloved Albert's great mind has conceived.'

Her enthusiasm was not universally shared. Hardly had Prince

Albert's grandiose scheme been announced than he was launched into a sea of troubles and criticism. With the government refusing to pay for such 'frivolities', he had to organize private guarantors. His choice of Hyde Park as a suitable site was bitterly attacked: Members of Parliament who had not made speeches for years suddenly showed touching concern for the fate of the trees and the grass. His plan to house the exhibition in a sort of giant glass greenhouse, to be designed by Joseph Paxton, led to prophesies of disaster: it would be shattered by hail, swamped by rain, shaken down by vibration.

It was claimed that the multitudes attending the exhibition would be a source of potential danger. They would spread disease, they would ruin the park, they would encourage criminals and prostitutes, they would go hungry for lack of adequate catering facilities, they would disseminate subversive literature and atheistic doctrines, they would harbour assassins. Members of foreign royal families proved especially apprehensive about visiting London. Those who had just survived revolution had no intention of risking regicide. King Bomba of Naples even went so far as to prohibit the sending of exhibits, lest they somehow become contaminated by British liberal ideas.

Not every fear proved groundless. Once Paxton's glittering glass exhibition building – happily described by *Punch* as 'The Crystal Palace' – had been erected, it was found that sparrows were still flitting merrily among the huge trees that had been enclosed within it. Who could tell what harm their droppings might inflict on the priceless exhibits below? The only practical solution came from the old Duke of Wellington. 'Sparrow-hawks, Ma'am,' he advised the Queen.

Never once did Queen Victoria lose faith in her husband's project. She regularly visited the site, marvelling at the 'hum of life' beneath the great glass roof as things began to take shape. But she was seriously worried about Prince Albert's health. He spared himself too little, and others too much, she complained. He was 'shamefully plagued' about the exhibition. 'My poor Albert is terribly fagged,' she wrote. '*All* day some question or other, or some difficulty, all of which my beloved one takes with the greatest quiet and good temper.' And all this in addition to his customary political and domestic work and worries. An intense and highly sensitive man, Prince Albert suffered severely from the criticisms and disappointments of his ambitious enterprise.

Yet, in the end, it all went off brilliantly. By the time the Great Exhibition closed in mid-October 1851 it had proved itself an immense popular, cultural and commercial success. The Queen was to count the opening day – 1 May 1851 – as one of 'the greatest and most glorious' of her life. Dressed in pink and silver, with the Koh-i-noor diamond blazing in her hair and the Garter ribbon slanting across her breast, she processed – on the arm of the uniformed Prince Albert and with their two eldest children on either side of them – up the central aisle to take her place under a blue and gold canopy.

She could hardly do justice to the splendour of the scene about her. Her Journal is a catalogue of delights: the glass arches shimmering in the sunshine, the palms and flowers, the towering crystal fountain, the myriads of people, the kaleidoscopic exhibits, the flourish of trumpets, the thundering of the organ, the sound of six hundred voices raised in song. It was all a sort of fairyland.

'It was the *happiest, proudest* day in my life and I can think of nothing else,' she wrote breathlessly to Uncle Leopold. 'Albert's dearest name is immortalised with this *great* conception, *his* own, and my *own* dear country *showed* she was *worthy* of it.'

The end of Exhibition year brought the royal couple a flurry of political excitement. Causing this flurry was a man destined one day to set the Queen's pulses pounding: Prince Louis Napoleon Bonaparte.

The Queen did not, at this time, know a great deal about Louis Napoleon. She was aware that he was the nephew of the great Napoleon; that his father was the Emperor's disgruntled brother Louis and his mother the Empress Josephine's daughter by her first marriage, the seductively mannered Hortense de Beauharnais. Louis Napoleon was born on 20 April 1808, during the halcyon days of Napoleon's empire. The Queen knew, also, that since the death of Napoleon's only son in 1832 Louis Napoleon had been a very active pretender to the throne of France.

Until the tumultuous year of 1848, however, the Prince's attempts to re-establish his uncle's empire had been not only unsuccessful, but also faintly comic. On each occasion the garrisons whom the young man had exhorted to rise up against the current French sovereign, King Louis Philippe, had refused to do any such thing. One of the Prince's attempts had ended in his banishment, another in his imprisonment. Not until 1848, following the overthrow of King Louis Philippe by revolution and the proclamation of a republic, was Prince Louis Napoleon presented with his opportunity. When it was announced that a president of the republic was to be elected by universal suffrage, he put his name forward as a candidate.

It was at this stage that Queen Victoria began to take Louis Napoleon's pretensions more seriously. That he would be elected to the presidency seemed certain (the name he bore guaranteed this), but that this softly-spoken, dreamy-eyed adventurer would prove to be anything more than a flash in the French political pan seemed extremely doubtful. The Queen's Prime Minister, Lord John Russell, imagined that Louis Napoleon's presidency would simply pave the way for the restoration of the legitimate monarchy. This was the Queen's own wish. 'In France, there really ought to be a Monarchy before long,' she told her Uncle Leopold.

The result of the presidential election put something of a damper on her pleasurable speculations. Louis Napoleon's majority was immense: he had polled the votes of almost three-quarters of the electorate. To Frenchmen thirsting, some for glory, some for order and some for an embodiment of the continuing spirit of the Revolution, the name Napoleon meant far more than all the electioneering promises of his rivals. As a result, on 20 December 1848 the forty-year-old Prince Louis Napoleon Bonaparte was proclaimed President of the French Republic.

'The success of Louis Napoleon is an extraordinary event . . .' wrote the Queen to King Leopold, adding, with characteristic realism, that 'it will, however, perhaps be more difficult to get rid of him again than one may at *first* imagine.'

She was right. Once Louis Napoleon had been elected president he set about, at first imperceptibly and then more boldly, consolidating his position. Not until he had been President of France for three years, during which time his popularity increased enormously, did he feel ready to make his next move. On 2 December 1851 – the anniversary of the battle of Austerlitz and of the first Napoleon's coronation – he staged a *coup d'état*. Overnight he established himself as complete master of France.

His bold stroke caused the Queen to forget, for a moment, her disapproval of Louis Napoleon and to dash off an ecstatic letter to King Leopold. 'I must write a line to ask what you say to the *wonderful* proceedings at Paris, which really seem like a *story* in a book or a play! What is to be the result of it all?'

As always, King Leopold's answer was carefully considered. 'As yet one cannot form an opinion,' he wrote, 'but I am inclined to think that Louis Napoleon will succeed.'

As one of the strengths of Queen Victoria's character was that her impulsiveness was tempered by her common sense, her first flush of excitement at Louis Napoleon's *coup d'état* was followed by a return to a more reasonable frame of mind. The great thing, she and Prince

Albert decided, was to keep cool and not *provoke* Louis Napoleon. When Lord John Russell (appreciating that there was nothing his government could do about the matter) assured the French ambassador in London that what Britain desired was the 'happiness and welfare' of France, she expressed wholehearted approval.

Yet the Queen remained on her guard. She was, after all, dealing with a Napoleon. With 'such an extraordinary man as Louis Napoleon,' she said, 'one can never be for an instant safe.'

Exactly how extraordinary a man he was, she was beginning to find out. From the reports of Lord Cowley, the British ambassador in Paris, she was able to learn something of Louis Napoleon's personality. He seemed a complete enigma. Lord Cowley professed himself utterly baffled. 'To fathom the thoughts or divine the intentions of that one individual, the Prince President of France, would sorely try the powers of the most clear-sighted,' he reported. In another dispatch he claimed that the President's personality seemed to be 'a strange mixture of good and evil. Few approach him who are not charmed by his manners. The patience with which he listens to those who differ from him is remarkable. I am told that an angry word never escapes him . . .'.[7]

That the Queen should be intrigued by this sphinx-like figure is understandable. Before long she was dropping hints that she found Lord Cowley's reports from Paris a little too dry, too lacking in intimate information about the Prince President and his circle. The ambassador duly enlivened his dispatches, even to the extent of reporting on Louis Napoleon's rakish private life. Thus the Queen was no doubt informed when the bachelor President – an accomplished philanderer – finally rid himself of his English mistress, Miss Howard.

As the year following the *coup d'état* unfolded and it became increasingly obvious that Louis Napoleon was planning to restore the empire, the Queen came to accept the inevitable. To England's Queen, any monarchy was better than no monarchy at all. Whatever her private opinion of Louis Napoleon might be, her official attitude was always sensible.

The question of his future title was a case in point. He planned to style himself Napoleon III, in recognition of the great Napoleon's only son who had died in exile in 1832. This infuriated Europe's more legitimate sovereigns. How dare this adventurer, elected to power, regard the Bonapartes as an established royal dynasty? They would refuse to recognize him.

Queen Victoria would have no truck with such pig-headedness. She impressed the Foreign Secretary, Lord Malmesbury, with the importance of Britain's *not* giving her Continental allies an undertaking that she would join them in refusing to acknowledge Napoleon III. For one thing it would offend France and, for another, the rest of them had no means of stopping him from doing 'exactly as he pleases'.

In this, she was proved correct. On 2 December 1852 – again, on the anniversaries of Austerlitz and Napoleon I's coronation – Louis Napoleon Bonaparte was proclaimed Napoleon III, Emperor of the French. A plebiscite on the question had given him an even bigger majority than that for his *coup d'état.*

In contrast to the other sovereigns of Europe, Queen Victoria lost no time in accrediting her ambassador to Napoleon III and in addressing him as 'my good Brother, the Emperor of the French.' In her formal letter of recognition she assured him of her 'invariable attachment and esteem' and of her 'sentiments of sincere friendship.' She signed herself 'Your Imperial Majesty's good Sister, VICTORIA R.'

To the Queen this was merely the language of diplomacy. Into the conventional phrases Napoleon III was ready to read a great deal more.

The generally accepted picture of Victoria and Albert as a devoted and perfectly matched couple, with the adoring Queen living only for her husband's happiness, is not quite accurate. It is true that they were happier than was the case with a great many married couples, but there were times – as in any marriage – when their relationship was less than harmonious. In fact, there were often violent scenes followed by long periods of tension.

In temperament the couple were very different. The Queen was a highly emotional woman, possessive, egotistical, quick-tempered. Honesty being her most outstanding quality, she always said what was on her mind. This did not make her easy to live with. The Prince, on the other hand, was almost incapable of showing his true emotions: he tended to bottle things up. Because he hated scenes and crises, he tried to play down their devastating effect on him by adopting a calm and distant manner. Yet this air of detachment masked a sensitive, vulnerable, kindly nature with a great capacity for love. Gradually this suppression of his genuine feelings took its toll. Prince Albert was frequently plunged into depths of melancholy and despair.

As the years went by, and as the Prince took over more and more of his wife's duties, so she became increasingly resentful of the time he was obliged to spend away from her. She often felt lonely and neglected. She missed the kind of whole-hearted attention that Lord Melbourne had once given her.

'Albert becomes really a *terrible* man of business,' she complained to King Leopold. 'I think it takes a little off the gentleness of his character, and makes him so preoccupied. I grieve over all this, as I *cannot* enjoy these things *much as* I [try to] interest myself in *general* European politics . . .'.[8]

But it was not only his absorption in political matters that she minded. He was interested in so many things from which she felt excluded: science, photography, economics, geology, agriculture. Proud of all his achievements and deeply resentful of the fact that his talents were not generally appreciated, she was none the less jealous of the interests and enthusiasms that took him from her side. Often, when they were together, she sensed that he was longing to get away to continue some unfinished bit of business. Nor was she consoled when he explained, in his always reasonable way, that everything he did was for her.

One of the most serious storms between them blew up in the spring of 1853. In April the Queen had given birth to her fourth son and eighth child, whom they named Leopold after the King of the Belgians. Although the Queen's labour had been eased, for the first time, by the use of chloroform, she hated the process of child-bearing as much as ever and, as always, resented the fact that her husband was exempt from its degradations and sufferings.

The baby, who at first seemed healthy enough, soon revealed that he was not. He remained worryingly puny. In fact Prince Leopold was a haemophiliac, a sufferer from the dreaded 'bleeding disease'. Although the true nature of the baby's malady was not yet apparent, his frailty became a contributory factor in the Queen's general feelings of anxiety and edginess.

One evening, as the couple were compiling a register of prints, the Prince rebuked the Queen for not paying enough attention to what she was doing. At this she flared up. For over an hour she was in hysterics – weeping, shouting, flinging wild insults and accusations at him. When he tried to reason with her, she became more violent still. The scene was followed by twenty-four hours of further sulks, snappings and tantrums.

Prince Albert tackled this, as all other such explosions, in the only way he knew: by writing his wife a long and closely reasoned letter about it. He was astonished, he said, at the effect which a hasty word on his part could produce. He appreciated her sufferings but denied that he was the *cause* of them; she simply used his occasional remonstrances to give vent to all her bottled-up resentments. Only afterwards, in her 'candid way', did she reveal the 'real cause' of her complaints.

How, he asked, was he to deal with her during these paroxysms? If he denied the validity of her accusations, she simply became more vehement. If he ignored her, she felt insulted and demanded a response. If he accused her of being self-obsessed and of not trying hard enough to control her feelings, it made matters worse. His most frequently employed method – of leaving her alone and retiring to his room – was the least effective of all. She simply followed him from room to room, determined 'to have it *all out*'. If he tried to forget the whole thing and behave normally, she claimed that he was being cold, heartless and indifferent.

It was an impossible situation. What Queen Victoria needed was a man who would argue back, shout her down, reduce her to tears and then make it up with a kiss and the reassurance that he still loved her. She did not want chilling, patronizing, painstakingly argued memoranda. But it was no easier for Prince Albert. So undemonstrative, so embarrassed by her tantrums and baffled by her accusations, so conscious of the fact that he often appeared indifferent, and yet temperamentally incapable of making the necessary loving gestures, he did not know what to do. In his analytical way, he appreciated that her unreasonableness had its roots in her love for him. There must have been times when he wished that her love was not quite so exclusive; that she could spare more of it for others, especially their children.

'It is indeed a pity that you find no consolation in the company of your children,' he once wrote. 'The root of the trouble lies in the mistaken notion that the function of a mother is to be always correcting, scolding, ordering them about and organising their activities. It is not possible to be on happy friendly terms with people you have just been scolding.'

Some of their most intense rows – or at least intense strains – concerned their children. The Queen was jealous, not only of the time the Prince spent on business, but of that which he devoted to his children. He was a far more patient and painstaking parent than she was. The Queen was becoming especially jealous of their eldest daughter Vicky, the Princess Royal. Of all their children, Vicky was the one who best lived up to their high expectations. Turned thirteen in 1853, she was a lively and intelligent girl, very much her father's favourite.

Not long after the Great Exhibition, the Prince began giving her lessons in the evenings. As Vicky was so eager to learn and the Prince so eager to teach, these lessons became a pleasure for them both. It was a pleasure from which the Queen felt firmly excluded. As a result – and quite unconscious, one may be sure, of the true reason for her dissatisfaction – Queen Victoria began to find fault with her daughter. Prince Albert, in turn, would accuse his wife of being unfair, and this would lead, inevitably, to yet more of those harrowing scenes.

Equally distressing, but for different reasons, was the couple's relationship with their eldest son Bertie, the Prince of Wales. One year younger than his sister Vicky but as backward as she was forward, Bertie showed no eagerness whatsoever to learn. This was particularly unfortunate as, in spite of Lord Melbourne's advice, the parents were subjecting the boy to a system of educational force-feeding. Known as 'The Plan', this system was designed to fashion him into a man worthy of his great destiny. Already the scheme was failing dismally. Bertie simply did not have the mental ability to live up to his parents' expectations. With each passing year their disappointment in him became more acute. The Queen became more strident in her dealings with him, the Prince more despairing.

It is important to see all these marital difficulties in perspective. The quarrels and tensions between the royal couple were the exception rather than the rule. At bottom, they loved each other deeply, to an extent very rare in many, and certainly in most royal, marriages. When the Queen was not in one of her occasional nervous crises and when the Prince was not too overwhelmed by the demands of his position, they were a close, compatible and affectionate couple.

'I feel very lonely without my dear Master', wrote the Queen to Stockmar when the Prince was away on some public duty; 'and though I know other people are often separated for a few days I feel habit could not make me get accustomed to it. Without him everything loses its interest. It will always be a terrible pang for me to separate from him even for two days; and pray God never to let me survive him.'[9]

8

'Princely Mind, Princely Person'

THE FALL of Lord John Russell's Whig ministry in February 1852 brought Queen Victoria a new Tory Prime Minister, in the person of the Earl of Derby. It also brought her a new Chancellor of the Exchequer and Leader of the House, in the person of Benjamin Disraeli.

Disraeli's appointment displeased the Queen considerably. Neither she nor Prince Albert approved of him. To them, this forty-seven-year-old politician was too flashy, too pushy, too irresponsible. The Queen once called him 'unprincipled, reckless and not respectable', and Prince Albert claimed that he 'had not one single element of the gentleman in his composition.'[1] Lord Derby's assurance that Disraeli had 'great ability and talent' did little to reconcile the royal couple to the appointment. Indeed, the reason why Derby had given Disraeli the post of Chancellor rather than the more important one of Foreign Secretary was in deference to the Queen's feelings: Her Majesty need not give as many audiences to the one as she would to the other.

To date contact between Queen Victoria and Benjamin Disraeli had been slight. As a Member of Parliament he had attended her coronation and, with the other members of the House of Commons, he had gone to Buckingham Palace to deliver an address on the occasion of her marriage. The Queen, for her part, knew that Mr Disraeli had written several colourful novels, that he was married to a woman years older than himself, and that his reputation for being socially *outré* and politically ambitious was richly deserved.

Did she know, one wonders, of the exchange that had taken place, many years before, between Disraeli and Lord Melbourne? Disraeli in those days had not yet entered politics, and Melbourne, although a leading light in the Whig cabinet, was still to become Prime Minister.

'Well now,' the worldly Melbourne had asked the equally worldly young man on first meeting him, 'tell me what you want to be.'

'I want to be Prime Minister,' Disraeli had answered unblinkingly.[2]

This exchange is a fascinating one, not only in the light of the political future of each man, but also as regards each one's relationship with the Queen.

That Disraeli could even dream of one day becoming Prime Minister was because he was, by then, a Christian. Only Christians could take the parliamentary oath. Before Benjamin Disraeli turned thirteen (he was born on 21 December 1804), his Jewish father – the skull-capped, scholarly, retiring Isaac D'Israeli – had quarrelled and broken with his local congregation, and with active Judaism. Although he was not himself converted to Christianity, Isaac D'Israeli was persuaded to have his children baptized into the Church of England. From then on Benjamin Disraeli (the spelling of his name was also changed in boyhood) was a professing, if not very convinced, Christian. A born Jew who had become a practising Christian, Disraeli seemed to belong to neither world. He was the blank page, he once quipped to Queen Victoria, between the Old and the New Testaments. But his Christianity at least allowed him to enter Parliament.

Now, twenty years after his exchange with Melbourne, Disraeli was, if not Prime Minister, certainly an important member of the new Tory ministry. And if his post as Chancellor of the Exchequer did not allow him frequent audiences of the Queen, it did allow him to communicate with her on paper. As writing was not the least of his many accomplishments, Disraeli was soon employing his pen to considerable effect. Indeed, there now began his first advance along the road that was ultimately to lead him to the Queen's heart.

Within days of Disraeli's assumption of his post, Queen Victoria was receiving the most interesting reports from him. Never before had she had parliamentary debates presented in so vivid and entertaining a fashion. Here was Mr Disraeli writing of speeches being 'elaborate, malignant, mischievous'; he describes Lord John Russell's speech as 'statesmanlike, argumentative, terse and playful'. It was all so delightfully different from the dry-as-dust accounts she was normally obliged to read. She even went so far as to copy out a few of his more scintillating observations into her Journal, in the same way that she had once noted down Lord Melbourne's pungent phrases.

'Mr Disraeli (*alias* Dizzy) writes very curious reports', wrote the Queen to her Uncle Leopold, '... very much in the style of his books.' It was all, she thought, so amusing. It helped take some of the drudgery out of politics.

In April 1852 the Queen moved a step closer to her entertaining Chancellor. She invited the Disraelis to dinner. This was the first time the Queen was able to study the couple at her leisure. She had met Mrs Disraeli once before and pronounced her to be 'very singular'. And so she was. Disraeli had married the wealthy widow Mary Anne Wyndham Lewis in 1839, when he was thirty-four and she forty-six. It was an age difference to which the skittish Mary Anne was not prepared to make the slightest concession. A few months short of sixty on the occasion of this dinner-party at Buckingham Palace, Mary Anne Disraeli was dressed in her usual youthful fashion. Her tinted hair was crowned with an extravagant wreath of diamonds, velvet leaves and feathers; her dress was an elaborate confection of white satin trimmed with looped-up flounces of gold lace and glittering with diamonds and turquoises.

By the Queen, whose own taste in clothes was uncertain, such outlandishness might pass unremarked; it was Mary Anne's frank and colourful conversation that astonished her.

'*She* is very vulgar,' noted the Queen, 'not so much in her appearance, as in her way of speaking.'

Dizzy, the Queen pronounced also 'most singular'. He was 'thoroughly Jewish looking, a livid complexion, dark eyes and eyebrows and black ringlets. The expression is disagreeable but I do not find him so to talk to.'

He had, she added, 'a very bland manner, and his language is very flowery.'

Not for long, though, was Disraeli able to employ his bland manner and flowery language on his Sovereign. Before the year 1852 was out, Derby's government had fallen. On retiring from office, the astute Disraeli took care to write letters of thanks to the Queen and Prince Albert for their help and kindness.

'I may perhaps', he wrote to the Prince, 'be permitted to say that the views which Your Royal Highness had developed to me in confidential conversation had not fallen on ungrateful soil. I shall ever remember with interest and admiration the princely mind in the princely person, and shall at all times be prepared to prove to Your Royal Highness my devotion. I have the honour to remain, Sir, Your Royal Highness's most obedient Servant, B. Disraeli.'

The princely mind in the princely person. The Queen could hardly have wished for better than that.

★

Seldom was the difference in temperament between Victoria and
Albert brought into sharper focus than during the Crimean War,
which broke out in March 1854. The Queen's mood of exultation
during this time was something which her husband, so dedicated to
the arts of peace-time and so conscious of the horrors involved, simply
could not share. He worked towards a successful conclusion of the war
as conscientiously as ever, but he was not spurred on by anything like
the same feelings of bellicose patriotism.

In the period leading up to the outbreak of the Crimean War – in
which Britain and France supported Turkey against Russia – British
public opinion suddenly turned against the Prince. As war fever
mounted, so was he accused of all sorts of misconduct: of interference
in military matters, of exercising undue influence over the Queen, of
assuming authority not rightly his, of being – as a foreigner – less than
whole-heartedly dedicated to the British cause. It was even rumoured
that he was about to be arrested for treason and locked up in the
Tower.

The royal couple were extremely upset by these calumnies, but
whereas they left the Prince feeling depressed, they left the Queen
feeling enraged. Although she defended her husband's good name with
characteristic vigour (she even chose this far from propitious moment
to suggest that he be awarded the title of Prince Consort), she could
not help being annoyed by the fact that he was nothing like as angry
as she was. She even accused him of timidity and cowardice. 'The
attacks on Albert', she wrote, 'have the result of making him afraid to
do what I should think right.'

The Queen, who had at first shared the Prince's apprehensions about
the possibility of war, dramatically changed her attitude once it had
been declared. The war, she assured her Uncle Leopold, was 'incredibly
popular'. Suddenly, she saw the times as 'stirring', the Tsar of Russia
as an ogre, and herself as a latter-day Boadicea. The British Army
became 'my Army', the fleet 'my Fleet, and the troops 'my children'.
It was as if the spirit of the great Queen Elizabeth I lived again in her
dumpy little figure.

Braving the icy dawn, she stood on the balcony of Buckingham
Palace to see a battalion of Guards march off to war. They 'cheered
us *very heartily* and went off cheering. It was a *touching and beautiful
sight* ...'. An equally 'splendid and never-to-be-forgotten sight' was
the sailing of 'our noble Fleet' from Spithead. The Navy and the
Nation, she assured her Uncle Leopold, 'were particularly pleased at
my leading them out.'

Her emotions see-sawed between agony at the sufferings of her troops and elation at such scant military successes as there were. When Britain's ally, the Emperor Napoleon III, announced that he was thinking of going out to the Crimea to take personal command of his armies, the Queen was appalled. What if the French troops, led by their Emperor, were to win a glorious victory and so steal the British thunder? That, she exclaimed, she *never* could bear.

In her new belligerent mood the Queen was even prepared to give her *bête noire* – her new Prime Minister, Lord Palmerston – his due. She was obliged to admit that by his courage and energy, the jaunty Palmerston was maintaining the 'honour and interests' of the country.

The longer the grossly mismanaged war dragged on, the stronger became what Charles Greville called the Queen's 'military mania'. She graduated from knitting scarves and mittens for the men and writing heartfelt letters of condolence to the widows, to visiting hospitals for the wounded. In mounting anguish she trailed through ward after ward, making gruesome note of the exact nature of the wounds. Dressed in a scarlet tunic and navy-blue skirt, she sat her horse to review her troops. Looking distinctly less dashing in a lilac dress and a green shawl, she distributed medals to the returned and often cruelly maimed heroes.

'The rough hand of the brave and honest private soldier came for the first time in contact with that of their Sovereign and their Queen' ran her emotional report on this medal-distributing ceremony at Horse Guards. 'Noble fellows! I own I feel as if they were *my own children*; my heart beats for *them* as for my *nearest and dearest*. They were so touched, so pleased; many, I hear, cried ...'.

It was all 'so *beautiful and touching*'; it was all so glorious.

Not, though, for Prince Albert. His more realistic, pessimistic nature could find precious little glory in the situation. Gazing one evening at the London crowds bellowing their 'terrible cry to arms' in the Mall below, he was filled with astonishment at this casting-off of their habitual reserve. He could only think of the risks being run, the hardships endured and the lives unnecessarily lost. He knew how badly prepared, equipped and led the armies were; he knew how wrong it could all go. Wrapped in a blanket because the Queen insisted on setting an example in economies by cutting down on fires (that she seldom felt the cold rendered her sacrifice a shade less noble), the Prince slaved from dawn until midnight: writing reports, making suggestions, thinking up military improvements. His contribution to the struggle may have been more valuable than the Queen's, but he could draw no consolation from that.

Of the war, he one day recorded in typically understated fashion, 'I do not like it myself.'[3]

Whatever may have divided Victoria and Albert in their reactions to the Crimean War, they were united in their distrust of their ally, Napoleon III. The Queen's prompt acceptance of his new imperial status in 1852 had not signalled her personal approval of him, nor of his regime. To Victoria and Albert, Napoleon III remained an adventurer. As upholders of the system of constitutional monarchy, they strongly mistrusted his illiberal and unstable empire.

But they were reckoning without the Emperor's shrewdness in overcoming this mistrust. Having achieved his life-long ambition to restore the great Napoleon's empire, this new Napoleon was determined to avoid the rock on which the First Empire had foundered: Napoleon I's rivalry with Britain. This was one feature of his illustrious uncle's reign he planned *not* to emulate. Subtly but surely, during the years between assuming the imperial crown and the outbreak of the Crimean War, Napoleon III set about courting Britain and, with her, Britain's Queen. He had always preferred to conduct affairs on a personal rather than an official level.

His first approach towards an *entente* with the Queen was the classic one: a royal marriage. In 1853 the forty-four-year-old Emperor sounded Queen Victoria out, indirectly, on the question of a possible marriage between himself and the seventeen-year-old Princess Adelaide of Hohenlohe-Langenburg. Princess Adelaide was the Queen's niece: her mother was the Queen's half-sister, daughter of Queen Victoria's mother's first marriage.

The request threw the Queen into a quandary. She had no wish to offend the Emperor by a refusal, but nor did she want to welcome him into her family circle. He was far too exotic a bird for the Coburg aviary. In any case, she could hardly be expected to allow her unspoilt niece to marry a notorious libertine whose regime might not last for more than a couple of years. In the end, the Queen neatly side-stepped the issue by suggesting, unofficially, that the matter should be decided by the Princess and her parents but that, as they were Protestants, she did not think their acceptance very likely.

Hardly had the Queen extricated herself from this awkward situation than she heard that the Emperor was on the trail of a quite different quarry. Through Lord Cowley, the ambassador in Paris, she heard of

Napoleon's infatuation with a certain Mademoiselle de Montijo. In letter after letter to London, Lord Cowley made much of Napoleon's obsession with the beautiful, red-haired Spanish countess. According to the cynical Cowley, Eugénie de Montijo was simply a flashy *femme du monde*, bent on trapping the Emperor into marriage. In this she was being actively encouraged by her mother – an ambitious busybody, well known in international society.

By the middle of January 1853, with the Second Empire barely six weeks old, Cowley was able to report the success of the Montijo ladies. 'The great one has been captured by an adventuress,' ran the lip-smacking phrases. 'To hear the way in which men and women talk of their future Empress is astounding. Things have been repeated to me, which the Emperor has said of her, and others which have been said to him, which it would be impossible to commit to paper. In fact she has played her game with him so well, that he can get her in no other way but marriage, and it is to gratify his passions that he marries her . . .'.[4]

If Queen Victoria had once complained about the dreariness of her ambassador's reports, she had no reason to do so now.

It was from highly-coloured reports such as these that Queen Victoria formed her opinion of the future Empress Eugénie. She learned that Eugénie's late father had been a grandee of Spain and her mother, less illustriously, the daughter of a wine merchant named Kirkpatrick. Eugénie's youth (she was now twenty-six) had been spent, it appeared, in flitting from one country to another in the company of her worldly mother. It was no wonder the Queen saw the future Empress as a showy *intrigante* ('beautiful, clever, very coquette, passionate and wild', was her description); a fitting match for a somewhat spurious Emperor.

Less than a month after the collapse of his plans to marry Princess Adelaide, Napoleon III married Eugénie de Montijo in the cathedral of Notre-Dame. By that time, the Queen was beginning to revise her opinion of the Empress somewhat. She was obviously not quite the brazen adventuress of Queen Victoria's first imaginings. In a letter to her Uncle Leopold, the Queen admitted that the 'description of the young Empress's character is an interesting one and also agrees with what I had heard from those who know her well. It may be in her power to do much good – and I hope she may. Her character is made to captivate a man, I should say – particularly one like the Emperor.'

But whatever the advantages of Napoleon's marriage to Eugénie may have been, it did not bring him any closer to his longed-for alliance with Great Britain.

And then, gradually, during the next few months, the situation began to change. What Napoleon III had been unable to achieve by diplomacy came about through the threat of war. Britain and France were drawn into a military alliance to defend Turkey against Russia. By March 1854 their combined armies were on their way to wage war against Russia in the Crimea.

But as muddle succeeded muddle in the Crimea, it was thought that some show of solidarity between the allies might not be out of place. Napoleon invited Prince Albert to visit him at the military camp at Boulogne for a few days in early September 1854. The Prince accepted.

The visit was a great success. The Emperor exercised his considerable charm to such an extent that even the normally impervious Prince Albert succumbed. Far from being a tyrant, Napoleon III revealed himself to Prince Albert as a man of almost gentle disposition – calm, indolent, humorous. The Prince was delighted at the ease with which the Emperor spoke German and the readiness with which he recited Schiller. He seemed more like 'a German savant' than a French emperor. Prince Albert might deplore Napoleon's lack of musical appreciation, his incessant cigarette-smoking and the general *ton de garnison* of the imperial entourage, but he welcomed the frankness with which his host discussed any topic and the apparently rapt attention with which he listened to Prince Albert's wordy advice.

. While Prince Albert returned home to write a ponderous memorandum on the visit, Napoleon employed his time in a more advantageous fashion. He bombarded the Queen with praise of her husband. To the Queen such flattery sounded sweet indeed. Not since Disraeli's delightful letter on relinquishing office had the Queen heard the Prince so highly spoken of.

The Emperor, reported the Foreign Secretary Lord Clarendon, 'had spoken with enthusiasm of the Prince, saying that in all his experience he had never met with a person possessing such various and profound knowledge, or who communicated it with the same frankness. His Majesty added that he had never learned so much in so short a time, and was grateful.'

To the gratified Queen, none of this sounded excessive.

Having heaped on the flattery, the Emperor got down to business. He was determined to be received by the Queen. During the visit to Boulogne Prince Albert had said something about the possibility of the Emperor and Empress visiting Windsor; he now pressed for a more definite invitation. The Emperor would be 'delighted to avail himself of the Queen's gracious kindness; nothing would give him so much pleasure ...'.

The Queen, refusing to be tied down, wrote back saying that the Emperor could come if he liked. The middle of November would suit her best. But Napoleon could not agree that November would be a good time. He suggested a later date, to prove that 'the friendship had suffered no diminution', and that it was not merely a manifestation of the political alliance.

The Queen reacted sharply. It was really not for the Emperor, she said, to be suggesting alternative dates. 'His reception here ought to be a boon to him and not a boon to us.'

The stalemate was broken, with dramatic suddenness, early the following year, when Napoleon III announced his intention of going to the Crimea to take personal command of his armies. The campaign having been bogged down for months, the Emperor was anxious to make a *grande geste*; to strike a spectacularly Napoleonic blow for his empire.

The news appalled the British government as much as it did the Queen. No more than she did they relish the idea of the French stealing British thunder. Lord Clarendon hurried across to France to try to dissuade the Emperor from his rash decision. Finding Napoleon ready to listen to reason but unable himself to convince him, Clarendon thought that a state visit by Napoleon to Britain might do the trick. Where British diplomacy had failed, British royalty might well succeed.

This was exactly what the Emperor wanted. He let Lord Cowley know that a visit to Windsor soon after Easter would be convenient. With this the Queen and Prince Albert were obliged to agree. A state visit was arranged to take place from 16 to 21 April 1855.

Part Three

NAPOLEON III

9

'A Very *Extraordinary* Man'

'I CANNOT say what indescribable emotions filled me, how much it felt like a wonderful dream,' wrote Queen Victoria of the moment that she welcomed the Emperor Napoleon III and his beautiful young Empress to Windsor. 'These great meetings of Sovereigns, surrounded by very exciting accompaniments, are always very agitating ...'.

The Queen, for all the apparent assurance of her manner, dreaded meeting strangers. Although she had been on the throne for almost eighteen years, she had still not conquered the inhibiting shyness which she had complained about to Lord Melbourne during the early days of her reign. True, by now she appreciated that Napoleon III was not the ogre of her earlier imaginings: Prince Albert's meeting with him had dispelled any such notions. Nor was the Empress Eugénie the *femme fatale* of Lord Cowley's first reports. In fact, Eugénie had a reputation for chastity; the Queen had been gratified to hear that the Empress admired the high moral tone of the English court. None the less, the visit of this somewhat unorthodox couple was bound to bring some strain.

That it did not was due, almost entirely, to the personality of the Emperor Napoleon III. With his hooded eyes, his hooked nose, his cat's-whisker mustachios and his top-heavy body he might not be considered conventionally handsome, but his air was very reassuring. In no time the Queen found herself responding to his soothing but fascinating manner.

'We got on extremely well at dinner,' she wrote, 'and my great agitation seemed to go off very early; the Emperor is very quiet; his voice is low and soft and *il ne fait pas de phrases*.' There was, admitted the Queen in a letter to her Uncle Leopold the following day, 'great fascination in the quiet, frank manner of the Emperor ...'.

Not for the first, nor for the last time in her life, was Queen Victoria falling under the spell of an accomplished seducer.

In many ways, Napoleon III epitomized the sort of man to whom Queen Victoria was irresistibly drawn. He looked like a buccaneer. His past had been unconventional – rakish, glamorous, adventurous. Something of the dashing, devil-may-care air of the early nineteenth century clung to him still. He was undeniably an exotic. Yet his manner was decorous, his expression impenetrable, his aura mysterious. He was, even to those who knew him well, an enigma: a man in whom ruthless ambition went hand-in-hand with high romanticism, realism with idealism.

He had, in addition, a perfect understanding of women. For Napoleon III – as for Lord Melbourne – feminine company was essential. His behaviour towards the opposite sex was confiding, attentive, flattering. He radiated, in the most gentlemanly way, an undeniable aura of sexuality. And as far as Queen Victoria was concerned, he fully appreciated the value of treating her as a woman first, a sovereign second. It was no wonder that in the plump, plain, normally sensible Queen he roused a strong undercurrent of excitement; that she should find herself becoming more and more attracted to him.

'She was charmed with the Emperor,' the suave Lord Clarendon afterwards told Charles Greville, 'who made love to her, which he did with a tact which proved quite successful. ... and the Queen was mightily tickled by it, for she had never been made love to in her life, and never had conversed with a man of the world on a footing of equality; and as his love-making was of a character to flatter her vanity without alarming her virtue or modesty, she enjoyed the novelty of it without scruple or fear ...'.[1]

Lord Clarendon's assessment is a shade too glib. This was not the first time the Queen had 'been made love to', in the sense that Lord Clarendon meant it. Both Lord Melbourne and Prince Albert, in their different ways, had paid her court. Nor did Napoleon III make love to her in even the generally accepted nineteenth-century sense of the phrase. But he certainly set out to fascinate, flatter and indeed flirt with her. It was not so much what he said, as how he said it. With characteristic astuteness the Emperor had made himself completely conversant with her past, her tastes and her personality. To Victoria, accustomed to Albert's artless manner, Napoleon's interest and attention were flattering in the extreme.

It was 'very extraordinary and unaccountable', she afterwards said to Lord Clarendon with charming naïvety, how the Emperor seemed to know everything about her since she was twelve years old: what she had done, where she had been, even what she had worn.

'Le coquin', thought Lord Clarendon to himself.

On the other hand, Queen Victoria was no fool. Had the Emperor been nothing more than a charlatan, she would have been very quick to discover it. The fact that he set out consciously to impress and captivate her did not mean that he was not impressive or captivating. His advances to the Queen may have been carefully calculated, but they were not forced. Naturally charming and considerate, Napoleon tended to treat every woman as though she were both beautiful and interesting. These things were second nature to him.

Once she had come to appreciate his real worth, Victoria allowed herself to meet him more than half way. She was ripe for the mild, almost unconscious flirtation he was offering her. In this spring of 1855 the Queen was thirty-five years old, quite young enough to believe that she was still a desirable woman. The high-spirited, pleasure-loving young Queen of Lord Melbourne's day had not been completely submerged in Prince Albert's serious-mindedness. By now she had been married to Albert for fifteen years and much as she adored him, there were times when she felt that he was taking her for granted. In any case, Prince Albert had never been one for the honeyed phrases of love-making. For Victoria, with her less disciplined temperament, a periodic flash of emotional colour was a necessity. So when Napoleon, with his dreamy eyes and dangerous reputation, began his subtle advances, Victoria abandoned herself to his attentions.

This skilful courtship was conducted along the most innocuous lines: it never went beyond an exchange of confidences. But then, Victoria had never exchanged confidences with a man like Napoleon III; to the urbanity of a Lord Melbourne, he brought all the swashbuckling air of the man who had so thrilled her girlhood senses, Charles, Duke of Brunswick. Everything Napoleon spoke about seemed tinged with romance and adventure.

Born into the splendour of the First Empire, he had been brought up in the poverty and uncertainty of exile. His first attempt to restore the empire had resulted in his banishment to North America; his second to six years in a French prison. He had spent many years in relatively humble circumstances in London. This had left him, he claimed, with a lasting admiration for all things English. The Emperor told the Queen how deeply impressed he had been by the sight of her, *une jeune personne*, opening Parliament for the first time, eighteen years before. Had she known, he wondered, that he had acted as a special constable

in London during the Chartist riots of 1848? He spoke of the occasion
on which he had paid forty pounds for a box simply to see her pay a
state visit to the theatre. He told her of how he had once been locked
up in a London park for two hours because he had forgotten the time.

Victoria listened and was enthralled. She found these glimpses of his
relatively humble past particularly intriguing. It seemed to her almost
incredible that only six years ago this powerful sovereign had been
living in obscurity. He now behaved, she thought, as though he had
been an emperor for most of his life.

The Emperor, she noted on the fifth day of the visit, 'is *very*
fascinating; he is so quiet and gentle, and has such a soft pleasant voice.
He is besides so simple and plain-spoken in all he says, and so devoid
of all phrases, and has a good deal of poetry, romance and *Schwärmerei*
in his composition, which makes him peculiarly attractive. He is
a most extraordinary, mysterious man, whom one feels excessively
interested in watching and knowing ...'.

In his dealings with Prince Albert, too, the Emperor managed to
strike exactly the right note. He seemed to become less French and
more German, less polished and more philosophical, when he was with
Victoria's husband. Dutifully he trudged round the Prince's model
farm at Windsor and was quite likely, in some quiet moment of the
day, to break into one of the German *Studentenlieder* which he professed
to admire so greatly. He had been educated, he took care to remind
his host, in Bavaria.

'The Emperor is as *unlike a Frenchman* as possible,' claimed Victoria,
'being much more *German* than French in character.' Higher praise she
could hardly bestow.

Napoleon's visit even produced one of Prince Albert's rare flashes
of humour. He would have to have precautions taken in the crypt of
St George's Chapel, quipped Albert on this arrival of a Bonaparte at
Windsor Castle, to ensure that King George III did not turn in his
grave.

The innocence of the Queen's obsession with Napoleon III can be
gauged by her attitude towards his Empress: she was almost equally
enchanted by Eugénie. But whereas Napoleon had set out deliberately
to win over the Queen, Eugénie managed it almost unconsciously.
Like Victoria herself, Eugénie was incapable of dissembling; there was
no hint of deceit or guile in her nature. Her manner was utterly natural.

Nevertheless, Victoria's first – and enduring – impression of Eugénie
was slightly inaccurate. To the Queen, the Empress was always a

beautiful, lively, delicate, gentle and self-effacing creature. Beautiful and lively Eugénie certainly was, but not even her most dedicated apologist could describe her as delicate, gentle and self-effacing. On the contrary, she was a woman of exceptional vitality, assertive manners and strong opinions.

But it is understandable that Eugénie should have created a somewhat different impression at Windsor in that spring of 1855. She was still in her twenties and had been an empress for just over two years. Previous to that, she had had very little contact with courts, having been raised in a quite different *milieu*. Regarded as a showy, shallow *arriviste* by the other crowned heads of Europe, she stood in considerable awe of so long-established and highly respected a monarch as the Queen of England. With so much depending on the success of this visit, the parvenue Empress would have been on her best behaviour. In addition, Eugénie's public manner always tended to be rather diffident, and this would have been accentuated during her visit to this strange and self-confident court.

This was why the Queen could say of the Empress that 'naturally, she felt the *gêne* of her position, from not having been brought up to it,' but that 'her manner is the most perfect thing I have ever seen – so gentle and graceful and kind . . . and so modest and retiring withal.'

About Eugénie's looks, Victoria was in raptures. There is no hint of jealousy here, either, in the Queen's attitude. Time after time, with a wealth of underlinings and capital letters, Victoria made enthusiastic note of the Empress's beauty. Although there was only seven years' difference in their ages, the contrast between them was pronounced. By day, Eugénie would wear some simple dress, uncluttered by any ornament, with her copper-coloured hair drawn well back from her face. This simplicity set off to perfection the translucency of her skin and the blue-green of her down-slanting eyes. Beside her Victoria, with her florid complexion and her rabbity mouth, looked like nothing so much as a middle-aged, badly dressed housewife. At night, the Empress would appear in breath-taking creations of white tulle, with skirts of enormous dimensions.

'*N'est-elle pas délicieuse?*' whispered Victoria to someone as the Empress, at a ball in the Waterloo Gallery, glided by in a crinoline of white net.

Even Prince Albert, usually so impervious to feminine charm, had nothing but praise for Eugénie. On one occasion, when the Empress appeared in a flounced dress of pale green silk, Albert was full of admiration. 'Altogether I am delighted to see how much he likes and admires her,' wrote Victoria, 'as it is so seldom that I see him do so with *any* woman.'

Napoleon III's state visit was divided into two parts: four days were spent at Windsor and three at Buckingham Palace. As far as Queen Victoria was concerned, it was all a brilliant success. At Windsor she enjoyed the dash and glitter of a military review as well as the more sedate ceremony of investing the Emperor with the Order of the Garter. The Queen, commented Lord Clarendon dryly as he watched Victoria fasten the Garter to the Emperor's outstretched leg, 'fumbled *ostensibly*, as she always does, to show her unfamiliarity with the slightly indiscreet article of male attire.'[2] 'At last,' murmured Napoleon to Victoria as they processed out of the Throne Room at the end of the ceremony, 'I am a gentleman.'

In London, the imperial visitors carried out the customary engagements – a Guildhall luncheon, an embassy reception, an attendance at the opera (where it was noted that while the Queen sat down without ever taking her eyes off the applauding audience, the parvenue Empress looked round to make sure of her chair), and a tour of Prince Albert's celebrated creation – the Crystal Palace, now transferred from Hyde Park to Sydenham. At a concert at Buckingham Palace the Queen and the Emperor chatted happily to each other, on 'several important subjects', throughout the performance.

So *causant* was Napoleon's mood, wrote the Queen afterwards, that had the concert been longer he would have been inclined 'to converse upon many *more* delicate subjects even ...'.

Leave-taking at the end of that momentous week left the Queen feeling desolate. Only the prospect of accepting the Emperor's invitation to visit Paris in the summer made the parting bearable. It had all been, she wrote in her Journal that evening, like a dream – 'a brilliant, successful and pleasant dream.'

For the Emperor personally, her enthusiasm knew no bounds.

'That he *is* a very *extraordinary* man, with great qualities, there can be *no* doubt – I might almost say a mysterious man,' she wrote. 'He is evidently possessed of *indomitable courage, unflinching firmness of purpose, self-reliance, perseverance and great secrecy*; to this should be added, a great reliance on what he calls his *Star*, and a belief in omens and incidents as connected with his future destiny, which is almost romantic – and at the same time he is endowed with wonderful *self-control*, great *calmness*, even *gentleness* and with a *power of fascination*, the effect of which upon all those who become more intimately acquainted with him is *most sensibly* felt.'

That the Queen was infatuated, there could be no doubt.

Queen Victoria's return visit to Paris for ten days from 18 August 1855, on which she was accompanied by Prince Albert and their two eldest children, Vicky and Bertie, merely confirmed the Emperor's many fascinations. He had spared no effort to make her stay as spectacular and as comfortable as he could. Although it would be an exaggeration to say that Napoleon III had actually rebuilt Paris for the Queen's reception, his plans for the aggrandizement of his capital were well under way by the time she entered it that summer. In honour of her arrival, the transformed city had been especially decorated as well; its new boulevards were bright with banners, flags, flowers and triumphal arches. The Queen writes of the 'blaze of light from lamps and torches – amidst the roar of cannon, bells and drums, and cheers ... I felt quite bewildered – all was like a fairytale, so beautiful and enchanting!'

Her apartments at the Palace of Saint-Cloud had been redecorated to resemble, as closely as possible, her own at Buckingham Palace. The zealous decorators had even gone so far as to saw the legs off an exquisitely proportioned table lest it prove too high for the diminutive Queen. All this gave her, she exclaimed in answer to the Emperor's solicitous enquiries, such 'a home feeling!'

If Napoleon was the perfect host, Victoria was no less the perfect guest. Everything was charming. Despite her 'home feeling', she had to admit that it was all very different from England. Saint-Cloud seemed so delightfully foreign: those *outside* shutters, those clipped avenues, those orange trees in tubs, that luminous atmosphere, that view of distant Paris, so white and glittery. The coffee was excellent and the cornices, gilded in *three* different shades of gold, quite splendid. The furniture was 'so well stuffed', noted the Queen, 'that by lying a little while on the sofa, you are completely rested.'

Hardly had the royal party settled in at Saint-Cloud than Napoleon was able to take up, once more, the threads of his subtle courtship. He saw to it that he was alone with Victoria as they drove in a phaeton through the dappled sunshine of the tree-lined avenues; it was on his arm that the Queen strolled through the formal gardens of the palace after the first day's luncheon; it was on her side of the barouche that Napoleon rode his horse when they all went for a drive in the newly laid-out Bois de Boulogne. And in no time she had once more fallen under his spell. Even she was at a loss for adjectives to do justice to his many qualities. 'He is so simple, so *naïf*, never making *des phrases*, or paying compliments – so full of tact, good taste, high breeding . . .'.

On and on ran the royal pen until the recipients of Victoria's letters must have wondered whether Napoleon were some sort of magician, or whether Victoria had indeed fallen in love. 'For the Emperor personally, I have conceived a real affection', admitted the Queen to Baron Stockmar; he had 'the power of attaching those to him who come near him, which is quite incredible.'

What Prince Albert referred to as 'the Parisian campaign' began on the second day of their stay and lasted for a week. They paid several visits to the *Exposition Universelle*, they toured the Louvre, they attended one ball at the Hôtel de Ville and another at Versailles (on both occasions the Queen amazed the onlookers by the energy of her dancing and the inelegance of her clothes) and paid homage to the remains of Napoleon I in the Hôtel des Invalides. 'There I stood,' the Queen afterwards noted in amazement, 'at the arm of Napoleon III, his nephew, before the coffin of England's bitterest foe; I, the grand-daughter of that King who hated him most, and who most vigorously opposed him, and this very nephew, who bears his name, being my nearest and dearest ally!'

Two aspects of Queen Victoria's behaviour during this state visit were especially striking; one was her almost boundless energy, the other her unfeigned enjoyment of things. Time and again she mani-fested these two admirable and endearing characteristics. She would not even allow the heat, which she admitted was like a 'furnace', to spoil her pleasure. One afternoon, following an exhausting morning at the *Exposition*, she spent several hours driving through the streets of Paris. The huge, good-natured crowd roared its approval as she sat in the merciless sunshine, responding gaily and tirelessly to the cheers. She, in turn, registered her approval of Paris and the Parisians.

'Everything so gay, so bright, and though very hot, the air is so clear and light. The absence of smoke keeps everything so white and bright, and this in Paris, with much gilding about the shops, green shutters etc., produces a brilliancy of effect which is quite incredible . . .' she enthused.

On passing the Conciergerie, Napoleon informed her that that was where he had been imprisoned after one of his attempts to overthrow the regime of King Louis Philippe. 'Strange, incredible contrast, to be driving with us as Emperor through the streets of the town in triumph!' exclaimed the Queen.

'I am *delighted, enchanted, amused* and *interested*, and think that I never saw anything more *beautiful* and gay than Paris – or more splendid than all the Palaces ...' she gushed to her Uncle Leopold. 'How beautiful and enjoyable is this place!'

Prince Albert's mood was not nearly as euphoric as his wife's. He was undoubtedly enjoying his stay in Paris, but he could not entirely overcome his reservations about Napoleon III's regime. For this earnest, liberal-minded Prince, devoted to the ideals of peace and orderly progress, the Second Empire was far too showy, too militant, too loosely rooted. He was deeply impressed by the improvements to Paris, he was intensely interested in the *Exposition*, he was even ready to believe, to a certain extent, in the Emperor's professed love of peace. But he remained uneasy. He could not share the Queen's uncritical enthusiasm for the regime, and for the French alliance.

Yet even he could not help being charmed by the Emperor personally. 'I have frequently talked with Albert,' wrote Victoria, 'who is naturally much calmer, and particularly much less taken by people, much less under *personal* influence than I am. He quite admits that it is extraordinary how very much attached one becomes to him when one lives with the Emperor, quite at one's ease and intimately, as we have done during the last ten days ...'.

The Emperor, she went on to claim, 'is so fond of Albert, appreciating him so thoroughly, and shows him so much confidence.' Indeed, when the visit was over, Napoleon wrote to tell Albert of his great esteem for his character and of his friendship for his person. 'Of this you must be convinced,' continued Napoleon, 'for we know by intuition those who love us.'

In the face of such unreserved admiration, even the wary Prince Albert was obliged to melt.

There was no hint of restraint in the response of the Prince's children to their host and hostess. Vicky and Bertie were besotted with the imperial pair: Vicky with the Empress and Bertie with the Emperor. The Princess Royal's crush on Eugénie, which had blossomed in England, was now in full flower. 'Vicky is never tired of praising the beauty, kindness and goodness of the Empress ...', wrote Queen Victoria. Only the fact that Eugénie was pregnant and therefore unable to accompany the party on every occasion disappointed Vicky.

As for Bertie, the Emperor was introducing him to a whole new world. Napoleon III, who loved children, knew exactly how to treat a boy like the Prince of Wales. So accustomed to the humourless, heavy-handed ways of his father and his tutors, Bertie found himself responding immediately. Here, in the person of the Emperor of the French, was a man who accepted him for what he was. Here was someone who seemed to take an unashamed delight in those things in which Bertie delighted; who loved show and colour and movement; who lived, quite naturally and unashamedly, for pleasure. To the young Prince, whose life had always been narrow, repressed and dedicated to self-improvement, Napoleon's tolerance, ease of manner and sense of enjoyment were a revelation. This, surely, was how life was meant to be lived.

It was during this visit to Paris that Bertie's great love of France was born. The beauty of the French capital, the liveliness of the French people, the *bonhomie* of the French emperor, the elegance of the French Empress, made an indelible impression on his young, pleasure-hungry nature. From the time of this first visit to Paris until the establishment, almost fifty years later, of the *entente cordiale*, he never ceased to work for an understanding between the two countries.

On the last night but one of the visit, the Queen and the Emperor, having returned to the Palace of Saint-Cloud from a ball at Versailles, sat up for another hour, loath to go to bed and so put an end to a magical evening.

'It's terrible that there's only one more night,' sighed the Emperor. In full agreement, Victoria begged him to come soon again to see her in England. 'Most certainly!' he answered.

'But *you* will come back, won't you?' Napoleon insisted. 'Now that we know each other, we can visit each other at Windsor or Fontainebleau without any ceremony, can't we?'

This would give her great pleasure, said the Queen. Laughingly, she told him that she would come back the following year as an ordinary traveller. With her bag in her hand, she would jump out of the train, take a cab and present herself at the Tuileries to beg some dinner. It was a delicious if wistful idea.

Here was Queen Victoria at her most endearing: a frank, charming and happy young woman, very much in love with life and – unknowingly – more than half in love with Napoleon III. No one seeing her flushed face, her bright eyes and her sweet smile would have doubted that she was enjoying herself to the full. It was so seldom that Queen Victoria was able to relax with anyone other than the members of her family. And few were able to put her at her ease as completely as this softly-spoken, worldly man sitting beside her.

But, of course, Napoleon's accomplishments did not end with putting the normally shy Queen at her ease. As valuable was his ability to create a heady, almost erotic atmosphere, an atmosphere to which her passionate nature was quick to respond. No wonder she claimed that she would always look back on this period as one of the most memorable of her life. Nor is it surprising that for days after she got back to England she felt 'dreadfully bewildered, excited, and unable to do anything but think and talk of everything . . .'.

Her final parting from this disturbing man was even more upsetting than most such partings. He had come to Boulogne to see them off and that night, having accompanied them out to sea on their yacht, took his leave. With 'a heavy heart' the Queen watched him climb down into the barge which was to carry him to his own yacht. As the little boat pulled away, Napoleon called out to her. *'Adieu, Madame; au revoir!'*

'Je l'espère bien,' cried the Queen in return.

She stood by the rail, watching the boat being rowed across the glittering sea, with no sound other than the splash of the oars to break the silence. She saw the Emperor climb aboard his own yacht and watched as it slipped away in the darkness. For a long time she stood waving her handkerchief until all hope of Napoleon seeing her had gone; 'and then *all* was still – all over . . .', she said.

She did not get to bed until a quarter to two, 'low, bewildered and excited'. The night that she left France, she afterwards admitted to Lady Cowley, she felt 'so unhappy'.

And on the very day that she arrived back home, she instructed Lord Clarendon to ask Lord Cowley to collect everything that the Emperor had 'said, thought or written about the visit and *herself*.'[3] Nothing, she insisted, would be too small or insignificant.

10

'We Really are *Great Friends...*'

IN HER customary end-of-the-year résumé, Queen Victoria noted that not least among the many joys of 1855 (the year in which she met Napoleon III) was the 'happy conviction that I have made great progress and am trying energetically to overcome my faults.' How, she continued, 'can I thank my dearest Albert for his unchanging love and wonderful tenderness, quite unchanged during these sixteen years!' She was being too sanguine. The following eighteen months were to bring several marital crises and to test Prince Albert's 'unchanging love and wonderful tenderness' considerably.

Much of the Queen's emotional turbulence during this period was associated with her eldest and youngest daughters: with the secret engagement of Vicky, who had turned fifteen in November 1855, and with the birth of Beatrice in April 1857.

Vicky's secret engagement, when still only fourteen, to the twenty-four-year-old Prince Frederick William of Prussia, in September 1855, was a love match. It also, though, served as a first step towards the realization of one of Prince Albert's most cherished dreams: the unification of the fragmented states of Germany under Prussia. By this linking of the royal houses of Great Britain and Prussia, Prince Albert hoped to provide a future united Germany with a ruling couple who reflected his own progressive ideals and who would ensure that this Greater Germany was a suitably liberal and peace-loving state.

In this high-minded goal, Albert was fully backed up by Victoria. Any doubts that the Queen may have harboured about the wisdom of encouraging a fourteen-year-old girl to become engaged were stifled by the conviction that she was furthering her beloved Albert's noble scheme. It was all in such a glorious cause. Even if Vicky was somewhat young, her parents could not run the risk of the handsome, affable twenty-four-year-old Prince Frederick William being snatched away by some other royal house. And it was not as if they were forcing the match. Fritz was clearly in love with Vicky and she, who as everyone agreed was very mature for her age, was no less enamoured of him. In any case, the marriage would not take place until after Vicky had turned seventeen, in over two years' time.

To square this projected child-marriage with her conscience, Queen Victoria began treating her eldest daughter as an adult. More and more often was Vicky allowed to join her parents as a fellow grown-up. The dinners and evenings which Victoria and Albert had always enjoyed *à deux* now became *à trois*, with the father's delight in the presence of his attractive and precocious daughter only too apparent.

Had this state of affairs lasted for a matter of weeks, or even months, the Queen would no doubt have coped with it, but the two-and-a-half-year stretch between Vicky's secret engagement and her wedding – set for 25 January 1858 – put a considerable strain on the Queen. It was not that she disliked Vicky. On the contrary, she was fond of her and proud of her and almost as excited about her forthcoming marriage as the girl was herself. But there was no denying that, deep down, the Queen was jealous of her. She resented the fact that Albert, of whom she saw so little during the day, devoted so much of his time to Vicky in the evenings. She resented the fact that Albert was so obviously impressed by Vicky's quickness and cleverness. And she resented, most of all, the fact that Albert loved Vicky so deeply. *She* wanted to be the chief object of her husband's attention, admiration and devotion; *she* wanted to be his 'child'.

The Queen's churning emotions were further upset by the realization that she was again pregnant: by the autumn of 1856 it was certain that she would be giving birth to her ninth child the following spring. The pregnancy, which as always rendered her depressed and irritable, was made worse by a series of flaming rows with Prince Albert. Significantly, in the course of them, her attitude to Vicky kept cropping up. The Prince accused her of being 'thankful' that she would soon be rid of Vicky; she made it clear that she did not want Vicky to spend her evenings with them.

These rows, which invariably started with the Queen flaring up at some remark of his, would be followed by a period of tension in which she would make a 'parade' of her suffering; as much as to say to her husband, 'See, this is *your* work.' Albert would then write her one of those maddeningly logical, analytical, eminently reasonable letters.

Instead of having the desired effect of calming her, they simply made matters worse.

As the time of the baby's birth drew nearer, the Queen became still more querulous. She begged the Prince to uphold her authority with the children and not to scold her in front of them. Her nerves, she said, were 'shaken'. Her condition left her with feelings of 'degradation, indignation etc. etc.' The whole business of child-bearing, she complained at a later stage, was humiliating. 'I think much more of our being like a cow or a dog at such moments; when our poor nature becomes so very animal and unecstatic...'. Child-bearing was 'such a complete violence to all one's feelings of propriety'; God knows, she added, those feelings of propriety received 'shock enough' in the intimate marital act.[1]

The birth of Princess Beatrice, on 14 April 1857, ushered in a period of domestic harmony, with the Queen making a conscious effort to control her emotions. Indeed, it marked the start of what she was later to call an 'epoch of progress'. During it, Victoria resumed her more characteristic pose: that, not of the petulant wife, but of the assured and resolute Queen. For instance, a demand by the Prussian royal family that Vicky be married in Germany rather than Britain brought forth one of the Queen's typically affronted replies.

The assumption, she thundered to Lord Clarendon, 'of it's being *too much* for a Prince Royal of Prussia to *come* over to marry *the Princess Royal of Great Britain* IN England is too absurd, to say the least ... Whatever may be the usual practice of Prussian Princes, it is not *every* day that one marries the eldest daughter of the Queen of England.'

That Victoria's scenes with Albert were surface matters only, born out of her deep and possessive love for him, was only too apparent from the determination with which she battled for the realization of one of her most cherished ambitions: the creation of her husband as Prince Consort. Ever since their marriage she had been trying to secure him an appropriate royal title, one that would define his status both in Britain and on the Continent. Now that almost all the members of the old royal family who had objected so strongly to any elevation of an obscure German princeling were dead, she felt that she could make another attempt. The current Prime Minister, Lord Palmerston, having read her lengthy memorandum of the subject, proved sympathetic. But with Parliament deciding that it could not confer the title, the Queen resolved the matter by creating him Prince Consort (even she appreciated that the title of King Consort might present difficulties) by letters patent on 25 June 1857.

Queen Victoria now had the satisfaction of knowing that her beloved husband was 'an Englishman, bearing an English title, and enjoying the legal position' which she need not defend 'with a wife's anxiety' against possible usurpation by 'her own children, her subjects and Foreign Courts'.

But Albert's new title meant more to her than this. In Queen Victoria's eyes it was an affirmation, not only of his exceptional qualities, but of her abiding love.

By the autumn of that same year – 1857 – Queen Victoria found herself succumbing, once more, to the fascinations of that altogether less worthy man, the Emperor Napoleon III. The successful conclusion of the Crimean War, leading to the signing of the Peace of Paris in the spring of 1856, had seemed to confirm not only the Anglo-French alliance but also the friendship between the two sovereigns. The Queen wrote enthusiastically of 'my brother and faithful ally – and *friend*, Napoleon III – I may add for we really are *great friends . . .*'. Although Victoria might complain, in private, that the peace treaty was not really favourable to Britain, she could not help congratulating Napoleon on his skilful handling of the delicate negotiations. The Emperor, in turn, was lavish in his praise of Britain's conciliatory attitude.

There was further cause for an affectionate exchange of letters between the sovereigns during that spring of 1856. On 16 March the Empress Eugénie gave birth to a son. It had been an extraordinarily difficult delivery. Victoria was told how the normally impassive Emperor's eyes filled with tears on describing his wife's sufferings. Napoleon had been deeply touched, reported the Foreign Secretary, by the Queen's letters of congratulation. Indeed, the Emperor lost no time in thanking the Queen personally. His wish, he wrote with customary adroitness, was that his newly born son might resemble Victoria's favourite child, 'dear little Prince Arthur', and that the Prince Imperial would develop the 'rare qualities' of the Queen's own children.

'I hope', he continued, 'my son will inherit my feelings of sincere affectionate esteem for the great English nation.'

But in the months following Napoleon's double triumph – the Peace of Paris and the birth of an heir – the Anglo-French alliance began to show the first signs of strain. Napoleon III's tentative advances towards the allies' recent enemy – Russia – alarmed the British government considerably. The Queen was no less alarmed. Was the Emperor planning to end the Anglo-French *entente*? She wrote several letters to

1. Queen Victoria receiving the news of her accession from the Archbishop of Canterbury and the Lord Chamberlain. From *V.R.I. Her Life and Empire* by the Marquis of Lorne.

2. The young Queen's first romantic attachment: the urbane Lord Melbourne.
Author's Collection.

3. A detail of a painting of Queen Victoria riding with Lord Melbourne at Windsor.
The Royal Collection.

4. The Queen's favourite painting of Prince Albert, as a knight in shining armour.
The Royal Collection.

5. Queen Victoria at the time of her marriage to Prince Albert. Author's Collection.

6. The Queen, Prince Albert and the young Prince of Wales in the Highlands. From *Sixty Years a Queen* by Sir Herbert Maxwell.

7. A sketch of Louis Napoleon in 1852, the year in which he assumed the title of Napoleon III, Emperor of the French. Author's Collection.

8. The Empress Eugénie, Spanish-born consort of Napoleon III. Author's Collection.

9. A drawing of Queen Victoria at the time of her first meeting with Napoleon III. Author's Collection.

10. Napoleon III, Queen Victoria, the Empress Eugénie and Prince Albert at the opera during the state visit to Britain in 1855. Author's Collection.

11. The Reality: The Queen and the Prince Consort photographed in 1861. Royal Archives.

12. The Ideal: Theed's statue of the Prince Consort 'alluring' his adoring wife to 'brighter worlds'. From *Sixty Years a Queen*.

13. 'The Queen's Highland Servant': the bluff and handsome John Brown. Author's Collection.

14. The Queen and John Brown photographed at Balmoral. Royal Archives.

15. The astute and silver-tongued Disraeli. Author's Collection.

16. A copy of the painting of Queen Victoria by Joachim von Angeli, given by the Queen to Disraeli. Author's Collection.

17. The romantic and political partnership: Queen Victoria and Benjamin Disraeli, Earl of Beaconsfield. Author's Collection.

18. Queen Victoria's last emotional obsession: the Munshi Abdul Karim. Royal Archives.

19. The controversial photograph of Queen Victoria and the Munshi which appeared in *The Graphic*. Royal Archives.

the Empress on the subject, but was assured by Eugénie that there was nothing to fear. Lord Clarendon, too, was able to put the Queen's mind at rest by reporting, on excellent authority, that 'the Emperor is as staunch as ever to the Alliance, and that he believes that all his personal interests as well as those of France are bound up with England.'

Queen Victoria's first stirrings of disenchantment with the Emperor must have been further heightened by rumours of his infatuation for the nineteen-year-old Italian beauty, the Countess de Castiglione. The Countess was the first of the many mistresses who were to make the Empress Eugénie's married life so embarrassingly difficult. Lord Cowley was forever passing on tit-bits about Napoleon's latest affair. The Emperor once absented himself from a fête for a *whole* evening, reported the ambassador, by spending it in 'certain dark walks' with the ravishing Countess. At a later stage Napoleon used to set out to visit her each evening between eleven and midnight: 'how long he stays', wrote Cowley with a hint of regret, 'I cannot tell you.'[2]

The Queen, who had so recently been the object of the Emperor's admiring, if chaste, attentions, cannot have found such information especially flattering.

Conscious of the slight slackening of those 'bonds of friendship' between France and Britain, Napoleon now decided that it was time for another meeting between the sovereigns. The French ambassador, in conversation with Lord Clarendon, spoke of the Emperor's earnest desire to come to England on a private visit 'in order to *éclairer* his own ideas, to guide his policy, and to prevent by personal communication with the Queen, His Royal Highness and Her Majesty's Government the dissidences and *mésintelligences* which the Emperor thinks will arise for want of such communications.'

The Queen, Prince Albert assured Clarendon, was quite ready to do whatever was best for the public interest. It was therefore agreed that the Emperor and Empress should visit Osborne from 6 to 10 August 1857. As this was a period during which the Queen was normally in residence, as well as the 'best yachting season', it was imagined that the imperial visit would appear 'less *forcé*'.

'I have no doubt', wrote Albert in a somewhat lukewarm strain, 'that good will arise from a renewed intercourse with the Emperor.'

In contrast to the state visit of 1855, this four-day stay at Osborne was extremely informal. Although the Queen's description of the house as 'poor, dear, modest, unpretentious Osborne' was a shade fanciful, the tone of the visit was decidedly domestic. With the exception of a dance

held in a marquee and a couple of large dinner-parties, there was
nothing in the way of formal entertaining. The party amused themselves by walking or driving about the estate and by sight-seeing on
the island. They explored Carisbrooke Castle, they sailed up the Solent,
they trudged around Albert's inevitable model farm, they drove, in
charabancs, to Ryde. The Empress wore simple cambric and muslin
dresses; the Emperor was never in uniform. A great deal of time was
spent in the company of the royal children. 'They were much admired,
including our dear little pet, Beatrice,' wrote the Queen. Princess
Beatrice was by then four months old. The weather for much of the
time was 'abominable', so that the Queen's Journal notes a succession
of postponed outings and scurryings-in out of the rain.

Yet they seem to have enjoyed these unsophisticated amusements
immensely. The island, despite grey skies, was looking its tranquil,
summery best; the sea was alive with yachts assembled for the regatta.
The Queen was able to make the satisfactory entry in her Journal that
they were 'all very merry – none more so than the Empress.'

Indeed, it was Eugénie who seems to have made the strongest
impression on Victoria during this visit. She was obviously enchanted
by the Empress. In contrast, the Queen had rather less to say about the
Emperor. It was not that she was disappointed in his manner in any
way, or that he had ceased to intrigue her; it was simply that the
emphasis had shifted. Whereas before she could never find enough
superlatives to do justice to his many qualities, she appeared to be
taking him for granted now and to be discovering Eugénie's many
fascinations. Napoleon's liaison with the Countess de Castiglione may
have had something to do with this. So devoted to her own unques-
tionably faithful husband, Victoria could not help but disapprove of
the Emperor's infidelity. Yet it is unlikely that the Empress was suffering from anything worse than loss of face; as Eugénie had never been
deeply in love with her husband, her pride rather than her heart would
have felt the hurt.

'Nothing escapes the dear Empress,' wrote the Queen, 'whatever it
is seemed to interest and please her. She really is quite charming, so
lovely, so graceful, so merry, so natural, clever and lively and full of
conversation . . .'.

The truth was that, since their first meeting over two years before,
the Empress had matured. The Queen was quick to notice the change.
She pronounced Eugénie to be 'very well-informed and read, much
more serious than people give her credit for – understanding all the
questions of the day.' Her opinions always made very good sense. The

Emperor, thought the Queen, would do well to follow her advice. Victoria went on to say that Albert 'is excessively fond of her, and I think few, if any Princess has pleased him as much'.

This might, indeed, have been one of the reasons for Victoria's championship of Eugénie. Albert had never really trusted Napoleon and, now that minor disagreements had broken out between their two countries, he was beginning to trust him even less. During the course of this Osborne visit Napoleon and Albert, with attendant ministers, held a series of political talks; the Emperor's views did little to allay the Prince's apprehensions. On the other hand, Albert often found himself in accord with Eugénie's opinions. Like Albert, Eugénie disapproved of the rumoured Franco-Russian *rapprochement* and did not really share her husband's faith in the theory of 'completed nationalities' to settle Europe's problems. Her outlook was more conservative, her manner less devious, than his.

Albert, reported Victoria to King Leopold, was the Empress's 'great ally'. And as the Queen usually looked to her husband for guidance, her attitude towards the imperial couple was beginning to echo his.

When the visit was over and the Queen answered Napoleon's letter of thanks, she tactfully but firmly advised him to take notice of his wife's opinions. 'In a position so isolated as ours,' she wrote, 'we can find no greater consolation, no support more sure, than the sympathy and counsel of him or her who is called to share our lot in life, and the dear Empress, with her generous impulses, is your guardian angel, as the Prince is my true friend.'

They all parted on the best of terms. Leave-taking was preceded by the usual exchange of gifts and by the usual floods of tears in the royal nursery. There were the usual promises to see each other again. Victoria, Albert, their three eldest children and their household boarded the imperial yacht and inspected it thoroughly. 'Not large or commodious', was the Queen's verdict. Having said their last farewells, they were rowed back to the shore. With the French sailors shouting '*Vive la Reine d'Angleterre*' and the Empress waving her white handkerchief again and again, the imperial yacht steamed away. The royal party returned to Osborne, feeling 'rather *désœuvrée*'.

'The Emperor and Empress so kind and civil, and so thoroughly pleasant and amiable,' noted Victoria, 'I know of no other royalties who are less *gênant*.'

Within six months the Queen was once more in contact with the

man who so closely resembled the Emperor Napoleon III: Benjamin
Disraeli. The fall of Lord Palmerston's government early in 1858 meant
that Lord Derby once again became Prime Minister and Disraeli
Chancellor of the Exchequer. In no time the Queen was receiving
those delectable reports from Mr Disraeli.

'Your Majesty once deigned to say that Your Majesty wished in
these remarks to have the temper of the House placed before Your
Majesty, and to find what Your Majesty could not meet in the newspapers,' ran his mellifluous phrases. 'This is the Chancellor of the
Exchequer's excuse for these rough notes, written on the field of battle,
which he humbly offers to Your Majesty.'

Once again the proceedings in the Commons were brought to vivid
life for the Queen. She knew when the house was 'tranquil and
interesting' or when it was 'wild and capricious'. She knew that a
statement had been 'clear, calm, courteous, persuasive, and full of
knowledge' or when a speech had been 'apt, terse and telling'. She
could smile at the story of the wife of the Governor of Singapore who
insisted on employing convicts in her nursery; when asked whether
she chose thieves or murderers, the lady's unhesitating reply was
'Always murderers'.

And there was closer contact than this. In April 1858 Disraeli was
invited – without his wife – to Windsor. He was able to assure Mary
Anne that the Queen was 'very gracious' and that Prince Albert 'talked
to me a great deal.' September of the same year saw him at Osborne
which, in his inimitable style, he described as 'a Sicilian Palazzo with
gardens, terraces, statues and vases shining in the sunshine, than which
nothing can be conceived more captivating'.

Disraeli's boast that Prince Albert had spoken to him a great deal
did not really signify very much. The Prince did not approve of
Disraeli. It was the Napoleon III story all over again. The charm and
the wit and the flattery which were beginning to melt the Queen's
previous hostility, the Prince Consort found less irresistible. Disraeli
might, when in office, be careful to keep the Prince fully informed,
and to be lavish with praise of his painstaking memoranda, but Albert
could never quite shake himself free of the notion that Disraeli was an
opportunist.

Yet in spite of the Prince's disapproval, the Queen's regard for Mr
Disraeli increased considerably during the parliamentary session of
1858. This saw the passing of a measure on which the hearts of Victoria
and Disraeli beat as one. This was the India Bill. The horrific Indian
Mutiny of the year before had underlined the fact that the days of

rule by the East India Company must end, and that India should be transferred to the British Crown. With satisfaction the Queen made note of the general feeling that 'India should belong to *me* . . .'.

This was certainly Disraeli's view. Things like chartered companies were incomprehensible to people of the East, he argued; one must appeal to their imaginations. He had no sympathy for those who wanted to westernize and 'civilize' the gorgeous East. Its glamour should be enhanced, not minimized: it needed the mystique of a monarch, not the bleakness of a chartered company. The Indians should understand that their 'real Ruler and Sovereign' was Queen Victoria and that she would respect their laws, customs and religions.

The India Bill received the Queen's assent in August 1858. She applied herself to her new responsibility with a customary sense of duty. Her Proclamation to her Indian subjects, drawn up in her name, she altered radically. In common with Disraeli, who had always spoken out strongly against any attempt to undermine the power of the princes or to convert the masses, Victoria was all for Indian traditions being respected and upheld.

Lord Derby must understand, she wrote, that she was 'a female sovereign who speaks to more than a hundred millions of Eastern people', so that her Proclamation 'should breathe feelings of generosity, benevolence and religious toleration'.

Her revised Proclamation was received by Lord Canning, the Viceroy of India, in October 1858. 'It is a source of great satisfaction and pride to her to feel herself in direct communication with that enormous Empire which is so bright a jewel in her Crown, and which she would wish to see happy, contented and peaceful,' she wrote to the Viceroy. 'May the publication of her Proclamation be the beginning of a new era, and may it draw a veil over the sad and bloody past.'

The passage might have been written by Disraeli himself.

Although the India Bill was not in fact Disraeli's creation (and was, as he described it to the Queen, 'only the ante-chamber to an imperial palace'), it set the two of them – Victoria and Disraeli – on the road that was to end so triumphantly eighteen years later when he made her Empress of India.

11

'The Universal Disturber'

ON THE night of 14 January 1858 Queen Victoria, just arrived at Buckingham Palace to welcome the first of the guests for the Princess Royal's wedding, was told some startling news from Paris. The Emperor Napoleon III and the Empress Eugénie had narrowly escaped assassination. The imperial couple had been driving in state to the opera when three bombs were flung at their carriage. Although the explosions had killed ten people and wounded over a hundred others, the Emperor and Empress had escaped serious injury. There were slight cuts on their faces from splintering glass, and Eugénie's white crinoline had been splattered with blood. Her calm, the Queen was told, had been exceptional. 'Don't bother about us,' she had said quietly to the frantic police, 'such things are our profession. Look after the wounded.' They had entered the opera house to be given a wild ovation by the audience and had remained in their box, noted the admiring Victoria, 'through the whole performance.'

This assassination attempt, serious enough in itself, sparked off a series of even more disastrous events that ended by straining the relationship between Britain and France, and between Victoria and Napoleon III, to the limits.

When arrests were made it was discovered that the bomb-throwers, led by an Italian by the name of Orsini, had all come from England. The plot had been hatched in London, and the bombs made in Birmingham. Thus, despite the fact that the reasons for the attack were tied up with a campaign for the liberation of Italy from Austrian rule, it was against Britain that the wrath of France was chiefly directed. In fiery addresses of congratulation to Napoleon on his escape, army officers openly insulted the British government for granting political asylum to the enemies of the Second Empire.

Not unnaturally, Britain took strong exception to these attacks. The Queen claimed that her subjects were 'very indignant here at the conduct of the French officers, and at the offensive insinuations against this country . . .'.

While, in France, Napleon was coerced into passing harsh legislation in the cause of public safety, from Britain he asked for an assurance that political refugees would be treated with more strictness in future. To this Palmerston – at that stage still Prime Minister – acquiesced by introducing a bill to make conspiracy to murder a felony. Parliament, aflame with national pride, refused to be dictated to by France, and the government was forced to resign. Palmerston was succeeded by Lord Derby, who with Disraeli as Chancellor headed a short-lived Tory government.

With the advent of Lord Derby's administration the agitation died down a little. Lord Malmesbury, the new Foreign Secretary, was able to assure the Queen that 'much of the excitement that prevailed on the *other* side of the water is subsiding . . .'. And a few days later Disraeli reported that his announcement in the House, about the 'painful misconceptions' between Britain and France having terminated in an honourable and friendly spirit, had met with cheers.

Taking advantage of the improved atmosphere, Napoleon decided that a little more personal diplomacy was called for. He invited Queen Victoria and Prince Albert to visit him at Cherbourg, in August 1858.

This would be the royal couple's second visit to Cherbourg within a year. In August 1857, soon after the imperial stay at Osborne, Victoria and Albert had paid an unofficial two-day visit to Cherbourg in the royal yacht. They had been deeply disturbed by what they saw. Napoleon III's new fortifications were alarming in the extreme. 'Cherbourg is a gigantic works that gives one grave cause for reflection,' the worried Prince Albert had reported to Baron Stockmar.[1] The royal couple returned home determined that British defences must be improved.

Now, a day or two before this second visit to Cherbourg, Queen Victoria wrote a strong letter to Lord Derby, impressing upon him the importance of building up Britain's sea power. What was required was 'action, and immediate action'. The plan recently put forward by the Surveyor of the Navy she dismissed as far too moderate and judicious. It was imperative that the cabinet spend more money on the building of a battle fleet. 'Time is most precious under these circumstances!' she declared.

In this troubled state of mind, then, did Queen Victoria and Prince Albert, with the Prince of Wales, cross the Channel for their visit. The so-called Cherbourg Fêtes, at which they were to be the guests of honour, were planned as a week-long celebration to mark, among other things, the inauguration of a vast new dock. The ambitious naval works at Cherbourg had been compared by the Emperor to the marvels of ancient Egypt. It was a curious comparison, and one which afforded *Punch* the opportunity of publishing a cartoon of a sphinx, with the fittingly inscrutable face of Napoleon III, rising out of the sea.

Although cordial enough on the surface, the meeting between the Queen and the Emperor lacked the usual warmth. On the first evening, while the Queen's yacht *Victoria and Albert* lay at anchor, a splendid barge canopied in green velvet and crowned by a golden eagle brought the Emperor and Empress on an unofficial, hour-long visit to their royal guests. The call was not a great success. Victoria found Napoleon '*boutonné* and silent', Albert felt aware of a change in his attitude, and even Lord Malmesbury the Foreign Secretary, who was an old friend of the Emperor's, could find nothing better to say than that Napoleon was friendly 'in his manner'.

The imperial couple were upset by certain attacks made on them by the London *Times* (Eugénie had come in for some especially strong criticism), and it was with difficulty that the freedom of the British press was explained to them. It was noticed that the Queen made a point of not giving the customary royal kiss to the young Madame Walewska, wife of Count Walewski – the illegitimate son of Napoleon I by Marie Walewska and one-time French ambassador in London – who was known to be the latest object of the Emperor's fickle affections. In more ways than one, it seemed, was the third Napoleon emulating the first. This latest *affaire* may have been one of the reasons for Eugénie looking, as Prince Albert noted, 'out of health'.

The rather strained visit over, Queen Victoria could hardly wait to get back to reading that 'most interesting' book, *Jane Eyre*.

For over an hour the following morning the Queen sat on deck beneath an awning, sketching the exciting marine activity in front of her. Their official landing was followed by lunch with the imperial couple at the *préfecture* and then a tour of the port and its surroundings. 'The nice caps of the *paysannes* were very numerous, transcendently white and they looked very pretty and picturesque,' noted the Queen. It was not, though, the quaintness of Breton national dress that most deeply impressed her. It was the all-too-apparent evidence of French naval might. The massive fortifications, the enormous dockyards, the vast French fleet riding at anchor in the bay, disturbed the royal visitors considerably.

'Cannons, cannons, cannons, wherever you turned,' wrote the correspondent of *The Times*. 'They poured upon you from every corner, they commanded every turning ... one could not help wondering what in the name of wonder they were meant to attack or defend.' On this score Prince Albert had very little doubt. The theory put forward by one British journal, that Napoleon III would never have shown Queen Victoria these warlike preparations had he intended to use them against her country, afforded cold comfort.

When Victoria and Albert returned to their yacht later that afternoon, it was they who were *boutonnés* and silent.

That evening the royal couple dined as the Emperor's guests aboard *La Bretagne*. The ship, reported one of the Queen's ladies, was 'magnificently furnished with crimson silk and filled with flowers, and dinner was laid on the second deck *à soixante couverts*'. But even among these sumptuous surroundings there seems to have been a disturbing emphasis on the arts of war. All the decorations, noted one of the English guests, were made of firearms: 'chandeliers of pistols etc. – most capitally done.'[2]

After dinner Napoleon made a reassuring little speech about the Anglo-French alliance. 'I am happy to show the sentiments we entertain towards them,' he declared. 'Indeed, facts speak for themselves, and they prove that hostile passions, aided by a few unfortunate incidents, did not succeed in altering either the friendship which exists between the two Crowns, or the desire of the two nations to remain at peace.'[3]

It was encouraging enough, but defensive.

To this speech Prince Albert was obliged to respond. Knowing how much the Prince loathed public speaking, the Queen afterwards wrote of 'the dreadful moment for my dear husband, which was terrible to me, and which I should never wish to go through again ... I sat shaking, with my eyes *cloués sur la table*'.

Her anguish was unnecessary; Prince Albert acquitted himself very well. Dinner over, the entire party went on deck to watch a breathtaking display of fireworks. Not only was the inky sky ablaze with cascades of colour, but all the ships in the bay were brilliantly illuminated. The *pièce de résistance* was supplied by the British. When the Emperor's canopied barge returned to the shore from delivering the Queen to her yacht at the conclusion of the display, an electric light from the royal yacht was trained on to it. This light, known as the Honourable Major Fitzmaurice's Life Light, followed Napoleon's barge all the way back, 'the light shining only on the barge, whilst all around remained in darkness'.

What the Emperor thought about having to sit in a merciless blaze of electric light for the entire slow progress back to the shore is not known.

The following morning Napoleon boarded the *Victoria and Albert* to take his leave. The two sovereigns parted on friendly if slightly preoccupied terms. Of that flood of adoring adjectives with which Queen Victoria had first described Napoleon III over two years before, there was now no trace. Napoleon returned to play his part in the various ceremonies connected with the Fêtes, while Victoria sailed back to England to urge her sluggish cabinet to spend more money on defence.

It was not, though, against Britain that the Emperor was preparing for war; it was against Austria. Much of Napoleon's adventurous youth – the recalling of which Queen Victoria had once found so romantic – had been dedicated to the cause of Italian patriotism: in effect, to the liberation of northern Italy from the reactionary rule of Austria. So when the Italian patriot Orsini flung his bombs at the Emperor's carriage, they served as a reminder to Napoleon III of his obligations towards Italy. In the footsteps of his uncle Napoleon I, who had won his first military laurels in northern Italy, Napoleon III would liberate the Italians from their Austrian overlords.

Although the Emperor made his plans in secret, Queen Victoria got wind of them. 'I really *hope* that there is no *real* desire for war in the Emperor's mind,' she wrote to King Leopold; 'we have explained to him strongly how *entirely* he would *alienate* us from him if there was any *attempt* to *disturb standing and binding treaties*.'

It was a vain hope. As the year 1859 unfolded and Napoleon – in spite of all protestations to the contrary – prepared for war, so did Queen Victoria become more and more agitated. Encouraged by Prince Albert, she saw the rumoured campaign in northern Italy as the start of a general European conflagration. It would be the wars of conquest of the first Napoleon all over again. Even if Napoleon III were not planning to re-establish Napoleon I's great Continental empire, he would never rest until he had redrawn the map of Europe in accordance with his ideas of 'completed nationalities'.

The Queen's Journal developed into a tirade against French iniquity; her letters became increasingly emphatic. With a wealth of underlinings she wrote off to Brussels declaring that 'the feeling against the Emperor here is *very strong*. I think *yet* that if *Austria* is *strong* and well *prepared* and *Germany strong* and *well inclined* towards *us* (as *Prussia certainly* is) France will *not* be so eager to attempt what I *firmly* believe would *end* in the *Emperor's downfall*.'

King Leopold lost no time in reinforcing his niece's views. 'Heaven knows what dance our Emperor *Napoleon Troisième de nom* will lead us ... I fear he is determined on that Italian war.'

Victoria wrote to Napoleon himself, reminding him that rarely had any man such an opportunity of keeping the peace of Europe as did he, and begging him to do his best to calm international anxieties.

It was all to no purpose. In the spring of 1859 Napoleon marched his armies into northern Italy. Within a couple of months he had been successful enough to open peace negotiations with the Austrian Emperor. He returned to Paris a hero. 'The Emperor Napoleon,' wrote the Queen sourly two days after the armistice, 'by his military successes, and great apparent moderation or prudence immediately after them, has created for himself a most formidable position of strength in Europe.' She had no doubt that Prussia would be his next victim. The time would come, she warned her cabinet, 'for us either to obey or to fight him with terrible odds against us.'

The Queen's customary end-of-the-year letter to the Emperor was distinctly cool. 'The year which has just passed has been stormy and painful and has made many hearts suffer,' she wrote. 'I pray God that the one upon which we are entering will permit us to see accomplished the work of peace-making with all its benefits for the tranquility and progress of the world. . . .'.

She was being too optimistic. The new year brought very little improvement in the relations between Britain and France. Indeed, British suspicions against Napoleon III, once aroused, became almost pathological. His annexation of Savoy and Nice as a reward for his campaign of liberation was strongly resented. King Leopold, in a characteristically ponderous *bon mot*, referred to the Emperor as '*Annex-ander*'. Victoria and Albert did not need any convincing on this score. The Prince Consort was especially apprehensive about the Emperor's reckless adventures. 'At the court of Napoleon,' he complained, 'they play, they make love, enjoy themselves, dream, and between sleeping and waking make decisions on matters of the greatest importance, *et la question ne s'examine qu'après* when things have happened.'

The Prince would not rest until he had goaded the government into overhauling Britain's somewhat ramshackle defence system. On this very subject he had once covered twenty manuscript sheets in his immaculate handwriting; now he had the long-delayed satisfaction of seeing his schemes materialize. In a frenzy of anti-French sentiment the Volunteer movement sprang into life. By the summer of 1860, over 130,000 men had been enrolled. In August over 20,000 volunteers paraded before the Queen in Hyde Park. The gratified Victoria hoped that this show of public enthusiasm would check the 'sinister designs of our neighbour.'

But she doubted it. 'Really it is too bad,' she exploded on hearing of Napoleon's proposal to land his troops on some peace-restoring mission in the Levant. 'No country, no human being would ever dream of *disturbing* or *attacking* France; everyone would be glad to see her prosperous; but *she* must needs disturb every quarter of the globe and try to make mischief and set everyone by the ears; and of course, it will end some day in a *regular crusade* against the *universal disturber* of the world. It is really monstrous!'

Her disenchantment was complete. No matter how personally attractive the Queen might once have found Napoleon III, any such attraction faded in the face of what she regarded as his menacing attitude towards Britain. With Queen Victoria, the interests of her country always came first.

The machinations of Napoleon III were merely one of the many problems besetting the Prince Consort. By the year 1861 he was in an almost continuously depressed and harrassed state; he could hardly cope with the strains of everyday living. Prince Albert had never been strong; to his life-long gastric troubles were now added rheumatism, toothache, nausea and shivering. He slept very badly. Every bout of illness left him more exhausted still. Yet he refused to spare himself. As conscientious, as involved, as finicky as ever, he allowed himself – cried his anguished wife – to be 'torn to pieces by business of every kind.' He was working himself, quite literally, to death.

His family life was hardly less troubled. He missed his beloved daughter Vicky – by now married to Prince Frederick William and living in Berlin – and he worried about the increasingly illiberal and militaristic tone of the Prussian court in which she was obliged to make her home.

His eldest son Bertie, the Prince of Wales, was a source of continuing disappointment and concern. Instead of developing into the diligent, intelligent, unsullied prince of his parents' fond hopes, Bertie showed no interest whatsoever in things of the mind and far too much in things of the body. In vain the Queen begged him to try and be more like his father, if only in *some* ways. She realized only too well that her son was developing into what *she* might have become had it not been for Albert's uplifting example. Bertie, she once claimed, was her caricature. Of any serious-minded Coburg characteristics he showed no trace. He was all Hanoverian.

Although Queen Victoria's conscious effort to control her own emotions had met with some success during the last two or three years, there were still occasions when they got the better of her; when she revealed herself to be as touchy, as possessive, as unreasonable as ever. Time and again Albert was obliged to turn from his own preoccupations to cope with her tantrums. The death of her once-despised mother the Duchess of Kent on 16 March 1861 led to so irrational an outburst of grief on Victoria's part that Albert was 'well-nigh overwhelmed'.

The faults were not all on one side. There was considerable jus-tification for the Queen's complaint, to Vicky, that dear Papa was often 'very trying – in his hastiness and overlove of business.'

Yet there were some shafts of sunlight among all these storm clouds. Their autumn holidays at Balmoral could still bring Victoria and Albert great happiness and contentment. Among the spectacular scenery and unsophisticated people of the Highlands, and away from the cares of their position, they were able to enjoy, and demonstrate, the great love they felt for each other. Here they were seen at their most affectionate: Victoria showing the generosity and vivacity that were far more typical than her occasional outbursts of petulance, and Albert full of tenderness and thoughtfulness.

In September 1860 they embarked on the first of what the Queen called their 'Great Expeditions': a two-day journey to Glen Feshie. Travelling incognito, with two members of the household, as 'Lord and Lady Churchill and party', the couple enjoyed themselves immensely. By carriage, on horseback, on foot, they climbed hills, splashed through streams, wound through woods, admired views, picnicked and slept in a humble inn. Their identity, it seems, was never guessed; although the crown emblazoned on the dog-cart might well have given things away. Seeing the many rings crammed onto the Queen's pudgy fingers, a woman did remark that 'the lady must be terrible rich', and one of the two gillies accompanying them inad-vertently called Victoria 'Your Majesty'.

The offending gillie was John Brown. On all these Great Expeditions, the Queen notes, 'Grant and Brown were on the box as usual'. As for Grant and Brown, she wrote after this first Great

Expedition, 'they are perfect – discreet, careful, intelligent, attentive, ever ready to do what is wanted; and the latter, particularly, is handy and willing to do everything and anything, and to overcome every difficulty, which makes him one of my best servants anywhere.'

Even to King Leopold the Queen sang the praises of her 'particular ghillie.' Brown combined, she said, 'the offices of groom, footman, page and *maid*, I might almost say, as he is so handy about cloaks and shawls . . .'. When he was not 'bashful' – that is, too drunk – he would even wait at table during their expeditions. Censorious in some things, Queen Victoria was very tolerant about the vast quantities of alcohol downed by her Highland servants.

Not the least of John Brown's many attractions for Queen Victoria was his outspokenness: his refreshing lack of unctuousness. One day at Balmoral, as the Queen and her ladies were making a hilarious, helter-skelter descent of Craig Nordie, Jane Churchill collapsed. John Brown, having picked her up, announced, 'Your ladyship is not so heavy as Her Majesty.'

'Am I grown heavier do you think?' asked the Queen laughingly.

'Well, I think you are,' was Brown's blunt reply.

In later years one of the gillie's attractions in the Queen's eyes was his close association with her happiest times at Balmoral. Long after the Prince Consort died, Brown was a living reminder of those Great Expeditions during which Victoria and Albert had enjoyed some of their most carefree, most intimate times together.

'To my dear Albert do we owe it,' wrote the Queen of the first of these journeys, 'for he always thought it would be delightful, having gone on many similar expeditions in former days himself.'[4] And at the end of the fourth Great Expedition, in October 1861, she noted that 'the moon rose and shone most beautifully, and we returned at twenty minutes to seven o'clock, much pleased and interested with this delightful expedition. Alas, I fear our *last* great one!'

By '*last*' the Queen meant the last great one of that year, but six years later, when she was preparing her notes for publication in her book *Leaves from the Journal of Our Life in the Highlands*, she added, poignantly, 'It was our last great one!'

Almost exactly two months after this Great Expedition, Prince Albert died.

'I do not cling to life,' Prince Albert said to Queen Victoria one day in November 1861. 'You do: but I set no store by it . . . I am sure that

if I had a severe illness I should give up at once, I should not struggle
for life. I have no tenacity of life.'

The Prince's habitual fatalism was deepened during this period by
a series of personal and political misfortunes. Early in November he
heard that his close Coburg relations – King Pedro V and his brother
Prince Fernando of Portugal – had died of typhoid fever. While
suffering from this blow Albert was dealt, from his point of view, a
worse one. He was told that Bertie had been involved in a sexual
escapade with an actress. Whereas most royal or aristocratic fathers
would have treated the episode, in a twenty-year-old, as perfectly
natural or even commendable, Prince Albert regarded it in the blackest
possible light. Shocking in itself, it seemed the final blow to Victoria
and Albert's dream of fashioning the perfect heir. What hope was
there now of presenting the country with that paragon who, by his
unimpeachable morals and high sense of duty, was to win the love and
respect of the people? The Queen, on being told the story (Albert
assured her that he was sparing her 'the disgusting details'), was equally
shocked. She would never again be able to look at Bertie, she declared,
'without a shudder'.

Having written his son an anguished letter on the subject and
received a suitably contrite reply, the Prince Consort travelled to
Cambridge (where the Prince was furthering his painful education) to
see him. He returned to Windsor cold, dispirited and exhausted. He
was immediately obliged to turn his attention to an international crisis
concerning two British envoys and the American Civil War. The
Prince's rewriting of the government's belligerent draft prevented the
crisis becoming more serious still. But the effort cost him a great deal.
He was so weak, he told the Queen, that he could hardly hold his pen.

By then – the last day of November 1861 – the Prince was already
suffering from typhoid fever.

During the following two weeks the Queen was in agony. For much
of this time the Prince was delirious; at other times there seemed to be
a slight improvement. Victoria see-sawed between wild hope and still
wilder despair. Yet no matter how hysterical her tears and prayers
when she was away from her husband, in his presence she always
showed a calm and cheerful face. This, the dithering doctors thought,
would help his recovery.

On the morning of his death, 14 December 1861, things seemed to
be a little better. She was led to believe that the crisis might be over.
But by afternoon hopes were fading. By nightfall it was clear that he
was dying. *'Est ist das kleine Fräuchen,'* whispered the Queen as she

leant over him. When she asked him for a kiss, he moved his lips.

'Two or three long but perfectly gentle breaths were drawn, the hand clasping mine, and ... *all, all* was over ... I stood up, kissed his dear heavenly forehead and called out in a bitter and agonising cry "Oh! my dear Darling" and then dropped on my knees in mute, distracted despair, unable to utter a word or shed a tear!'

The Prince Consort died at a quarter to eleven that night. He was only forty-two years of age.

Queen Victoria was inconsolable. 'My *life* as a *happy* one *ended*! The world is gone for *me*...', she cried out in her anguish. 'But oh! to be cut off in the prime of life – to see our pure, happy, quiet, domestic life, which *alone* enabled me to bear my *much* disliked position, CUT OFF at forty-two – when I *had* hoped with instinctive certainty that God would *never* part us, and would let us grow old together ... it is too *awful*, too cruel!'

Part Four

JOHN BROWN

12

'The Queen's Highland Servant'

'HOW ONE longs to cling to one's grief', Queen Victoria had once written. Now, clinging to it with all the intensity of her nature, she plunged her court into its long period of mourning. Had this unrelieved sorrow lasted several months, a year, or even a couple of years, it might have been appreciated and forgiven; but year succeeded year and there seemed to be no light bright enough to pierce the cloud of the Queen's unhappiness.

Although in private she worked almost as conscientiously as ever, in her public life – perhaps the more important part of her monarchical duties – she would make no effort at all. She withdrew from the public gaze almost completely. Not until three years after Prince Albert's death did the Queen show herself in London; and that was for the length of the carriage-drive from Paddington Station to Buckingham Palace and back. She pronounced the experience 'very painful'. One week a year, after that first painful visit, was as much as she was prepared to spend in the capital.

In 1866 she agreed to open Parliament, but only because she was anxious to secure from the House adequate allowances for two of her children. She agreed to it, though, with the worst possible grace. 'The Queen must say that she feels *very bitterly* the want of feeling of those who *ask* the Queen to go to open Parliament . . . why this wish should be of so *unreasonable* and unfeeling a nature as to *long to witness* the spectacle of a poor widow, nervous and shrinking, dragged in *deep mourning* ALONE *in* STATE as a *Show* where she used to go supported by her husband to be gazed at, without delicacy of feeling, is a thing *she cannot* understand, and never could wish her bitterest foe exposed to.'

The Prince Consort had by then been dead for over five years.

At the Prime Minister's request, the Queen opened Parliament again the following year. She hated it even more. On such occasions she might spend one night at Buckingham Palace, but more often than not she would hurry back to the seclusion of Windsor Castle. So for most of the time the palace stood empty. 'These commanding premises to be let or sold in consequence of the late occupant's declining business', read a prankster's notice outside the palace. The joke was not entirely good-natured.

Only fifteen or sixteen weeks of the year were spent at Windsor. The castle was like a morgue during the half-dozen or so years following the Prince's death. The Queen, who wore only black, insisted that her ladies do the same. Her maids-of-honour were allowed half-mourning: white, grey, mauve or purple. For days on end no one other than her dressers or a single lady-in-waiting would set eyes on her. Even with members of her household she would communicate by letter; and these always carried a half-inch mourning border.

An appearance at the dinner-table was about as much effort as she was prepared to make towards entertaining her guests. Not that this did anything towards dispelling the gloom; on the contrary, it became gloomier still. The rooms were always ice cold; no one spoke above a whisper and any sound of merriment, no matter how subdued or distant, was likely to bring a strongly worded rebuke from Her Majesty. Her secretary Henry Ponsonby, who joined her service in 1865, describes one such dinner. There were, he says, 'prolonged silences, broken by the Queen's, Leopold's and C's respectable coughs, Cowley's deep cough, S's gouty cough and all the servants dropping plates and making a clatteration of noise.'[1] After-dinner smoking, of which the Queen strongly disapproved, had to be confined to certain times in the smoking-room.

The winter (part of December and all of January and February) and the summer (July and August) the Queen spent at Osborne. As the sea crossing, particularly in winter, was something which her ageing ministers would do almost anything to avoid, the Queen felt relatively safe from her cabinet. She always imagined that they were going to force her to undertake more than she was capable of; that they wanted to push her beyond her limits. Any suggestion, no matter how tactfully put, that she fulfil some public duty, was immediately countered by a letter from her complaisant doctor forbidding that she do any such thing. By now her need for seclusion and her self-pity had been compounded by hypochondria: the Queen had convinced herself that her health was in a precarious state. It was most important, she assured her Uncle Leopold, 'that I should have *no* excitement, *no* agitation, IF I am to live on.'

Balmoral she liked best of all; or rather, it was here that she was least unhappy. Six hundred miles from London and twenty from the nearest railhead, Balmoral suited her very well. To the annual autumn visit from early September to late November, she added a late spring visit lasting through May and June. Amidst the desolate moors and rugged hillsides, she could get right away from the public contact which she hated so much. For even greater seclusion she retreated to little lodges among the pine trees, where she would take tea or sit sketching. No matter how tempestuous the weather, she ventured out. In spite of the fact that her May and June visit took place during the parliamentary session, she was always adamant about not changing her dates of arrival and departure. Only a crisis of the most serious nature would induce her to alter her plans by perhaps a day or two.

Yet any criticism of the Queen's withdrawn life she dismissed as '*ill-natured* gossip . . . caused by dissatisfaction at not forcing the Queen *out*. . . . It is very wrong of the world to say that it is merely her *distaste* to go out and about as she could when she had her dear husband to support and *protect* her,' she cried out, 'when the *fact is* that her shattered nerves and health *prevent* her doing so.'

The one thing Queen Victoria's 'shattered nerves and health' did not prevent her from doing was perpetuating her late husband's memory. In this, she was extraordinarily active. So great a loss, she thought, demanded a commensurate amount of immortalization.

She saw to it that the Blue Room at Windsor, in which he had died, was kept undisturbed. His bust dominated the two wreath-strewn beds; his clothes, fresh towels and hot water were laid out each day. She slept with his night-shirt clutched to her breast; she had a cast of his hand within reach.

In spite of the late Lord Melbourne's advice that one should never waste money on memorials, she spent – or coerced various public bodies into spending – vast sums on the erection of monuments, statues, pyramids, obelisks, cairns and plaques in the Prince's honour. She lost no time in arranging for the building of a grandiose mausoleum at Frogmore to house his remains. For his tomb she commissioned a recumbent figure of him in white marble, sculpted by Carlo Marochetti. Among the paintings and statuary that gradually filled the mausoleum was a marble representation of Victoria and Albert by William Theed in which the Prince, with one arm circling the Queen's waist and the other raised to Heaven, appears to be encouraging and inspiring his docile and adoring wife. She distributed engravings of his likeness, she presented copies of his speeches, she encouraged the composition of countless poems and eulogies and tributes.

Inevitably, she began to distort his image; to remember him, or at least to present him, as some saint-like creature who had been too good for this wicked world. Forgotten were her complaints about his preoccupation with work and his indifference to her sufferings. He was now a noble, flawless, virtuous intellectual, who had worn, as Tennyson graphically put it, 'the white flower of a blameless life'. No praise of the Prince could be too fulsome for the Queen's ears. In the weeks and months following his death, every tribute was scrutinized and analysed; every politician assessed by his particular peroration.

And of all the paeans that poured in, few were more lavish than those of the man whom the Queen had hitherto treated with no more than official civility: Benjamin Disraeli. Indeed, it was through his extravagantly expressed reaction to the Prince Consort's death that Disraeli finally captured the Queen's full attention. He now took a giant stride along the road that was to end with him all but taking Prince Albert's place.

Disraeli's tributes to the Prince Consort, for all their superlatives, were not insincere. He had always thought very highly of the Prince. Although the two men were very different types, there were some points of similarity. Both were seen as outsiders. 'No Englishman', maintained Frederick Greenwood, editor of the *Pall Mall Gazette*, 'could approach Disraeli without some immediate consciousness that he was in the presence of a foreigner.'[2] And Prince Albert, with his German accent and German ways, had never been accepted as an Englishman. Neither man felt at ease in the hard-drinking, fox-hunting, philistine society of so many members of the aristocracy; they were far more interested in things of the mind. Both were highly intelligent men; both had a thorough understanding of, and absorbing interest in, politics. Disraeli, even in private, claimed that the Prince Consort had 'great ability' and one of the 'most richly cultivated minds' he had ever come across.

'This German Prince', wrote Disraeli on Albert's death, 'has governed England for twenty-one years with a wisdom and energy such as none of our Kings have ever shown ... we have buried our Sovereign.'[3]

A few weeks after Prince Albert's death, the leaders of the various political parties paid formal tribute to the late Prince. Disraeli's was particularly moving. He spoke of Prince Albert as the 'prime counsellor of the realm'; he drew attention to his great services towards cultural affairs, where 'the want of culture had been a great deficiency in the national character'. The Prince Consort, he declared, had been no mere figurehead. 'His contributions to the cause of the State were more powerful and far more precious. He gave it his thought, his time, his toil; he gave to it his life.'

The Queen devoured every word. In a letter to Lord Derby she wrote that 'The Queen would be glad that Mr Disraeli should also be made aware of H.M.'s grateful sense of his testimony to the worth and character of the Prince – perhaps as discriminating in the characteristics pointed out, and certainly as eloquent in the language employed, as any of those beautiful and glorious orations . . .'.

Disraeli wasted no time following up this lead. 'What I attempted to express on Thursday night I deeply felt', he answered. 'During those conversations with which, of late years the Prince occasionally honoured me, I acquired much, both in knowledge and in feeling, which will ever influence my life.'

This tribute brought him still further royal favour. The Queen sent him two engravings of pictures of herself and Albert. These Disraeli acknowledged as 'a hallowed gift'.

'Mr Disraeli', Victoria is reported to have said, 'was the only person who appreciated the Prince.'

But it was not until over a year later that the couple met face to face. In March 1863, in strict accordance with the late Prince Consort's wishes, the twenty-one-year-old Prince of Wales was married to Princess Alexandra of Denmark. With what the Queen considered to be the 'ordeal' of the wedding over, she granted audiences to a few selected ministers and politicians. She received Disraeli, as Conservative leader in the Commons, at Windsor.

He was ushered into the late Prince Consort's study. The room was exactly as Albert had left it; even his writing materials were laid out on his desk. After a five-minute wait, the Queen entered. In her black crinoline and veiled widow's cap she looked plumper than when last he had seen her, and her face was folded in sadness. Disraeli bowed. In her astonishingly sweet and musical voice the Queen said, 'It is some time since we met.'

Although the couple discussed various topics, both personal and political, the Queen did not raise the one issue which must have been uppermost in her mind: a suitable memorial to the Prince Consort, to be erected in London. Knowing that the matter was to be debated in the House that very afternoon the Queen, 'with great delicacy', avoided the subject.

Characteristically, during that afternoon's debate Disraeli pleaded for some dramatic monument rather than a utilitarian hall or hospital. 'It should be something direct, significant and choice,' declared Disraeli, 'so that those who come after us may say: "This is the type and testimony of a sublime life and a transcendent career, and thus they were recognized by a grateful and admiring people!" '

Having taken care to send the Queen a copy of this eulogy, Disraeli was rewarded by his sovereign with a copy of the Prince Consort's speeches, bound in white morocco and inscribed in the Queen's own handwriting: 'To the Right Honourable Benjamin Disraeli. In recollection of the greatest and best of men, from the beloved Prince's broken-hearted widow. Victoria R.'

The gift was accompanied by a letter, tied up with a black silk ribbon. In it the Queen wrote of her 'deep gratification' at Mr Disraeli's tribute to her 'adored, beloved and great husband. The perusal of it made her shed many tears, but it was very soothing to her broken heart to see such true appreciation of that spotless and unequalled character . . .'.

Disraeli's reply was even more flowery. 'The Prince', read the honeyed phrases, 'is the only person, whom Mr Disraeli has ever known, who realized the Ideal . . . there was in him an union of the manly grace and sublime simplicity, of chivalry with the intellectual splendour of the Attic Academe.' On and on flowed the sentences to detail the Prince's 'high tone, his universal accomplishment, his blended tenderness and vigour, his rare combination of romantic energy and classic repose.'

With royalty, as Disraeli was fond of saying, one had to lay it on with a trowel.

To the Queen, none of this sounded excessive. Disraeli's letter was shown round the court. 'I need not tell you', wrote Lady Augusta Bruce with just a hint of amusement as she passed the letter on, 'how Her Majesty has been affected by the depth and delicacy of these touches, or how soothing it is to the Queen to have this inexhaustible theme so treated . . .'.[4]

The subject which had given rise to this perfervid exchange of letters – the proposed monument to the late Prince – eventually took tangible shape in Kensington Gore: it was that extravagantly mock-Gothic confection, the Albert Memorial.

★

But it was not Queen Victoria's contacts with the colourful Mr Disraeli which initially revived her interest in life. It was her obsession with an altogether different sort of man: her Highland gillie, John Brown. Of all the Queen's romantic attachments, this was the most curious. It was also the most sexually charged. At the time, and to this day, it was and is widely believed that the bond between Queen Victoria and John Brown was physical; that the Queen was either his wife or his mistress. At the opening of the year 1865, John Brown was simply one of her Highland servants; within three years the Queen was being talked about as 'Mrs Brown'.

In the period immediately after the Prince Consort's death the Queen did not see a great deal of her 'particular gillie'. He attended her at Balmoral, where his unflustered behaviour during a couple of carriage accidents confirmed her admiration for his skills, and he was in charge of her pony-chaise when she visited the scenes of the Prince Consort's Coburg childhood in 1862. It was not until the end of 1864 that Brown began to assume a more significant role in her life. The Queen was at Osborne for the winter and as her personal physician, the obliging Dr Jenner, was anxious for her to take up riding again, it was agreed that John Brown should be sent for. A strange groom, protested the Queen, would never do. So to Osborne came good, dependable, resourceful Brown.

Born on 8 December 1826, John Brown was just thirty-eight when he arrived at Osborne that year. Queen Victoria was forty-five. If she looked the very picture of broken-hearted widowhood, he epitomized the rude health and unashamed heartiness of the Highlander. His handsomeness was of a particularly Scots variety: he had clear blue eyes, a resolute chin and vigorously curly red-gold hair and beard. He always wore the kilt. He wore it, apparently, with more success than the late Prince Consort had. The Prince's 'want of whipcord in his thews proclaims that he is no Highlander', noted one contemporary. 'It needs the feline cleanness of build and muscularity of the mountain Celt for the bare knees and legs to look well.'[5] John Brown certainly had that.

The qualities which the Queen always admired in Brown – his honesty and his bluntness – did not mean that he was naïve. John Brown was nobody's fool. Although the Queen's secretary Henry Ponsonby might refer to Brown as a 'child of nature', he recognized and respected his canny good sense. Brown's father later became a farmer but had at one time been a teacher, and it was he who was responsible for his son's education. One of the Queen's lords-in-waiting, the Marquis of Huntly, went so far as to claim that 'Brown was shrewd, a great reader, and was capable of giving a considered opinion on most matters'.[6]

It did not take the Queen long to come to an appreciation of Brown's additional qualities. Within a couple of months of his arrival at Osborne she was assuring King Leopold that Brown was 'so intelligent, so *unlike* an *ordinary* servant', and to her daughter Vicky, now the Crown Princess of Prussia, she claimed that 'he is so quiet, has such an excellent head and memory . . . is besides so devoted and clever.'

She began passing on examples of his homespun philosophy. 'Brown's observation about a cross person seems to me very applicable here', she wrote to Vicky apropos the bad-tempered Prussian ambassador; 'it can't be very pleasant for a person themselves to be always cross.' It was 'so true and original. His observations upon everything he sees and hears here are excellent and may show how superior in feeling, sense and judgement he is to the servants.'

Brown may have been all this, but from what one knows of Queen Victoria, one can be fairly certain that what initially attracted her were his rugged good looks. Those, and his assertive, reassuring, undeniably masculine air. No unattractive man, no matter how worthy he might have proved himself to be, would have won the Queen's confidence and affection to the same extent.

By the beginning of February 1865 – less than two months after Brown's arrival – the Queen had decided that he must remain permanently by her side. Just to attend to her while she was at Balmoral was no longer enough; he must be with her at all times. A new post was especially created for him. He was to be known as 'The Queen's Highland Servant'. He would take orders from no one but the Queen, and would attend her both indoors and out. The few menial tasks he was initially expected to perform – such as cleaning her boots and seeing to her dogs – were soon dropped.

In these early days Brown reported to the Queen twice a day: after breakfast and after luncheon. Gradually, these instruction-giving sessions developed into something more intimate. The Queen found herself taking more and more comfort in Brown's company. It was not only that he was so reliable, plain-spoken and intelligent; he was ready to devote himself entirely to her. It was the old story: the Queen had once again come across a man who was prepared to give her his undivided attention, as Lord Melbourne had, as Napoleon III once had and as, in the early days of their marriage, Prince Albert had. She felt herself, once again, to be the most important person in someone's life.

Brown became another in that series of men to whom the Queen could look for support, guidance or gallantry.

'I feel I have here, always in the House, a good, devoted Soul ... whose only object and interest is my service,' she wrote to Vicky, 'and God knows how much I want to be taken care of.'

But she was prepared to see Brown in an even more elevated light than that of personal guardian and consoler. He soon developed into another of her father-figures. Someone like Brown was invaluable, she confided to Vicky, because – with the Prince Consort dead – there was no longer a 'Male head of the House'. What the other, more deserving members of her household – people like her private secretary and her senior equerries, not to mention her grown-up sons – would have thought of the Queen's high estimation of a servant who had been in his present position for a matter of three or four months only, may be imagined.

Indeed, before long it did not need to be imagined. First the household and then the press began to make their opinions of this extraordinary relationship between the Sovereign and the servant only too clear.

Having elevated John Brown's status, Queen Victoria decided to do the same for his background. Or, rather, to confirm that so admirable a character must, as a matter of course, come from commensurately admirable stock. She commissioned Dr Andrew Robertson, the Balmoral factor, to trace Brown's ancestry.[7]

The canny little doctor supplied exactly what was wanted. Skirting over some ancestors and concentrating on others, he was able to link John Brown, if somewhat tenuously, to several important Scottish clans and to imply that – like the Queen herself – Brown had Stuart connections. In his grandiloquent praise of the sterling qualities of the Highlanders Dr Robertson almost outdid his Sovereign. The gratified Queen circulated Dr Robertson's memorandum among the members of her family and household. How many of them read it, or were impressed by it, is uncertain.

Yet it was precisely for his un-aristocratic and un-courtier-like qualities that the Queen was so drawn to John Brown. Indeed, from the time of her close association with him dates the Queen's ardent championship of the worthy 'Lower classes' against the frivolous 'Higher classes'. Time and again she contrasts the industry, morality and nobility of 'the ordinary people' with the idleness, self-indulgence and vulgarity of the aristocracy.

'The Lower Classes are becoming so well informed – are so intelligent and earn their bread and riches so deservedly that they cannot and ought not to be kept back – to be abused by the wretched ignorant Highborn beings, who live only to kill time', she wrote to the Crown Princess.

That John Brown was a shining example of 'a man of the people' (as she subsequently described with less accuracy, another man with whom she became equally besotted, Disraeli), she had no doubt. Brown's naturalness was like a breath of fresh air in the affected, hot-house atmosphere of London society.

The Queen, who was shy in aristocratic or intellectual company (her ladies noticed how she gave a quick, nervous laugh on meeting anyone new), had always felt at ease among the poor and the unsophisticated. With the Highland crofters and peasants she was particularly relaxed. So for her, it was a tremendous solace to have one of these rough-hewn, plain-spoken men by her side; someone with whom she could be utterly natural and whom she could trust.

Brown's physical strength, too, was an advantage. By now the widowed Queen, who had experienced several attempted assassinations and who had suffered several carriage accidents, was nervous about driving out. With Brown sitting four-square on the box she felt more secure. Time and again he saved her from danger or even death: by grabbing pistols from the hands of madmen, by steadying runaway horses, by rescuing her from toppled carriages.

He protected her in other ways as well. As the days were now long gone when his duties had been confined to accompanying her on her rides and drives, he was constantly at her elbow. When she sat working, he kept guard over her. He saved her from being unduly pestered; he saw to it that she was warmly wrapped up; he took care that she did not tire herself. Like Prince Albert, Brown could be almost motherly. The Queen felt herself to be, once again, someone's 'Child'.

But it was for Brown's treatment of her as a woman, rather than as a child, that Queen Victoria was chiefly attracted to him. This was the secret of his success. He was not overawed by her status; he was not afraid of her. Perhaps adroitly, but more probably instinctively, John Brown behaved as though his Sovereign were a helpless female who needed cosseting, protecting, even ordering about. He appreciated that in that dumpy and increasingly intimidating figure there beat an intensely feminine heart. Elderly courtiers or eminent statesmen, committing some slight breach of etiquette, would earn one of the Queen's most thunderous frowns; Brown, no matter how irreverently he addressed her, would always be rewarded with a smile.

It was, indeed, the irreverence with which Brown treated the Queen that was one of the most curious aspects of their relationship. This 'child of nature' took – and was allowed to take – his gruff behaviour very far indeed. In private, he almost always addressed his Sovereign as 'wumman'; the extent to which he bossed her about was astonishing. She was to stop complaining about her awkward sketching table, he once commanded, 'for I canna mak one for ye'. During the course of a holiday at Baveno on the Italian lakes, Brown was late in joining the Queen and her ladies in the hotel garden. 'I have been waiting for you', she said with uncharacteristic mildness when he finally appeared. Anyone else would have apologized profusely. But not Brown. To the consternation of her ladies, he merely looked at his Sovereign, as she sat there in her straw hat and white cape, and remarked, 'Well, I must say you look very summery.'[8]

He was not always so complimentary. 'What are ye daeing with that auld black dress on again? It's green-moulded', he once grumbled. Meekly, she returned upstairs to change. Often he would upbraid her for not knowing her own mind 'for two minutes together'.

On one occasion a tourist, walking in the vicinity of Balmoral Castle, suddenly stumbled across the Queen and John Brown out together. Brown was busily fastening the Queen's cloak under her chin.

'Hoots then, wumman,' the startled tourist heard Brown bark, 'can ye no hold yerr head up?'[9]

As her relationship with John Brown developed, so did Queen Victoria gradually realize that her grief for Prince Albert was becoming less acute. This worried her. Was she wrong in drawing comfort from Brown's presence? In her dilemma she turned to Dean Wellesley. Of her various spiritual mentors, the Queen preferred Wellesley (Dean Stanley, she confided to her daughter Vicky, was too cold 'and to me as if he were of no sex') because – like Brown – Wellesley was 'tender-hearted' under a 'rough exterior'. But not even Wellesley, she went on to say, was as much comfort to her as 'honest Brown'.

Dean Wellesley was reassuring. There was no need for Her Majesty to reproach herself because her grief for her late husband was 'less violent'. A 'settled mournful resignation' was 'a more lasting proof of affection than active grief'. If the good Lord saw fit to bring one into contact with a sympathetic, congenial and comforting fellow being, one should not analyse one's reactions too deeply but simply treat the appearance of this person as providential. To allow oneself to be comforted by someone else did not imply disloyalty to the memory of a loved one.

'When one's beloved Husband is gone and one's Children are married,' wrote the Queen to her daughter Vicky, 'one feels that a friend ... who can devote him or herself entirely to you is the one thing you do require to help you on – and to sympathise entirely with you. Not that you love your children less – but you feel as they grow up and marry that you can be of so little use to them and they to you (especially in the Higher Classes) ...'.

Just how much of a friend John Brown was proving to be is apparent from a letter unearthed by the writer Tom Cullen which the Queen wrote, after John Brown's death in 1883, to Brown's brother Hugh.

Referring to this very time, in 1866, when she was mourning the death of one of her daughter Vicky's little sons, the Queen told Hugh Brown that she had held his brother's 'dear kind' hand and had said that she hoped he might long be spared to comfort her. 'But we all *must* die', Brown had answered.

'Afterwards,' continued the Queen, 'my beloved John would say: "You haven't a more devoted servant than Brown" – and oh! *how* I felt *that*!

'Afterwards so often I told him no one loved him more than I did or had a better friend than me; and he answered "Nor you – than me."

' "No one loves you more." '[10]

13

'Mrs Brown'

IF JOHN BROWN'S peremptory manner had been confined to his dealings with Queen Victoria in private, all might have been well. It was when it extended to her family, her household, even to officials and politicians, that it caused increasing resentment, and eventually widespread gossip.

On first being appointed 'The Queen's Highland Servant', Brown had been expected to act as a link between the Queen and the other Highland servants. It was through him only that her orders were to be transmitted to his fellows; no one else, decided the Queen, could be entrusted with this sensitive task. 'It will never do to speak harshly and dictatorially to Highlanders', she explained to Sir Howard Elphinstone, her son Prince Arthur's governor; 'their independence and self-respect and proper spirit ... make them resent that far more than an ordinary English servant.'[1]

Before many months had passed, however, the Queen was using Brown for transmitting her commands not only to those servants who were not Highlanders, but also to members of her household. The words 'Her Mad-jesty says', officiously rapped out by Brown, came to be dreaded throughout the various royal residences. He treated everyone, including the Prince of Wales (who loathed him) with equal brusqueness. Lord John Manners, for instance, was astonished by the way in which members of the household and guests were informed that they had been selected to join the Queen at dinner: thrusting his head round the door of the billiard room, Brown scanned the various faces and said, 'All what's here dines with the Queen.'[2]

On one occasion the mayor of Portsmouth was waiting in the equerries' room at Osborne for an answer to his request that the Queen attend some function, when Brown burst in. 'The Queen says sairtenly not', declared Brown. On another occasion he horrified a director of the Great Western Railway by summoning the sons of the Prince of Wales with an abrupt 'The Queen wants the boys in her carriage.' The director could hardly believe his ears. 'He calls them boys', he gasped.

A complaint from Brown that he had been overworked or over-looked or insulted would earn the culprit Her Majesty's grave dis-pleasure. She always took his side. Brown 'must not be made "a man of all work" – besides it *loses* his position', the Queen once complained to Lady Biddulph, the wife of her Master of the Household. And when Brown grumbled about the royal smokers keeping him up too late, the Queen immediately indicated that 'for the sake of the *servants*', the smoking-room should be closed at midnight. When the young officer who had been appointed as governor to the Queen's youngest son, Prince Leopold, treated John Brown's brother Archie with insufficient deference, he was promptly dismissed.

One day General Sir John McNeill, one of the Queen's recently appointed equerries, was at his desk when Brown came in with a message about some carriages that were to be ordered. Having deliv-ered the message, Brown remained standing by the General's desk. McNeill, who had as short a way with servants as he had with private soldiers, commanded Brown to wait outside; he would send for him when the order had been written. Incensed by the equerry's curt manner, Brown complained to the Queen. That very evening McNeill received a letter from Her Majesty. In it she offered him a new posting: an unimportant command in a remote part of India. Puzzled by what amounted to a threat of dismissal, McNeill consulted Henry Ponsonby. Ponsonby understood the situation only too well. He advised McNeill to reply to the effect that, of course, he would be only too pleased to accept any command that Her Majesty might offer him, but that as people would be bound to ask why he was giving up his post in the royal household, he would like to know what reason he should give. McNeill heard no more. The Queen could not tell him the real reason. He retained his post as equerry for several years after that, but the Queen never spoke to him again.

Mutter as the household might about the increasing arrogance and importance of John Brown, the Queen was anxious to enhance his status even further. She considered giving him, in addition to an increased salary, a grander title. 'You will see in this the greatest *anxiety* to show *more and more* what you are to me and as time goes on this *will* be more and more seen and known. Every one hears me say that you are *my friend* and most confidential attendant.'

As not even she could consider ennobling a man who was, after all, a servant, the Queen revived the ancient title of 'Esquire'. By this, apparently, she meant to transform rough-hewn Brown into some sort of medieval figure: a shield-bearer, a knight's companion, a gentleman.

Although by early 1866 the bizarre relationship between the Sovereign and the gillie was being widely discussed in court circles, it was not until later in the year that the general public came to hear of it. At first the press merely noted the constant presence of the kilted Brown on the box of the Queen's carriage; the *Morning Post* compared him to Roustam, the famous Mameluke servant of Napoleon I. But in July 1866 *Punch*, to emphasize both the Queen's withdrawn way of life and the prominent part played in it by John Brown, boldly published an imaginary Court Circular.

Balmoral, Tuesday.
Mr John Brown walked the slopes.
He subsequently partook of a haggis.
In the evening Mr John Brown was pleased to listen to a bagpipe.
Mr John Brown retired early.

What the item lacked in wit, it more than made up for in audacity: to have named and ridiculed the Queen's favourite so openly was a significant move.

The example of *Punch* was followed by other attacks on John Brown's position and character. 'I suppose all my readers have heard of the great court favourite John Brown', wrote the London correspondent of the *John-O'-Groat* journal in August 1866. 'His dismissal some weeks ago was generally talked about at the time, and I observe that the fact has now found its way into print, coupled with the suggestion of John Brown's probable restoration to power before long.

'The reason assigned for his dismissal is an inordinate indulgence in the national taste for whisky, and the restraining of that appetite is mentioned as a likely condition of his readmission to favour ...'.

Within two months the *Pall Mall Gazette* published a tantalizing little paragraph to the effect that the British Minister at Berne had been obliged to lodge a complaint against an article in the *Gazette de Lausanne* because of certain 'calumnies against Queen Victoria'.

What these calumnies were no one in the royal household knew: 'I believe,' wrote Henry Ponsonby, 'that the Queen is as ignorant as any of us.' This was just as well, for the 'Special Correspondent' of the

Gazette de Lausanne had some startling revelations to make about the private life of the Queen of England.

'They say', he reported, 'that with Brown and by him she consoles herself for Prince Albert, and they go even further.

'They add that she is in an interesting condition, and that if she was not present for the Volunteers' Review, and at the inauguration of the monument to Prince Albert, it was only in order to hide her pregnancy.

'I hasten to add that the Queen has been morganatically married to her attendant for a long time, which diminishes the gravity of the thing.'

The British Minister at Berne would have been wiser to ignore this slanderous item, for in making an official complaint about it he ensured its wider circulation. *Reynold's News*, always ready to pass on items of royal gossip, was delighted to report that the Swiss authorities had refused to prosecute the offending newspaper. 'We do not care to reproduce in our columns', claimed *Reynold's News* in mock disapproval, 'the many extraordinary causes that are assigned for the Queen's seclusion' in the pages of various Continental newspapers.

Not for a moment, though, was Queen Victoria going to allow these innuendoes to drive her association with John Brown underground. On the contrary, she welcomed every opportunity to display their special relationship. In the 1867 Spring Exhibition at the Royal Academy the most sensational painting was Edwin Landseer's equestrian portrait of the Queen. Dressed in black, like a nun, and sitting side-saddle on a black horse, she is pictured reading a dispatch; on the ground below lie scattered, for some obscure reason, more official-looking papers. Perhaps it was meant to show that, even when out riding, the Queen was attending to her many duties.

But the chief interest of the picture lies in the figure of John Brown. Dressed in a black kilt he stands, in a masterful pose, holding the bridle of Her Majesty's horse. The Queen was delighted with the picture. However, for the engraving that was to be made from it she suggested one improvement: to render the already handsome Brown even more so, his beard needed to be shortened. A batch of photographs of the favourite, with shorter beard, was sent to Landseer to reinforce the Queen's suggestion.

The painting caused a considerable stir; the public flocked to see it. For all the demureness of the Queen's pose and the respectfulness of Brown's, their association was made only too apparent. 'We respect the privacy of Her Majesty,' commented *The Saturday Review*, 'but when Sir Edwin Landseer puts the Queen and her black favourites into what are, during the season, the most public rooms in England, he does more harm to her popularity than he imagines.' One had only to listen to the knowing comments of the public to appreciate 'how great an imprudence has been committed'.

The *Illustrated London News* was equally censorious. 'We trust it will be deemed no disloyalty either to the sovereign or to the reputation of the painter to say ... there is not one of Her Majesty's subjects will see this lugubrious picture without regret.'

Tomahawk, the new satirical magazine, put it more succinctly. 'All is black', it quipped, 'that is not Brown.'

An even more telling comment came from *Tomahawk* later that year. It published a cartoon which sent its hitherto modest circulation figures soaring. Entitled 'A Brown Study', it showed two unused symbols of monarchy – the crown under a glass dome and an empty throne – together with a British lion in a subservient posture. Over all presided the assured figure of John Brown, pipe in hand, leaning nonchalantly against the throne and looking down on the lion in lordly fashion. The message – that John Brown occupied the place neglected by the Queen – was only too clear.

And in the pages of *Tinsley's Magazine* a visiting American professed himself shocked by the way in which Englishmen spoke of the Queen's association with John Brown. Some said that she had gone mad and that Brown was her keeper; others that she was a spiritualist and Brown her medium. But most – and they were all 'gentlemen of rank and position' – claimed that she had succumbed to lust and that Brown was her lover. The Queen was invariably referred to, he continued solemnly, as 'Mrs Brown'.

One of the many public incidents in this strange affair occurred in the summer of 1867. The Queen had reluctantly agreed to attend a review of troops in Hyde Park. Lord Derby, Conservative Prime Minister for a third term, had heard that a hostile demonstration was being planned against John Brown who would, of course, be seated on the box of the Queen's carriage. Understandably, Lord Derby dreaded the impact of such a demonstration on the foreign diplomats, official guests and troops. Writing in strict confidence to Her Majesty's secretary, General Sir Charles Grey, Derby suggested that Brown develop 'some slight ailment' on the day and excuse himself.

Grey knew better than to pass this suggestion on to Brown; he would only complain to the Queen. So the secretary approached Her Majesty directly. By implying that the Prime Minister's only concern was for Brown's feelings and safety, Grey talked the Queen into agreeing to leave Brown at home on the day of the review. She certainly did not want her faithful servant exposed to any public humiliation.

Hardly had the Queen agreed to leave him behind than she had second thoughts. What if, by giving in to pressure, she had allowed a dangerous precedent to be set? Might this not be the first move in a campaign to deprive her of Brown's comforting presence? Was it all part of a plot to get rid of him? She was 'much astonished and shocked', she wrote to her favourite equerry, Lord Charles Fitzroy, 'at an attempt being made by some people to prevent her faithful servant going with her to the Review in Hyde Park, thereby making the poor, nervous, shaken Queen, who is so accustomed to his watchful care and intelligence, terribly nervous and uncomfortable . . . what it all means she does not know.'

The more she thought about it, the more outraged she became. It was all 'the result of *ill-natured* gossip in the Higher classes, caused by dissatisfaction at *not forcing* the Queen *out* of her seclusion . . .' ran the over-excited phrases, 'and probably seizing hold of those wicked and idle lies about poor, good Brown . . .'.

The Queen would not, she concluded, 'be dictated to.'

What course of action she planned to take, one does not know. Having by now decided that she would not go to the review without Brown, she would either have to defy her Prime Minister and take Brown with her, or plead, as she had so often done before, an attack of 'nerves' and stay home. In the event, she was not put to the test. The impasse was resolved by the receipt of the dramatic news that the Emperor Maximilian of Mexico (husband of the Queen's cousin Charlotte – King Leopold's daughter) had been executed by a firing squad in Queretaro. Thankfully, Lord Derby cancelled the review; while the Queen, no less thankfully, ordered her court into mourning.

There was only one way in which Queen Victoria's dearest friend fell short: he could not set fire to her romantic imagination. Their relationship, for all its advantages, lacked one essential ingredient – magic. But there was magic in abundance during the year 1868. From February to November that year, Benjamin Disraeli was Prime Minister.

The Queen had in fact been partly responsible for Disraeli's elevation. The good impression which he had created by his tributes to the late Prince Consort had been strengthened by his parliamentary battle for Reform – an extension of the franchise. In this, Disraeli had had the full support of the Queen. She was all for Reform. Her conviction came partly from the shade of the progressively-minded Prince Albert, and partly from her ever-growing distaste for the frivolity of the aristocracy. The Reform Bill, by which the franchise would be extended to include the 'respectable Lower classes', might well provide the shock which she considered necessary to bring the idle upper classes to their senses and so avoid some 'dreadful crash' along the lines of the French Revolution. The Queen fully agreed with Disraeli's convincingly argued theory that the bill would win still more adherents to the cause of Crown and Empire.

The triumphant passing of the Reform Bill, in April 1867, strengthened the Queen's conviction that Mr Disraeli must be the successor to Lord Derby. So when by the beginning of the year 1868 it became apparent that the ailing Lord Derby could not carry on as Conservative Prime Minister much longer, the Queen asked him to resign. On 25 February 1868, Disraeli became Prime Minister. He had climbed, as he put it – but not to Queen Victoria – 'to the top of the greasy pole.'

To her, he wrote one of his courtly letters. All he could offer, he declared, was devotion. It would be his duty and delight to render His Sovereign's work as easy as possible. Even had Her Majesty not been gifted with great ability ('which all now acknowledge'), her experience had given her a judgement which few living persons, and probably no living prince, could rival.

The Queen's answer was hardly less complimentary. It must be a proud moment, she wrote, for him to feel that 'his own talent and successful labours in the service of his Sovereign and country' had earned him his present 'high and influential' position. When he went to Osborne for his first audience, all, he enthused, was 'sunshine'. With 'a very radiant face' the Queen entered the room and invited him to 'kiss hands'. The sixty-three-year-old Disraeli, his sparse and improbably black ringlets carefully arranged across his brow, went down on one knee. Taking the Queen's plump and beringed little hand in both of his, he kissed it and pledged his 'loving loyalty and faith.'

He was as good as his word. Within days the Queen was expressing her delight in her new Prime Minister. While admitting to her daughter Vicky that Mr Disraeli was 'very peculiar', the Queen described him as 'full of poetry, romance and chivalry'. Audiences, which had hitherto been such a trial, suddenly became something to look forward to. With his engaging blend of deference and intimacy, Mr Disraeli seemed to be solely concerned with what the Queen called her 'comfort'. He was so attentive, so considerate, so obliging. He never lectured her, never badgered her, never tried to push her beyond her limits. He never even seemed to disagree with her. (He never contradicted, he never denied, he sometimes forgot, was how Disraeli once summed up his political discussions with the Queen.) In his soothing presence, the Queen found her own shyness disappearing. Mr Disraeli seemed to be so interested in everything she had to say. And he was so ready to discuss things that were not strictly business. Quite often, audiences overran their time while the Prime Minister diverted her with the latest political, or even social, tit-bit.

And when he was not chatting to her, he would be writing to her. 'Dizzy writes daily letters to the Queen in his best novel style,' reported Lady Augusta Stanley to the disapproving Lord Clarendon, 'telling her every scrap of political news dressed up to serve his own purpose, and every scrap of social gossip cooked to amuse her. She declares that she has never had such letters in her life, which is probably true, and that she never before knew *everything!*'[3]

Disraeli described the new Chancellor of the Exchequer as having 'the sagacity of the elephant as well as its form.' The Opposition he compared to 'a company, a *troupe*, like one of those bands of minstrels one encounters in the sauntering of a summer street'. Although it was highly unlikely that Her Majesty had ever encountered a troupe of minstrels, much less sauntered along a summer street, she was enchanted.

He took care to coat every possibly unpalatable suggestion in the most honeyed language. When he ventured that the Prince of Wales should visit Ireland on the grounds that Ireland 'yearned for the occasional presence and inspiration of Royalty', she could hardly refuse. The 'inspiration of Royalty' was such a gratifyingly perceptive way of putting it. 'There for the first time,' says one of Queen Victoria's biographers, 'like some Oriental Pan in the thicket, he sounded that flute-like note which she found irresistible.'[4]

But not quite irresistible; not yet, at any rate. If on a personal level the Queen and Disraeli were in accord, politically there remained a gap between them. The Queen's views were still coloured by those of the late Prince Consort and however sweetly Dizzy might pipe his tune, she was not yet ready to be enticed down his particular political path. His beliefs were too hazy, too eccentric, too inconsistent.

Like everything else about him, Disraeli's brand of Conservatism was unorthodox. Since becoming a Member of Parliament in 1837 – the very year that Victoria ascended the throne – Disraeli had come to regard Conservatism in a highly romantic light. He saw it, not as a philosophy of privilege, but as a noble alliance between the aristocracy and the people. Toryism should be a popular movement: a working together of the nobility and the masses in support of the monarchy and the church. It should be a revival of the loyal, chivalrous, idealistic spirit of the days before the Whig triumph in the revolution of 1688. He wanted an enlightened triumvirate – of monarchy, clergy and aristocracy – to dedicate itself to the general good of all the people. What Disraeli dreamed of, in fact, was a type of aristocratic paternalism.

In short, and as far as the Queen was concerned, Disraeli hardly fitted into that gallery of upright, earnest, liberally minded men so favoured by Prince Albert.

But then with the man who did – William Ewart Gladstone, leader of the recently formed Liberal Party – the Queen felt distinctly ill at ease. She had not yet come to loathe Gladstone but even now, given the choice between Gladstone and Disraeli, she would have chosen the latter.

Having heard her Prime Minister say that he was so fond of flowers, the Queen sent him some that spring. Back came a letter in which Dizzy declared that 'their lustre and perfume were enhanced by the condescending hand which had showered upon him all the treasures of spring'. She promptly sent him more. To his home in Grosvenor Gate, in their moss-lined boxes, came primroses from Windsor and then violets from Osborne.

When he presented her with a set of his novels, she gave him her recently published *Leaves from the Journal of Our Life in the Highlands*. 'There is a freshness and fragrance about the book like the heather amid which it was written,' he enthused, and in future conversation with the Queen he would delight her by speaking of 'We authors, Ma'am'.

Although one could not claim that at this stage Disraeli was drawing the Queen out of her seclusion in the way that John Brown was drawing her out of her mourning, it was certainly the first time for many years that she ventured abroad on holiday. She decided to spend a few weeks of that summer of 1868 in Switzerland. The fact that she travelled incognito as the Countess of Kent (an alias which allowed Disraeli to refer to her as 'our dear Peeress') fooled no one; her black-clad shape was unmistakable, particularly as the by now highly controversial figure of John Brown, kilted and uncompromising, was to be seen everywhere with her. He was 'insufferably bored and made himself intensely disagreeable,' complained Henry Ponsonby.[5]

That September Disraeli went to Balmoral. For all its attractions, remote and rain-lashed Deeside – with its obligatory picnics and wind-buffeted walks – hardly suited him. Not for a moment, though, did he allow the Queen to suspect this. Dear Mr Disraeli 'seemed delighted with his stay and was most grateful,' she noted in her Journal. 'He certainly shows more consideration for my comfort than any preceding Prime Ministers ...'. When he left, she loaded him with presents: the inevitable portrait of the late Prince Consort, a box of family photographs, a shawl for his wife Mary Anne and two books of views of Balmoral. In his adroit letter of thanks, Disraeli assured her that, because of those books of views, 'he will be able to live, as it were, in Your Majesty's favourite scenes.' But that, quite frankly, was as near as he ever wanted to get to them.

Hardly had Disraeli arrived back in London that autumn when he was plunged into the turmoil of a general election. Despite his optimism, the Conservatives were soundly beaten by the Liberals. Gladstone was to be the next Prime Minister; Disraeli's term had lasted a mere ten months.

But during this term, Disraeli had laid the foundations for his next premiership. The 1868 term was in the nature of a prelude: a prelude to his more spectacular premiership half a dozen years later and a prelude to his romantic partnership with Queen Victoria. With the Queen still tied, politically to Prince Albert and emotionally to John Brown, Disraeli had had to move with circumspection. All he had been able to do was to ingratiate himself with the Queen; he had yet to bring their association into full flower.

14

'Our Life in the Highlands'

'MORE CURIOUS things go on here', wrote Lord John Manners on visiting Balmoral for the first time, 'than I should have dreamed of.'[1] Among the many curious aspects of life at Balmoral was the startling contrast between the propriety expected of the Queen's family, guests and household, and the licence which she allowed her Highland servants. Indeed, the Queen often seemed to be more concerned about the feelings of her Scottish staff than she was about those of her entourage. When her book *Leaves from the Journal of Our Life in the Highlands* was published in 1868, some members of her household resented the fact that, in its pages, the Queen treated courtiers and servants alike; as though, grumbled one affronted lady-in-waiting, 'all are on the same footing.'[2]

The Queen's children and grandchildren were expected to share her unsnobbish and tolerant attitudes. When people were well-bred and well-educated, she explained to one of her grandsons, they should know better than to make mistakes, whereas humbly born people should always be forgiven. Once, when a servant who had been under threat of dismissal for years for drunkenness started a fire by toppling down a flight of stairs with a lamp in his hand, a report of his long history of transgressions was laid before the Queen. Expected to dismiss him, she merely wrote 'poor man' in the margin, and forgave him.

Her grandchildren, arriving to stay with her at Balmoral, would always be sent, 'before anything else', to shake hands with the servants and gillies. Not all of them, though, approved of this fraternization. When Princess Charlotte of Prussia – Vicky's little daughter – arrived at the castle, the Queen instructed her to 'Say how de do' to John Brown. Grudgingly, the girl obeyed. 'Now go and shake hands,' continued the Queen. But Charlotte refused. 'No,' she explained,

'Mama says I ought not to be too familiar with servants.' This led, reported Henry Ponsonby to his wife, 'to no end of a row' with the Prussian Crown Princess about her children's upbringing.[3]

It was, of course, the Queen's attitude to John Brown that was the most curious aspect of life at Balmoral. And seldom was this more apparent than at the annual gillies' ball. The general public, led to believe that their Sovereign was a pathetic, nervous, broken-hearted creature, would have been astonished at the sight of her presiding over this annual romp. There were few occasions she enjoyed more; no sign here of the Queen who was not amused. The drunken revelries of what Ponsonby calls this 'rough and tumble affair' were organized by Brown. 'What a coarse animal that Brown is ...' remarked Lord Cairns after attending one gillies' ball; 'I do not conceive it possible that anyone could behave so roughly as he does to the Queen.'[4]

Nor was she the only one to be roughly treated. Those whooping Highlanders, flushed with whisky, soon got out of hand. On one occasion Lord Cowley, Master of the Queen's Household, was tripped by a cavorting groom and sent sprawling; on another Prince Leopold, the Queen's haemophilic son, was crashed into by some beefy dancer. Even Brown, says Ponsonby, saw that this was unseemly and ordered the music to be stopped.

That Brown was more usually drunk than sober at these gatherings did not bother the Queen. She was extraordinarily tolerant of his excessive drinking. If he was discovered at her door in a hopelessly befuddled state, he would simply be carted off to bed. If the Queen's doctor dared suggest that for the sake of his health Brown should substitute claret for whisky, Her Majesty would show grave displeasure at her doctor's effrontery. On one occasion the Queen, having already seated herself in the carriage for her customary afternoon drive, was kept waiting for Brown to take his place on the box. Ponsonby, suspecting the reason for the delay, went upstairs to find Brown dead drunk on his bed. Without a word to the Queen, the private secretary took Brown's place on the box. Her Majesty, likewise, made no comment. She simply sat, bolt upright and impassive, as the royal carriage went spinning off down the gravelled driveway.

Meeting Brown with a basket on his arm on his way to accompany the Queen on an outing, one of the maids-of-honour asked if it were tea that he was taking out. 'Wall, no,' replied Brown, 'she don't much like tea. We tak oot biscuits and sperruts.'[5] He made the best cup of tea she had ever drunk, the Queen once told Brown. So it should be, he explained bluntly: he put 'a grand nip o' whisky' in it.

It was these outings, *à deux*, which gave rise to so much speculation and gossip. As early as 1865 Lord Derby was making mention, in his diary, of the 'strange and disagreeable stories' about the Queen and the gillie. She 'will have no one else to wait upon her, makes him drive her out alone in a pony carriage, walk with, rather than after her, gives orders through him to the equerries, allows him access to her such as no one else has, and in various ways distinguishes him beyond what is customary and fitting in that position.'[6]

What Ponsonby called the Queen's 'marked and sustained in-fatuation' for Brown made it impossible for anyone, even members of her family, to warn her of the inadvisability, even danger, of spending such long periods with her handsome servant. By 1866 Lord Derby was noting yet more gossip about Brown, and although he professed not to believe it, he made it plain that the Queen's behaviour was lending it credibility.

'Long solitary rides, in secluded parts of the park; constant attendance upon her in her room; private messages sent by him to persons of rank; avoidance of observation while he is leading her pony or driving her little carriage: everything shows that she has selected this man for a kind of friendship which is absurd and unbecoming in her position.'[7] Her daughters, he added, very wisely made a joke of the matter, speaking of Brown as 'Mama's lover'.

The jokes were not confined to the princesses. Georgie Sumner, recently mistress to that colourful poet and traveller, Wilfrid Scawen Blunt, met Queen Victoria while they were both guests at Dunrobin Castle. 'The Queen's visit', she reported to Blunt, 'was a great success. I fell in love with John Brown and almost made Her Majesty jealous.'[8]

It is in the pages of Wilfrid Scawen Blunt's 'Secret Diary', a confidential record not opened until 1972, fifty years after his death, that one is given a still more intimate glimpse into the relationship between Queen Victoria and John Brown. Blunt had in his youth been one of the many lovers of the famous Victorian courtesan, Catherine Walters, more usually known as 'Skittles'. In later life Skittles, who remained friendly with Blunt, regaled him with a great deal of gossip about the royal family (the Prince of Wales had also been one of her lovers), all of which he noted down. Although both Blunt and Skittles tend to be unreliable witnesses, there seems no good reason to think either of them is lying: Skittles did not know that Blunt was recording her memories, and Blunt did not intend his diary to be published until long after his death. As what Skittles had to tell him about Queen

Victoria and John Brown was so scurrilous, and as 'the story was so important historically', Blunt 'cross-questioned her pretty closely so as to test its accuracy'. He decided that 'in all essentials it held well together'.

The Prince of Wales once commissioned the fashionable Hungarian-born and Viennese-trained sculptor Edgar Boehm to do a head of Skittles, and it was from Boehm that Skittles heard about the curious goings-on at Balmoral. In 1869 or 1870 Boehm was commanded to the castle to create a bust of John Brown. During the three months that he worked at Balmoral, Boehm saw a great deal of Brown, his model, and of the Queen. 'Brown was a rude unmannerly fellow', reported Skittles, 'and [Boehm] had much ado to keep him in order during the sittings, but he had unbounded influence with the Queen whom he treated with little respect, presuming in every way upon his position with her ... he was a fine man physically, though coarsely made, and had fine eyes ...'.

The situation was considerably complicated by the fact that the Queen's fourth daughter, the vivacious and artistic Princess Louise, then in her early twenties and still unmarried, seems to have developed a passion for the handsome Boehm. In the course of the modelling lessons which he was giving her 'they became intimate, though not to the extent of actual love-making'. One day when the Queen, accompanied by Brown, arrived unexpectedly to see how the bust was getting on, she discovered Louise in what may have been a compromising position with Boehm. A 'violent scene' occurred between mother and daughter. The hot-tempered Louise accused Brown of carrying tales to the Queen (all the Queen's children complained of this), and informed her mother that she would stand his 'impertinence' no longer. She threatened to make a public scandal of 'the whole matter'.

The scene, possibly exaggerated by Boehm and Skittles, may well have spurred Queen Victoria on in her efforts to find Louise a suitable husband. However, in the Marquis of Lorne, later Duke of Argyll, Princess Louise seems to have gained a particularly unsuitable husband. One less likely to satisfy her highly sexed nature would have been difficult to find: Lorne, in the expression of the day, was 'unsatisfactory as a husband'. He was, apparently, a homosexual.

After her marriage, Princess Louise's name was coupled with at least two men in the Queen's household: her sister Beatrice's husband, Prince Henry of Battenberg, and Arthur Bigge, the Queen's private secretary. But one must always allow for the fact that in the cloistered, hot-house atmosphere of the court, even innocuous friendships between men and women could be transformed by gossip into passionate love affairs.

On Princess Louise's marriage, Brown ostentatiously contributed thirty guineas – more than a month's salary – towards a fund for a present from the staff; Ponsonby, the private secretary, could only afford ten. If Brown's gesture was meant to impress the Princess, it failed to do so. 'I don't want an absurd man in a kilt following me everywhere', announced Princess Louise to Ponsonby when discussing her future servants.[9]

About the Queen's relationship with Brown, Boehm was revealing. She allowed her muscular gillie, he was told, 'all privileges.' It was 'to be with him, where she could do more as she liked, that she spent so much of her time at Balmoral. . . . She used to go away with him to a little house in the hills where, on the pretence that it was for protection and to look after her dogs, he had a bedroom next to hers, the ladies-in-waiting being put at the other end of the building . . . Boehm saw enough of his familiarities with her to leave no doubt of his being allowed "every conjugal privilege".'

It was the 'talk of the household' that John Brown was 'the Queen's Stallion'.[10]

By now the widespread gossip about the Queen and Brown – that they were lovers, that they were husband and wife, even that she had gone to Switzerland to have his baby – was causing increasing unease among the members of the royal family. When added to the seclusion in which the Queen lived, the stubbornness with which she avoided her public duties and the growth of a republican movement, this talk was seriously undermining her position. Her eldest daughter Vicky (once described as 'always clever, never wise') composed a letter, to be signed by all the Queen's children, in which she lamented her mother's continuing withdrawal and warned her of the dangers her way of life was posing for the monarchy. Fortunately, the letter was never sent. Queen Victoria's probable reaction to this piece of self-righteous if well-intended meddling may be imagined.

The Queen's serious but vaguely diagnosed illness at Balmoral in the autumn of 1871 merely worsened the situation. In contrast to the members of her family, Brown was allowed full access to the Queen's sickroom. Whether in lifting her from her bed to her couch or in transmitting her stream of orders, he proved invaluable. His privileged position was bitterly resented by the Queen's sons and daughters. Her relations, admitted Ponsonby to his wife, were 'the very people the Queen is least inclined to send for'.

The Queen's second daughter, Princess Alice, Grand Duchess of Hesse, complained to Ponsonby about Brown's great influence. Although 'quite unfit for more than menial work', Brown alone 'talks to her on all things while we, her children, are restricted to speak on only those matters which may not excite her or which she chooses to talk about.'[11]

Occasionally this simmering family hostility towards Brown boiled over. Arriving at Balmoral that autumn, the Queen's sailor son Prince Alfred, Duke of Edinburgh, pointedly refused to shake hands with Brown. The immediate reasons for the Prince's churlishness were highly complicated, but the outraged Queen insisted that the row between the two men be patched up without delay. Prince Alfred agreed to see Brown, but only in the presence of a witness. This, he declared, was the way things were done on board ship. 'This is not a ship,' thundered the Queen on hearing of her son's conditions, 'and I won't have naval discipline introduced here.'[12]

In the end, a meeting was arranged between the protagonists and Brown forced himself to make an apology to Prince Alfred. The Prince pronounced himself satisfied, upon which the incorrigible Brown, determined to win the last round, announced that he, too, was satisfied.

Within a few weeks of this contretemps, the Queen was gratified to find her stubborn championship of Brown triumphantly vindicated. One day, when she was returning to Buckingham Palace from a drive, a youth named Arthur O'Conner pointed a pistol at her. He apparently hoped to frighten her into releasing certain rebel Irish prisoners. In a flash Brown, who had just alighted from the box, grabbed hold of the young man and kept him pinned. The Queen was greatly shaken, and although her third son, Prince Arthur, had behaved as bravely if not quite as quickly as Brown (the pistol, in any case, was unloaded), the Queen was convinced that it was to Brown's 'wonderful presence of mind' alone that she owed her escape.

So selfless an act of heroism, decided the Queen, deserved a tangible reward. Fobbing off the equally gallant Prince Arthur with a mere gold pin (the Prince of Wales was furious about this), the Queen set about creating a special award for Brown. It was to be an award for service to the Sovereign beyond the call of duty. It carried a £25 annuity for life and, more importantly, a gold medal with a relief portrait of Queen Victoria on one side; on the other, a wreath surrounded the words: 'To John Brown Esq., in recognition of his presence of mind and devotion at Buckingham Palace, February 29, 1872.'

Known as the Devoted Service Medal, it was irreverently referred to as 'The Greater Order of Brown'. He seems, at any rate, to have been its sole recipient.

A poignant reminder of the period when Queen Victoria had been attracted to an altogether more romantic man than John Brown came in the spring of 1871. For the first time in thirteen years she met the Emperor Napoleon III. Much had happened to him in the intervening years. Queen Victoria's long period of mourning had coincided, almost exactly, with the most brilliant days of the French Second Empire. During the decade between 1860 and 1870, Paris had become firmly established as the world's most spectacular capital: *la ville lumière*, the Queen of Cities, an appropriately glittering centre for the showiest regime in Europe. In contrast to the secluded life of the widowed Queen Victoria, the Emperor Napoleon III and the Empress Eugénie had lived in a blaze of public attention; they had presided over an apparently endless succession of military parades, royal visits, exhibitions, fêtes and balls.

That Queen Victoria disapproved, not only of the militarism and dazzle of the French imperial court but of its celebrated licentiousness, was only to be expected. To her, it was 'that Sodom and Gomorrah'. She ensured that the time spent there by her sons, particularly her all-too-susceptible son Bertie, was kept to a minimum. The Queen was in full agreement with the more serious-minded Vicky, who could only bemoan the mischief which the imperial court was doing 'to society, to the stage and to literature'.

Although the Queen did not meet the Emperor throughout those years, she did have three brief meetings with the Empress. She found Eugénie to be as charming as ever – and even more assured and well-informed – but in her disinclination to make any sort of social effort, the Queen was always relieved when these visits were over.

In September 1870, Napoleon III's tinselly Empire came crashing down. Cornered into declaring war on Prussia by the astute Chancellor, Bismarck, who needed a war with France to complete his plans for the unification of Germany, Napoleon III was obliged to surrender to the enemy after his defeat at the battle of Sedan. The Second Empire collapsed, the Empress fled to England, France was declared a republic, and for six months the Emperor was sent into relatively luxurious captivity by the victorious Prussians.

In March 1871 Napoleon III was released. He travelled to England to join the Empress and their only child, the fourteen-year-old Prince Imperial, then living in exile in a house known as Camden Place, in Chislehurst, Kent.

A week after the Emperor's arrival at Camden Place, Queen Victoria invited him to Windsor. For the Queen, the meeting was fraught with emotion. She could not help drawing a parallel between this doleful occasion and their first, enchanting meeting in 1855. Then he had come 'in perfect triumph, dearest Albert bringing him from Dover, the whole country mad to receive him ...'. Now, as she stood by the door, it was a very different Napoleon whom she watched alight, rather painfully, from the carriage. Gone were the dashing uniform, the cat's-whisker moustaches, the dyed chestnut hair: 'he had grown very stout and grey and his moustaches are no longer curled and waxed as formerly,' she noted. The Queen must have been conscious of the change in her own appearance as well. No longer was she the alert, brightly dressed young woman who had responded so eagerly to his flattering attentions; who had once laughingly threatened to arrive in Paris by train, bag in hand, to beg dinner and a night's lodging at the Tuileries.

For Napoleon III, the occasion was no less poignant. He looked depressed and his eyes were wet with tears. Victoria embraced him '*comme de rigueur*' and he, pulling himself together, remarked quietly, 'It's been a very long time since I have seen Your Majesty.'

As the two of them sat talking in the Audience Room, so did the Queen find herself falling, once more, under the spell of his personality; not quite all the old magic had worn off. She was soon responding, as she always had, to that 'pleasing, gentle and gracious manner'. They spoke about the Emperor's captivity (he had no word of complaint about his German captors), about the present regrettable state of France, and about Napoleon's 'renewed' admiration for England.

Their discussion on the Franco-Prussian war had to be conducted with considerable finesse, for it was on the ruins of the French Second Empire that the new German Empire had been declared; an empire over which Crown Prince Frederick, the husband of Queen Victoria's daughter Vicky, would one day reign as German Emperor. They were still busy on the origins of the war when their discussions were interrupted. The Queen considered this 'most provoking'.

The royal household had been assembled in the corridor, and before taking his leave the Emperor passed along the line, pausing to say a few kind words to each of them. Again it was, for the Queen, a heart-breaking echo of the triumphant imperial visit sixteen years before.

The Queen returned the Emperor's visit a few days later. She was met at the door of Camden Place – a three-storeyed, red-brick mansion set in a large park – by the young Prince Imperial. Inside waited the Emperor, the Empress and their suite. This was Queen Victoria's second visit to Camden Place. She had already called on the Empress Eugénie soon after the Empress's flight from Paris. The Queen on that occasion considered the house to look, for some obscure reason, 'very French' and had claimed, with her uncertain taste, that there were 'many pretty things about'. In fact, Camden Place had merely been rented, fully and tastelessly furnished, by the imperial couple.

Now, as the three of them sat in the small drawing-room, they spoke about the situation in Paris. With the Franco-Prussian War over, another battle was raging in the French capital – this time between the radical Communards, who had seized control of Paris, and the Republican government troops, stationed at Versailles. It was proving an extremely bloody insurrection. It lasted for two months and was crushed by the Republican government with the utmost ruthlessness. Over twenty thousand people were killed during 'Bloody Week' alone, and half Paris, including the Tuileries Palace, was gutted by fire. That other scene of Queen Victoria's enchanted visit in 1855 – the Palace of Saint-Cloud – had already been destroyed during the war.

The Empress, declared Queen Victoria, was greatly excited by the revolution, but the Emperor was more restrained. In fact, if there was one feature of the Emperor's behaviour which the Queen found especially striking during this exchange of visits, it was his stoicism. His fellow-exiles were no less amazed by this characteristic. Whereas Eugénie railed almost continuously against those whom she considered had betrayed the Empire, Napoleon said nothing. He never complained. There was never a murmur against those who had misled him, deserted him, or were now covering him with abuse. Nor did he complain about the little things: the food or the weather or the same sad faces. On that bored, irritable and often despairing company at Camden Place, his presence had a soothing and inspiring effect. His self-control was an example to them all.

'He bore his terrible misfortunes', wrote the admiring Queen Victoria, 'with meekness, dignity and patience.'

Not only was Queen Victoria once more warming to Napoleon III's relaxed and gentlemanly manner; she was reverting to her former political opinion of him as well. That he was not so much to blame for the Franco-Prussian war as she had originally assumed was gradually becoming clear to her. Her son-in-law Crown Prince Frederick visited the Queen soon after the war, and from him she learned something of its origins. The Crown Prince revealed that Bismarck's part in promoting the conflict had been considerable. The Prussian Chancellor had been as much to blame for the outbreak of war as had the Emperor. 'This corroborates and justifies what many people have said,' wrote the Queen.

After Napoleon III's death, the Queen assured the sceptical Henry Ponsonby that the Emperor was 'a most faithful ally to this country, much attached to it and most hospitable to the English and, to those who trusted him, most lovable, charming and amiable'. Forgotten, apparently, were her outbursts against him as the *'universal disturber* of the world'.

Once the Emperor had settled permanently in England, the Queen went out of her way to make him feel welcome. No one would ever believe, said the Empress in old age, how many 'delicate attentions' the Queen had lavished on them during the first years of exile. She always treated them as sovereigns. If the Emperor and Empress happened to be visiting some member of the royal family near Windsor Castle, the Queen would drive over to see them. On the occasion of her state drive to St Paul's Cathedral to give thanks for the Prince of Wales's recovery from a serious illness, the Queen invited the imperial couple to view the procession from the privacy of Buckingham Palace. Once when she visited Camden Place she delighted her hosts by assuring them that she had no wish to visit Paris, now that they were no longer there.

When, early in January 1873, the Emperor underwent an operation to remove a stone from his bladder, the Queen was kept fully informed. At luncheon on 7 January – the day on which the Emperor was operated on for a second time – the Queen was handed a bulletin in which Napoleon III's doctor admitted that the case was still serious. The news alarmed the Queen considerably. For the following two days the thought of the Emperor's suffering was almost continuously on her mind. On the afternoon of 9 January she received a telegram to say that he had died that morning.

'Had a great regard for the Emperor, who was so amiable ...' wrote the Queen in her Journal that evening. 'He had been such a faithful ally to England and I could not but think of the wonderful position he had, after being a poor, insignificant exile, of the magnificent reception given him in England in 1855, and his agreeable visit here in '57, and ours to Paris in '55! And now to die like this from the results of an operation, though it may have been inevitable, seems too tragic and sad.'

The Emperor's death had one remarkable effect on Queen Victoria: it converted her to Bonapartism. 'The Queen does *not* [think] the Bonapartist cause will lose by the poor Emperor's death,' she wrote to Theodore Martin, then busy writing his monumental life of the Prince Consort; 'on the contrary *she* thinks the reverse. *For* the peace of Europe, she thinks ... that it would be best if the Prince Imperial was *ultimately* to succeed.'

That France might just possibly manage to drag itself along without some form of monarchy was unthinkable to the Queen of England.

By the year of Napoleon III's death, 1873, the John Brown scandal was dying down. This did not mean that the Queen was seeing any less of her gillie or that her affection for him had in any way weakened; it was simply that people had come to accept him as a permanent part of her life. Dr Jenner, by now Sir William Jenner, admitted as much to Henry Ponsonby. 'He alluded to the Brown question and said how they all tried to press the Queen to send him away ...', reported Ponsonby to his wife. 'But the Queen would not be coerced, she held her own way and now the thing runs smoothly and we wonder there ever was a row about it. One thing resulted and that was that the Queen knew she had only to make a stand to carry her point.'[13]

So what, exactly, was the true nature of this enduring, and ultimately accepted, relationship between Queen Victoria and John Brown? At the time, and since, a great many people believed that the link between them was psychic: that Queen Victoria was a spiritualist and Brown the medium through which she contacted the dead Prince Consort. 'The real secret about John Brown and the Queen', noted William Rossetti in his diary in 1870, 'is that Brown is a powerful medium, through whom Prince Albert's spirit communicates with the Queen; hence Brown remains closeted with her alone sometimes for hours together.'[14] Rossetti's authority was the celebrated spiritualist Signor Damiani.

The sculptor Boehm – according to the evidence of Skittles by way of Scawen Blunt – was prepared to go even further. While working on his bust of Brown at Balmoral, Boehm was apparently told that 'the Queen, who had been passionately in love with her husband, got it into her head that somehow the Prince's spirit had passed into Brown and four years after her widowhood, being very unhappy, allowed him all privileges ...'.[15]

The spiritualist press was always claiming Queen Victoria as one of their own and, after the Queen's death, a story – much repeated since – was put about that the spiritualist Robert James Lees often attended seances at Windsor Castle where he acted as the Queen's medium. When on the first of these occasions the Queen suggested appointing young Lees as her Resident Medium, the spirit of the Prince Consort made a counter-suggestion: he could communicate equally well, he indicated, through John Brown. So Brown became the official medium with Lees occasionally standing in for him.

It is not surprising that, in a period of intense interest in the occult, these stories should have gained credence. Given the Queen's over-whelming grief at the loss of her husband, her withdrawn way of life and the, to some, inexplicable presence of John Brown, it was all too easy to believe that the Queen imagined herself to be in contact with the Prince through Brown's mediumship.

There is no proof that this was the case. Like many others Queen Victoria was superstitious, she believed in an after-life, she was intrigued by coincidences, portents and the apparently unaccountable, she indulged in a little experimental table-turning, and was interested in hearing about people like the famous Daniel Dunglas Home, whose psychic exploits so impressed Napoleon III and Eugénie. But not even by her closest associates – like the cynical Henry Ponsonby – was Queen Victoria ever suspected of meddling in the occult. Nor, in her thousands of unguarded letters to her daughter Vicky, does the Queen ever mention a seance.

In the final analysis, the Queen – even at her most vulnerable, in the years immediately after the Prince Consort's death – had too much common sense to be taken in by any spirit messages from the other side. Nor can one imagine bluff, gruff, four-square John Brown sitting down to deliver any such messages.

If the link was not spiritual, was it physical? Was Queen Victoria in love with John Brown in the generally accepted sense of the phrase? Was her undeniable infatuation with him taken to its obvious, sexual, conclusion? Were they lovers? Were they married?

Quite clearly, they were not married. Late in 1870 Ponsonby was writing to his wife in connection with a rumour that John Brown had just married – not the Queen, but someone else. Ponsonby thought it unlikely. If, however, the rumour were true, then Ponsonby imagined that Brown must have married Miss Ocklee, one of her Majesty's dressers. The story would hardly have been put about if Brown were already married to the Queen. In any case, a few months later Queen Victoria made her customary entry to mark her birthday, on 24 May 1871. 'My poor old birthday, my 51st!' she wrote. 'Alone, alone, as it will ever be!' The tone of this private observation was hardly that of a woman who had recently acquired a new husband.

Nor, even allowing for the fact that the Queen was not quite as hidebound as some of her royal contemporaries, would she ever have considered marrying a gillie, no matter how strong the attraction might be. The Queen of England held, she once claimed quite unself-consciously, 'the greatest position there is'; it was certainly not one to be shared with a servant.

But if they were not married, were they lovers? Such of the Queen's intimate letters to John Brown as have been seen by researchers into her life have been described as 'compromising'. The writer E. E. P. Tisdall — admittedly an unreliable witness — claims that he once owned a letter, retrieved by a royal footman from a waste-paper basket and inexplicably lost while moving house during the Second World War, in which the amorous nature of the Queen's relationship with Brown was made only too apparent. In her book *Unquiet Souls* Angela Lambert tells of 'a university professor who, working in the Windsor Castle archives, was by error brought a pile of letters between Queen Victoria and her gillie. From them he deduced that the affair was far from platonic.'[16]

Michaela Reid, in her biography of her husband's grandfather, Sir James Reid, personal physician to the Queen, reveals that Dr Profeit, the factor at Balmoral, had a trunkful of over three hundred letters written by him to the Queen on the subject of John Brown: many of these letters were 'most compromising'. After the Queen's death, Dr Profeit's son George threatened to blackmail King Edward VII with these letters. Sir James Reid was asked to negotiate in the affair, and after George Profeit had been bought off the letters were handed over to the relieved King who, a great destroyer of revealing correspondence, no doubt had the letters burned. Dr Reid confided the substance of these letters into his 'green memorandum book' which, in turn, was destroyed by his son on Reid's death in 1923. So it is highly unlikely that their 'most compromising' contents will ever be known.[17]

On the other hand, sentiments that seem compromising to others might not be considered so by the one writing them. This was par-ticularly true of Queen Victoria. To her daughter Vicky she once admitted to her 'very violent' feelings of affection and, being by nature utterly honest, the Queen never hesitated to put these feelings into words. Deeply attached to Brown, she never hesitated to transmit this attachment to paper. Nor, more significantly, did she make any secret of it. In that letter discovered by Tom Cullen, written by the Queen to John Brown's brother Hugh, the Queen quite openly refers to Brown as 'my beloved John' and declares that 'no one loved him more than I did.' In yet another letter, written to Brown himself on some everyday business, the Queen addresses him as 'darling one'.[18]

Elizabeth Longford, in researching her biography of Queen Victoria, came across valentines of eyebrow-raising archness which the Queen had sent to John Brown. 'My faith and love, to you my heart's best treasure', reads the verse under one saucy-looking serving maid; 'Then smile on her and let your answer loving be.' Her many gifts to him were always affectionately inscribed: from 'his true friend' or 'his faithful friend'. On one occasion, the two of them seem to have had a tiff which was followed by a reconciliation. 'Forgive and Ye shall be Forgiven: St Luke VI.37', read the printed message on her New Year card to him; to this she added, in her own hand, 'From a devoted grateful friend.' She once described John Brown to a member of her family as 'her *dearest* best friend who no one in *this world* can *ever* replace.'

That such terms of endearment should be misconstrued is only to be expected. When, after Brown's death, the Queen decided to publish a memoir in tribute to him, her household was appalled. At the risk of incurring her wrath, one after another of those closest to her either advised her to abandon the project or refused to have anything to do with it. 'Your Majesty's innermost and most sacred feelings ...', protested the anguished Ponsonby, would be 'misunderstood if read by strangers.'[19] Eventually, in the face of this concerted disapproval, the Queen gave up the idea.

But the very fact that she was prepared to make public her devotion to Brown must surely be proof of its innocence. If the Queen had been involved in a clandestine sexual relationship she would hardly have subjected her family and household to all those paeans to his many virtues. She would not have allowed herself to be seen with him so often and so publicly. The Queen's love for John Brown must have been chaste for her to have wished to proclaim it to all the world.

It would, in any case, have been almost impossible for her to conduct an illicit love affair. Even her exceptionally secluded life was never entirely private. She was still hedged about with maids, footmen and ladies-in-waiting. Nights spent with John Brown in her rooms would have been quickly discovered and talked about. Furthermore, as Tom

Cullen has pointed out, her ladies were all women of high standards and unimpeachable morals, not the type to turn a blind eye to any suggestion of sexual impropriety on the part of their mistress. They would have found excuses to resign their position. The only occasions on which the Queen was entirely alone with Brown, safe from any possibility of interruption, were when they were on their walks or rides at Balmoral; and one really cannot envisage the plump, corseted and overdressed Queen Victoria engaging in a little dalliance in the damp and spiky heather.

Moreover, the Queen did not need surveillance to prevent her from committing sins of the flesh; a deeply religious woman, her standards and morals were as high as those of any of her entourage. Utterly without guile, she would have been temperamentally incapable of any sexual double-dealing. Queen Victoria never dissembled, she could never live a lie. Infatuated with, indeed besotted by John Brown the Queen certainly was, but it is highly unlikely that he was ever her lover in a carnal sense.

Queen Victoria, on her own admission was 'naturally very passionate', but her passions were not of the body; they were of the senses, and of the emotions, and of the heart.

To Queen Victoria, John Brown was what so many members of a royal family lack – a friend. Although it was his handsome masculinity that first attracted her, it was for his companionship that she came to value him so highly. As far as she was concerned, he was a disinterested and devoted companion, entirely dedicated to her interests and 'comfort'. He was boundlessly understanding, boundlessly sympathetic. Tears would roll down his weather- or whisky-worn cheeks if he felt she was sad or suffering. If she had to be given any bad news, the household would entrust the task to Brown. He was her protector, her guardian, her confidant; even – in his homespun way – her counsellor. Once the scandal had died down he remained as a permanent, accepted and very important part of Queen Victoria's life.

When in the mid-1870s the Queen drew up her 'private written instructions' for what was to be done in the event of her death, she commanded that her 'faithful and devoted personal attendant (and true friend) Brown should be in the room and near at hand, and that he should watch over her ... remains and place them in the coffin ...'. In a second set of instructions she made clear that, in the event of serious illness, 'she *absolutely forbids anyone* but her *own* four female attendants to nurse her and take care of her, as well as her faithful *Personal*

Attendant, John Brown whose strength, care, handiness and gentleness make him invaluable at *all* times, and most *particularly* so in illness ... The Queen wishes no one therefore but J. Brown, whose faithfulness, tact and discretion are not to be exceeded, to help her female attendants in anything which may be required for her.'[20]

Part Five

DISRAELI

'Whatever I Wished SHOULD be Done'

THROUGHOUT THE years during which John Brown was finally being
accepted as her permanent companion, Queen Victoria was embroiled
in an increasingly bitter battle with her Liberal Prime Minister, William
Ewart Gladstone. Indeed, her gillie's qualities of sympathy and loyalty
merely emphasized, in the Queen's mind, the lack of any such qualities
in her Prime Minister. Fifty-nine years of age when he assumed office
in 1868, the tall, craggy-featured Gladstone, with his tendency to
lecture, complicate and insist, undermined the Queen's self-confidence.
Where Brown treated her like a woman Gladstone, it is said, treated
her like a public meeting.

The Queen and her Prime Minister clashed on many issues, but the
one on which they clashed most seriously was on what he called 'the
Royalty Question'. This question – of the declining popularity of the
monarchy – could only be solved, claimed Gladstone, by the Queen
emerging from her seclusion. She must shake herself out of her
lethargy, she must make more public appearances, she must spend less
time at Osborne and Balmoral, she must establish a residence in Ireland,
she must allow the Prince of Wales to play a more active part in public
affairs. In letter after letter, each one longer and more pedantic than
the last, Gladstone urged the Queen to play a more positive role. At
audience after audience, he reminded her of the need for her to be seen
fulfilling more public engagements.

It was all to no purpose. The more Gladstone insisted, the more
firmly Queen Victoria dug in her heels.

'She must say to General Ponsonby,' the Queen once wrote to her
secretary, 'though he may hardly like to believe it, that *she* has felt that
Mr Gladstone would have liked to *govern* HER as Bismarck governs the
[German] Emperor. Of course not to the same extent, or in the *same*

manner; but she always felt in his manner an overbearing obstinacy and imperiousness (without being actually wanting in respect as to form) which she never experienced from *anyone* else, and which she found most disagreeable.'[1]

How different, how delightfully different, was dear Mr Disraeli's attitude during these years. At the very time Gladstone was hectoring the Queen to make a greater effort, Disraeli was expressing public sympathy for her condition. He made unctuous speeches about the onerousness of her burdens; he even, in his novel *Lothair*, published in 1870, argued one of the Queen's most firmly-held convictions: that in forgetting its sense of duty, the aristocracy was degenerating into an indulgent and worthless caste. At the same time, Disraeli was fashioning his Conservative Party into something after her own heart. As, in the Queen's eyes, Gladstone's Liberal Party seemed to be becoming more and more radical, so did Disraeli's Conservative Party seem to be developing along lines of which she was coming to approve.

In a series of great public speeches, Disraeli clarified Conservative policy. It supported the monarchy, the House of Lords and the Church. It believed in a consolidation of Britain's overseas possessions. It recognized the importance of social reform. It stood for a strong foreign policy, for the greatness of Britain as opposed to Gladstone's 'Little England' theory. In contrast to the internationalism of the Liberals, the Conservatives were a truly national party. The working classes were conservatives in the best sense; they were proud of belonging to a great country and wished to maintain its greatness.

These were the sort of sentiments which Queen Victoria was coming to appreciate.

By the year 1873 it began to look as though Disraeli would soon be able to put his freshly defined theories into practice. Gladstone's Liberal administration, which had started well four years before, was running into trouble: it was being caught up in a tangle of mistakes and scandals. Early in 1874 Gladstone decided to dissolve Parliament and call a general election. The result was a resounding success for the Conservatives; they won just over one hundred more seats than the Liberals.

On 17 February 1874 Queen Victoria sent for Disraeli. Their meeting was ecstatic. 'He repeatedly said *whatever I wished* SHOULD *be done*,' declared the gratified Queen, and when Dizzy fell to his knees before her to kiss her little hand, his words could hardly have been more romantic. 'I plight my troth to the kindest of *Mistresses.*'

One really could not imagine Mr Gladstone saying that.

*

'My nature', Disraeli once wrote, 'demands that my life should be perpetual love.'[2] It did indeed. For just as Queen Victoria always needed the support of a man, so did Benjamin Disraeli depend on the love, encouragement and sympathy of women. 'A female friend,' he claimed, 'amiable, clever and devoted, is a possession more valuable than parks and palaces; and without such a muse, few men can succeed in life, none be content.'[3]

Yet Disraeli's romantic relationships had always been, and would always be, of a somewhat unorthodox variety. For whether as wife, mistress or friend, Disraeli invariably sought out women older than himself. They alone seemed capable of giving him the uncritical affection and admiration his egotistical nature so ardently craved. In fact, they were more like mothers than lovers. If Queen Victoria spent much of her life in search of a father-figure, Disraeli spent his in search of a substitute for his mother.

Benjamin Disraeli, who had so much to say about everything else, had surprisingly little to say about his mother. Quite clearly, there had been very little affection, very little rapport between them. Perhaps she had felt closer to her only daughter, Sarah; perhaps she had lavished more affection on her two younger, more dependable sons; perhaps she did not give Benjamin the admiration he felt he deserved. Ben, she would sigh, was a clever boy but 'no prodigy'.

But if Mrs Disraeli had not been prepared to concede her son's genius, there had been other women who were. And they had all been mature, maternal women.

During the course of his flamboyant, hedonistic bachelorhood, Disraeli had been seriously embroiled with at least three married women, all older than he; when he finally married, at the age of thirty-four, it was to a forty-six-year-old widow. Before long, he was referring to Mary Anne as his 'mother' and to himself as 'your child'. Their marriage was extremely happy. Disraeli was the most romantic, attentive and courtly of husbands, and Mary Anne, for all the bizarre girlishness of her appearance, the most loyal and supportive of wives. Both in public and in private they behaved like young lovers: he would kiss her hand, she would ruffle his ringlets.

'Well, my dear,' he had said to her as they sat over a bottle of champagne and a Fortnum and Mason's pie to celebrate the triumphant passing of the Second Reform Bill in 1867, 'you are more like a mistress than a wife.'[4] She was in her seventy-fifth year at the time.

Yet the felicity of his marriage did not prevent Disraeli from at one time becoming involved with another of those apparently indispensable dowagers: a rich, also eccentric widow in her eighties by the name of Mrs Brydges Willyams. For year after year Disraeli paid her gentlemanly court. It was not that he was in love with her, or that he was any less in love with Mary Anne. It was simply that Disraeli could no more resist an entanglement with a mature and devoted female than Queen Victoria could withstand the attentions of a flamboyant man. Dizzy's flattering blandishments bore fruit. When Mrs Brydges Willyams died, at well over ninety, she left him £30,000 in her will.

The death of Mary Anne Disraeli at the age of eighty in December 1872 by no means marked the end of Disraeli's pursuit of 'perpetual love'. Hardly had Mary Anne been buried than the sixty-eight-year-old Dizzy was once more moving in an aura of high romance. And, in truth, this was exactly what the selfless Mary Anne would have wanted for him.

In the summer of 1873 Disraeli fell in love with a fifty-four-year-old grandmother, Selina, Countess of Bradford. Unable to propose marriage, for the very good reason that she was already married, Dizzy did the next best thing: he proposed to her seventy-one-year-old sister, Lady Chesterfield, instead; but only because this would bring him closer to Lady Bradford. Not unnaturally, Lady Chesterfield refused. So Dizzy had to be content with writing colourful letters to both sisters and, as far as Lady Bradford was concerned, running 'the whole gamut of half-requited love – passionate devotion, rebuff, despair, resignation, renewed hope, reconciliation, ecstasy.'[5]

No wonder Disraeli could sigh that there must be no greater misfortune 'than to have a heart that will not grow old'.[6]

What more opportune time, then, for Disraeli to be thrown into the company of Queen Victoria? 'I am fortunate in serving a female sovereign,' he said not long after assuming office. 'I owe everything to women; and if in the sunset of my life I still have a young heart, it is due to that influence.'[7]

Not only was Dizzy serving a female sovereign; more significantly, he was serving a middle-aged female sovereign. Whereas for Lord Melbourne it was important that Queen Victoria was little more than a girl, for Disraeli it was an advantage that she was by now a mature woman. The Prime Minister's woman friends, remarked the amused Russian ambassador, were 'toutes grand'mères'. How much more rewarding, then, for Disraeli to be dealing with the greatest grandmother of them all? This, surely, was the culmination of a lifetime's association with matrons. Here was the matron to end all matrons; the mother-figure to end all mother-figures.

Disraeli had very little difficulty in adhering to his promise to do whatever the Queen wished 'SHOULD *be done*'. By now, there were few political questions on which they were not in fundamental agreement. Although, after Gladstone, almost any prime minister would have been welcome, Disraeli's somewhat idiosyncratic political views made him doubly so. Prince Albert's lessons in liberalism had served their day; the conservative creed of her new and infinitely more entertaining teacher was what Queen Victoria now wanted to hear. During Disraeli's term of office, their ideas became ever more closely interwoven. He brought her what she was coming, more and more, to value: his faith in the working together of the aristocracy, the squirearchy and the lower classes, his belief in a strong foreign policy and his dreams of imperial grandeur.

Nor, when their views did not coincide, did each feel equally strongly about the issue involved. In Church affairs, for instance, on which Queen Victoria held firm opinions, Disraeli was not particularly interested; and with Disraeli's great programme of social reform – his manifestation of Tory democracy – the Queen was not deeply concerned. Personally she was kind-hearted, sympathetic, even sentimental, but her social conscience was never strong. She was still inclined to subscribe to Lord Melbourne's theory that all dissatisfaction was caused by agitators; that, left alone, social injustices would sort themselves out. When Queen Victoria praised the 'lower classes' so extravagantly, she was thinking of those cap-doffing Highland crofters and ruddy-cheeked farm labourers, rather than of the unhealthy, exploited and badly housed urban masses.

But even on the rare occasions when the Queen and her Prime Minister did not see eye-to-eye on some political question, she could not argue with him for long. 'He had a way when we differed ...', she later told Lord Rosebery, 'of saying "Dear Madam" so persuasively, and putting his head to one side.'[8] Where Gladstone's bullying behaviour had achieved nothing, Dizzy's more adroit handling worked wonders. He had, claimed one member of the royal household, 'got the length of her foot exactly.'[9] Those who saw the Queen only as the stubborn and self-obsessed Widow of Windsor would have been astonished by Dizzy's behaviour with her. He coaxed her, he deferred to her, he paid her the most extravagant compliments on her political judgement and expertise.

As always with Disraeli, the froth of flattery contained a core of truth. He had been quick to appreciate that the Queen was a woman of considerable ability. Encouraged by Disraeli to think for herself and not always to wonder how Prince Albert would have reacted to a particular situation, Queen Victoria began to follow her own intuition and to put her trust in her own judgement. Her opinions – once freed of the Prince Consort's inhibiting insistence on impartiality – became more firmly held and more emphatically voiced. Her particular traits – her sagacity, her shrewdness, her common sense, her toughness – came into full play. Encouraged by Disraeli, she became more and more convinced that what she felt was always right.

There were other ways in which Disraeli was enticing her out from the Prince Consort's shadow. No longer did Queen Victoria feel that she must always be improving herself, that she must strive to be cultured or intellectual or serious-minded. Quite clearly, Mr Disraeli appreciated her for what she was; he made her realize that there was no need for her to be self-conscious about her intellectual shortcomings. Her self-confidence, undermined by Prince Albert's studiousness and badly shaken by Gladstone's erudition, was restored by Dizzy's blandishments; he never made her feel foolish.

As well as giving her an added self-confidence, Disraeli was giving her a renewed sense of vocation. The Queen began to take a livelier interest in political affairs. Instead of complaining that she was overworked, and having to be urged to make an effort, she began to busy herself as never before.

Where, with several other prime ministers, and certainly with Gladstone, the Queen had kept her audiences as short as possible, with Disraeli they often overran the customary hour. Sometimes luncheon would be delayed for as much as twenty minutes while the Queen sat in lively discussion with her Prime Minister. Nor was she the only one to be sitting: in contrast to Her Majesty's audiences with Mr Gladstone, whom she always kept standing, the Queen often had a little gilt chair brought in for Mr Disraeli; And there were times when no business was discussed at all; when these audiences were 'all milk and honey': entirely given over to 'the most animated, interesting and confidential gossip.'[10]

On one occasion, at Windsor, when Disraeli was due to board his special train back to London at five minutes past five exactly, the conversation proved so absorbing that Dizzy quite forgot to keep his eye on the time. Suddenly the clock struck five. Unceremoniously, he leapt to his feet and explained the situation. 'Run away, run away directly,' laughed the Queen. So he went scampering out of the room, hardly aware, he afterwards reported, that 'instead of being dismissed, I dismissed my Sovereign.'[11]

Dear Mr Disraeli was hardly less entertaining on paper than in person. While Gladstone's memoranda had been so ponderous that the Queen had to have a précis made before she could understand them, Dizzy's were pithy, airy, scintillating. 'Mr Disraeli has a wonderful talent for writing in an amusing tone while seizing the points of an argument,' noted Ponsonby.[12] And every now and then, the richness of his prose would be rendered richer still by the introduction of some daringly intimate observation. Writing to the Queen on the occasion of her fifty-sixth birthday in May 1875, Disraeli assured her that 'you live in the hearts and thoughts of many millions, though in none more deeply and more fervently than in the heart of him who, with humble duty, pens these spontaneous lines.'

It was often wondered how Queen Victoria – so astute, so honest and so sensible – could tolerate Dizzy's outrageous flattery. Surely she must suspect him of insincerity? She was no fool, she had a sharp eye for character, she was quick to recognize a charlatan. But it was precisely because of these qualities that she was able to appreciate Disraeli's flowery style. She realized that it was simply an expression of 'something poetic' in his temperament, that behind the baroque façade was an essentially honest structure. If it suited him to behave more like a silver-tongued courtier than a serious-minded prime minister, then well and good. She knew that he was both these things.

The political field in which the Queen and her Prime Minister were in complete accord was foreign policy. On the question of the enhancement of British prestige, their hearts beat as one. Here were opportunities for the sort of *grande geste* they both appreciated. For too long, argued the Queen, had people like Gladstone allowed Britain to 'swallow insults' and play a negative role; while Disraeli was itching for an opportunity to reassert British power in Europe.

Yet it was in what was loosely termed the East – the Balkans, the Levant, India – that Disraeli achieved his most spectacular successes. Whereas his knowledge of these areas was in truth of the scrappiest, Disraeli was always – not least in Queen Victoria's mind – associated with the East. His Jewish blood, his exotic appearance, his oblique, almost oriental manner, allied to the fact that he had made a youthful tour of the Middle East, tended to link him with those colourful, sun-steeped areas of the world. This somewhat inaccurate impression was strengthened by the coincidence that one of the great set-pieces of the Victoria–Disraeli partnership was concerned with the Near East: with that romantic waterway between the Mediterranean and the Red Seas – the Suez Canal.

Queen Victoria's interest in the success of Disraeli's manoeuverings to prevent the Suez Canal from coming entirely under French control was hardly less intense than his own. As much as he, did she appreciate the prestige and strategic importance of the canal. With the waterway providing the shortest route between Britain and India, over three-quarters of the ships using the canal were British. When early in November 1875 the debt-ridden Khedive of Egypt decided to sell his shares in the canal (of which he owned just under half) it was to a French syndicate that he offered them. Were they to acquire them, then the control of the canal would be entirely in French hands.

Alive to this danger, Disraeli was determined that the British government must buy the Khedive's shares. What a *coup* that would be; what a fillip for British prestige. But he had to move fast. 'Scarcely breathing time!' he scribbled to Queen Victoria. 'But the thing must be done.' Exercising all his celebrated daring, panache and sense of timing, Dizzy talked round his less enthusiastic cabinet, warned off the French government and, having borrowed £4,000,000 from Baron Lionel de Rothschild's banking house, bought the Khedive's shares.

The thing accomplished, Disraeli's first thought was for the Queen. 'It is just settled', he wrote triumphantly on 24 November 1875; 'you have it, Madam.' He promised to tell her, at the earliest opportunity, 'the whole wondrous tale' of the acquiring of the shares.

Like some exotic gift, the Suez Canal was laid at the feet of the Queen by her loyal Prime Minister.

Whether the two of them actually believed this, one does not know. Not only was Disraeli in no position to present the canal as some sort of personal present to Queen Victoria, but Britain had not even acquired a controlling interest in it. The Khedive had held less than half the total shares. But what Dizzy had done was to prevent the canal from becoming entirely French-owned, and this was no mean achievement. The buying of the Suez Canal shares had been, as the Queen put it, 'an immense thing'.

To Theodore Martin, then busy on the second volume of his monu-mental *Life of the Prince Consort*, the Queen declared that the Suez Canal feat was '*entirely* the doing of Mr Disraeli, who has *very large ideas and very lofty views* of the position the country should hold. His mind is so much greater, larger and his apprehension of things great and small so much quicker than that of Mr Gladstone.'

And when she saw Mr Disraeli in person she was, he reported, 'in ecstasies about "this great and important event".' She received him immediately; she was all smiles and coquetry; she swore that she had never seen him looking so well; she showed him all her telegrams of congratulation. At dinner that night, the Queen was in 'the tenth Heaven' – amusing, interesting, excited.

'Nothing could be more successful – I might say triumphant – than my visit,' boasted Disraeli.[13]

Whatever the truth of the matter, Victoria and Disraeli were happy enough with the myth that the loyal Prime Minister had presented his Sovereign with this great waterway linking Britain to India, the Mother Country to its Empire, West to East. It was the sort of gesture to set the Queen's pulses pounding; it was spectacular proof of her country's greatness.

The next gift to be laid at the Queen's feet by the imaginative Mr Disraeli was an imperial crown. In doing so, he was able to pander to two of her current preoccupations: with the great sub-continent of India, and with the question of whether the title of Empress was superior to that of Queen.

Of all Britain's possessions across the seas, India exerted the strongest fascination for Queen Victoria. Where the inhabitants of those other large British territories such as Canada, Australia and New Zealand were Englishmen enjoying a certain measure of self-government, the Indians were a subject people belonging, as the Queen was apt to put it, 'to me'. More so than with any other colonies, the Queen felt personally associated with India; she regarded herself as being directly responsible for that enormous country which was 'so bright a jewel in her Crown'.

Disraeli shared her views. The thought of India, with its clamorous cities, its exotic peoples and its fabulously rich princes had always excited him. It had even at one time been suggested that he might become Viceroy of India; what a bizarre vice-regal couple he and Mary Anne would have made. No less than the Queen did Disraeli regard this crowded sub-continent as the monarch's personal domain; the more British rule could be personified by the Sovereign, the better. Disraeli had once assured the Queen that the India Bill of 1858, whereby the British Crown had taken over the administration of the country from the East India Company, was 'the mere ante-chamber to an imperial palace.' The time had surely come for the entering of the imperial palace itself.

The first step was taken by the Prince of Wales. By the beginning of the year 1875, the thirty-three-year-old Bertie had decided that he wanted to visit India. Knowing that his mother's instincts were always to forbid him to do anything that he wanted to do, the Prince set about winning Disraeli's support for the project. This the Prime Minister was only too ready to give. A royal tour of India was exactly the sort of imperial gesture Disraeli might have thought up himself. But the Queen – as the Prince of Wales had suspected – was not nearly as enthusiastic. It needed all Dizzy's celebrated tact to persuade her to agree to the plan. Only by promising to take over the entire management of the affair did he still the Queen's apprehensions. She was worried about the cost, about the possibility of Princess Alexandra accompanying her husband, about the unsuitability of the Prince's proposed travelling companions and, above all, about the likelihood of the notoriously lecherous Prince getting into what were euphemistically termed 'scrapes'.

But in spite of the Queen's continuing unease (which took the form of advice, often by telegram *en clair*, for Bertie to be careful of what he ate and for him to be in bed by ten if possible) the tour was a great success. The Prince carried out his many engagements, both public and private, with his customary gusto. He was rightly regarded, not as a representative of the British government, but as a symbol of the Monarchy; his presence suggested that the Queen was as much the Sovereign of India – and not merely of India's rulers – as she was of Great Britain.

All this contributed towards Queen Victoria's growing conviction that it was time she assumed the title of Empress of India. Although she might, at one moment, dismiss the notion that a queen was somehow less than an empress, at another she would be admitting that Empress *sounded* more impressive than Queen. No one could deny that all the leading monarchies of Europe – Russia, Germany and Austria – were empires and that, until the regrettable fall of Napoleon III in 1870, France had been an empire. Her assumption of an imperial title would put paid, once and for all, to the infuriating Continental conviction that arch-dukes, grand-dukes and crown princes were more important than mere princes.

With the Queen's wishes Disraeli was in full accord. And, as Prime Minister, it would be up to him to see that this wish was granted. There were, in fact, sound political reasons for the introduction of the Royal Titles Bill. It was not all a matter of personal, or even national, vanity. The title would give an air of stability and permanence to British rule in India. A British Empress of India might make the

Russian Emperor think twice before advancing more deeply into Asia. Not only in the drawing-room, but across the North-West frontier, could Queen Victoria face Tsar Alexander II as an undisputed equal. If the Prince of Wales's tour had struck the first blow for British prestige in India, the Queen's assumption of the title of Empress would strike the second.

On 1 May 1876, after a surprisingly choppy passage through the House (and this despite the fact that Disraeli had talked the Queen into opening Parliament in person), the Royal Titles Bill was passed and Victoria declared Queen-Empress. She was highly delighted. Blithely ignoring the fact that she was Imperial only as far as India was concerned, the Queen signed herself 'V.R. & I.' on every possible occasion. Disraeli was rewarded with a larger-than-lifesize portrait of his Sovereign: a copy of a painting by Joachim von Angeli.

'Now,' she said one day to Dizzy after their usual audience, 'I will show you your picture.' She led him into an adjoining room. 'There it stood ...', he reported to Lady Bradford, 'a very large picture in a gorgeous frame with, I suppose, the Crown of an Empress at the top.'

Having admired the somewhat stony-faced but undeniably imperial likeness of his royal mistress, Dizzy fell to one knee. 'I think I may claim, Madam, the privilege of gratitude,' he breathed. 'She gave me her hand to kiss which I did three times very rapidly,' he said, 'and she actually gave me a squeeze.'[14]

Disraeli having made the Queen an empress, she now made him an earl. Feeling that his always precarious health could stand the hurly-burly of the House of Commons no longer, Disraeli told the Queen that he must either resign or continue his premiership from the House of Lords. As she would not hear of his resigning – and one suspects that he never seriously contemplated any such thing – she elevated him to the peerage. He became the Earl of Beaconsfield. (Disraeli always pronounced the name Beaconsfield as it was spelt: it was field of the beacon, he would maintain, not a beckoning field.) On 11 August 1876 Disraeli made his last speech in the House of Commons. From then on he ran his government from the relative tranquillity of the House of Lords.

It was as Earl of Beaconsfield, then, that Dizzy gave his blessing to the Queen's official assumption of her title on 1 January 1877. While at noon that day in far-away Delhi Queen Victoria was proclaimed Empress of India by the Viceroy, Lord Lytton, the occasion was celebrated that evening at Windsor by a sumptuous banquet. Plump, imperious and all adazzle in her Indian jewellery, the Queen heard the newly-created Earl make a speech so florid that it could have come straight out of the pages of one of his novels.

Its effusions excited an unheard-of reaction from the Queen. After he had cried out 'Your Imperial Majesty' and the toast had been drunk, the new Empress of India astounded the company by rising to her feet and half-curtseying to her Prime Minister.

'Do you', as Disraeli was fond of saying, 'call all this nothing?'

These two great flourishes of the Victoria–Disraeli partnership – the buying of the Suez Canal shares and the passing of the Bill that made the Queen Empress of India – was followed by a third: the British triumph at the Congress of Berlin in 1878.

Just over a year before, in the spring of 1877, Russia had declared war on Turkey. One might have imagined, from Queen Victoria's reaction, that Tsar Alexander II had declared war on her. She was incensed. It was like the Crimean War all over again, but this time there was no Prince Albert to temper the Queen's bellicosity. On the contrary, there was Disraeli to encourage it. He 'has skilfully described the situation', wrote a disapproving Ponsonby to his wife, 'as a struggle for mastery between England and Russia and that the point at issue is who shall be first, the Queen or the Tsar ...'.[15]

It was, of course, a great deal more complicated than this. The war between Russia and Turkey had its origins in the long-standing 'Eastern Question'. At its simplest, the Eastern Question amounted to the rivalry between Russia and Britain over the body of 'The Sick Man of Europe' – Turkey. Russia was anxious to see the sprawling Turkish Sultanate dismantled; Britain was determined to keep it shored up. In the eyes of both Victoria and Disraeli, Turkey was a safeguard against Russian designs on India. To surrender to the Russians one inch of Turkish territory would be to jeopardize both the land and the sea routes to India. To see the Russians in Constantinople was tantamount to seeing them in Calcutta.

Rendering the Queen more anti-Russian still was the fact that Gladstone was so anti-Turk. With each passing day the Queen's tirades against Gladstone became more and more shrill. From being merely tiresome and obstinate, he became a 'mischief-maker', a 'fire-brand', a 'half-madman'. Her hatred of him become almost pathological.

The Queen's attitude suited Disraeli perfectly. Indeed, many believed that it was he who not only encouraged, but instigated, the Queen's near-hysterical loathing of Gladstone. Knowing how his Sovereign always saw politics in terms of personalities, Disraeli had every reason to stimulate her antipathy towards his great rival. The more she hated Gladstone, the more she would support Disraeli's anti-Russian policies.

So it was hardly surprising that the Queen was so outraged at the Russian declaration of war against Turkey. And, as the Russians moved forward from victory to victory, so she became more outraged still. 'Oh, if the Queen were a man,' she exclaimed, 'she would like to go and give those horrid Russians ... such a beating.' Even her loyal Disraeli seemed, from the Queen's point of view, to be dragging his feet. She was forever exhorting him to act more boldly, more quickly, more aggressively. She simply could not understand why he did not tell Russia that Britain was resolved to declare war if she reached, and refused to quit, Constantinople.

But Disraeli, although hardly less Russophobe than his Sovereign, was not really prepared to fight. He wanted to be in a position to threaten Russia with war if she showed any signs of occupying Constantinople, but he did not actually want war.

As often before, Disraeli was making use of the Queen to further his own ends. Having worked her up into a warlike state, he used it to coax his divided cabinet into a more belligerent attitude, while depending upon their hesitancy to keep the Queen in check. Yet all the time Disraeli was assuring Victoria that he lived only for Her, and worked only for Her, and that without Her, all would be lost.

The signing of an armistice between Russia and Turkey on the last day of January 1878 did little to calm the Queen's hysteria. A rumour that Russia had ignored the terms of the armistice and was marching on Constantinople finally enabled Disraeli to jolt his irresolute cabinet into action. War credits were passed, arrangements made to move troops from India to the Mediterranean, and the reserves called up. Much to the Queen's satisfaction, two of Disraeli's more pacific cabinet ministers resigned. It looked as though Victoria was about to get her war after all.

Disraeli kept his head. This show of force was what he had all along been wanting: but he wanted nothing more. It alone would convince Russia of Britain's determination to stand firm; he was certainly not going to be stampeded into war.

He was proved right. The arrival of the British fleet off Constantinople halted the Russians. Hastily imposing the Treaty of San Stefano on the retreating Turks, Russia concluded the war.

How much easier she must be feeling, wrote Vicky to her mother, now that England 'has a policy'. Easier, certainly, but still not easy enough. There were aspects of the San Stefano Treaty that the Queen and her Prime Minister were not quite happy about. So the ironclads remained off Constantinople until Russia agreed to the holding of a conference of the Great Powers. After a flurry of preliminary agreements between Britain and Russia, it was decided to hold a congress in Berlin, under the presidency of Prince Bismarck. Russia might have won the war, but the Queen and Disraeli had the satisfaction of knowing that Britain was winning the peace.

The Congress of Berlin opened in mid-June 1878. The Queen was able to follow this month-long, magnificently staged affair in some detail because Disraeli, representing Great Britain, kept her fully informed. In a series of amusing, incisive and colourful letters and in a diary which he called 'a rough journal for One Person only', Dizzy regaled the Queen with the multiple glories of the Congress: the grandeur of the newly imperial German capital; the 'ceremonious and costumish' opening in the sumptuous decorated hall of the Radziwill Palace; the 'singularly various and splendid' costumes at a gala banquet in the Old Schloss, a 'splendid Rococo hall, which would have driven old Lord Malmesbury, with his frigid Ionic taste, quite crazy'; Bismarck's 'Rabelasian monologues: endless revelations of things he ought not to mention'; the pretty Countess Karolyi's extraordinarily hearty appetite ('I never refuse a dish' was her far-from-idle boast); the huge pilaff at a banquet at the Turkish Embassy.

When Bismarck, afloat on a mixture of champagne and stout, advised the British Prime Minister not to put his trust in princes, Dizzy replied that 'he served one who was the soul of candour and justice, and whom all her ministers loved'. That, at any rate, is what he told the Queen.

All in all, Disraeli achieved a great deal in Berlin. If the Congress did not prove quite, as Dizzy so graphically put it to the Queen, a surrender by the Emperor of Russia to the Empress of India, it was undoubtedly a triumph for British diplomacy. 'Peace with Honour' is what Disraeli claimed to have brought back. The cheering crowds that greeted him on his return to a triumphantly decorated London were ready to believe it.

And so, of course, was the Queen. She was ecstatic. She sent Ponsonby to Downing Street with a huge bouquet of 'Windsor flowers' to present to the returning hero. 'From the Queen' bellowed Ponsonby above the roar of the crowd as Disraeli alighted from his open carriage at the door of No. 10.

Windsor flowers were not the Queen's only reward. She offered him a positive shower of honours: the Garter, a dukedom, a peerage for his brother or his nephew. Rather than 'Peace with Honour', quipped one cynic, it was 'Peace with Honours'.

Disraeli accepted only the Garter. 'He will not trust himself now in endeavouring to express what he feels to your Majesty's kindness,' he wrote. 'He thinks he is ennobled through your Majesty's goodness quite enough, though with infinite deference to your Majesty's gracious pleasure, he would presume to receive the Garter; but, as he always feels, your Majesty's kind thoughts are dearer to him than any personal distinction, however rich and rare. The belief that your Majesty trusts, and approves of him is more precious than rubies!'

Three days after his return from Berlin, he was at Osborne. The Queen gave him a rapturous welcome. Never, since the days of Melbourne and Prince Albert, and perhaps not even then, had she been in such close political rapport with anyone. With the sentiments of *The Times* of London she would have been in complete agreement. The Prime Minister, it declared, was now 'at the pinnacle of Ministerial Renown, the favourite of his Sovereign and the idol of Society'. And as she conferred the Garter she must have felt, with the *Journal des Débats*, that 'the traditions of England' did indeed live on 'in the hearts of a woman and an aged statesman'.

'The Faery Queen'

CLOSER, EVEN, than their political rapport was the personal relationship between Victoria and Disraeli. During the six years of Disraeli's premiership, their association developed into something of an idyll – a partnership that was as much romantic as political.

In 1874, at the start of Dizzy's second term as Prime Minister, the Queen was fifty-four and Disraeli sixty-nine. Where, to others, the dumpy Queen Victoria in her black, elaborately bustled dresses and white widow's veil could be intimidating, to Disraeli she was invariably charming. Thomas Carlyle, meeting her at this time, considered the Queen attractive, and Disraeli would certainly have appreciated her more appealing features: her kindly blue-grey eyes, her beautiful voice, her silvery laugh, her graceful movements, her extraordinarily sweet smile. Never, claimed Madame Waddington, wife of the French ambassador, had she ever seen a face more transformed by a smile. Without losing a shred of her celebrated dignity, Queen Victoria could be extremely animated, even gay.

That the Queen found Disraeli attractive there is no doubt. To others he might look old and odd and sphinx-like; to her he was merely poetic, exotic, interesting. The rouged cheeks, the single dyed curl on the forehead and the many rings worn over the white gloves might look singular to some, but not to the Queen. Any word of criticism, says Ponsonby, was 'out of the question'. In fact, the Queen was so intrigued by her Prime Minister's appearance that she commissioned the fashionable Jabez Hughes to take a series of photographs of him. In them – with his straggly imperial beard, his hooked nose and his hooded eyes – Disraeli looked astonishingly like that other figure who had once captured her imagination, the fascinating Emperor Napoleon III.

She also had him painted. For this important commission Victoria employed yet another of those fashionable contemporary figures, Joachim von Angeli. Although Dizzy hated having his portrait done, he could hardly refuse. For several days he sat on a gilt, crimson-upholstered chair in one of the rooms at Buckingham Palace while Angeli painted and Montagu Corry, Disraeli's young secretary, read out dispatches. To the Queen Disraeli reported the picture to be a great success, but to his friends he was more frank. 'Oh,' he would say, 'is it not hideous — and so like.'[1]

He was also painted by Millais. As the Queen was not entirely happy with the likeness, she sent to Millais — as she had done to Landseer when he was working on the engraving of John Brown's likeness — some photographs of Disraeli. 'The photograph looking down at the newspaper gives the form and also something of the peculiar expression about the corner of the mouth, suggesting a keen sense of humour, which contrasts with the extreme seriousness of the upper part of the face,' ran the royal instructions. 'It prevents the whole expression being sad . . .'. When the picture had been altered to her satisfaction, the Queen was full of praise. 'Mr Millais has given the peculiar, intellectual, and gentle expression of his face.'[2]

One Christmas time she honoured her Prime Minister by allowing him to wear the 'Windsor uniform': that special dark-blue uniform with red facings worn by the men of the royal family and the members of the household in personal attendance. Lord Melbourne was the only previous prime minister to have been similarly honoured. She was giving it, wrote the Queen to Disraeli, 'as a mark of personal regard and friendship'.

As Queen Victoria refused to spend more than a night or two at Buckingham Palace, and Disraeli refused to expose himself to the vagaries of the Balmoral climate, it was against the backgrounds of Windsor Castle and Osborne House that the scenes of their close association were enacted. Most often they met, for official audiences, in one of the Queen's overfurnished sitting-rooms; sometimes the Queen would receive him in the more intimate Royal Closet, formerly the private room of the Prince Consort. To Disraeli, the cheerful lack of elegance in the Queen's surroundings would have been in no way offensive: the rooms of his own country house, Hughenden, looked very like this.

Although it remained unsuspected by the Queen, Disraeli never really enjoyed the longer periods that he was occasionally obliged to spend in one of her homes. To him, Windsor was 'the Temple of the

Winds'. The Queen's passion for fresh air was something he could not share. While she complained 'terribly of the sweltering clime of the realm she rules', Dizzy was never warm enough.[3] He seemed, he grumbled, to spend half his time being buffeted by the icy blasts in what he maintained was the thousand-foot-long corridor.

He soon tired of all the formalities of the court. 'All is well as long as I can keep to my room, or a morning walk,' he confided to Lady Bradford, 'but *toilette* and evening mannerisms destroy me.' There were even times when he found the Queen exhausting. 'What nerve! What muscle! What energy!' he groaned. 'Her Minister is very deficient in all three.'[4]

Yet, in Queen Victoria's eyes, her minister was never anything less than charming and amusing. Both in the audience chamber and at the dinner-table, she delighted in his company. 'What is he saying?' she would smilingly demand in German if she saw one of her children – Princess Christian or Prince Leopold – laughing at one of Disraeli's drily expressed witticisms. But one had to be careful. No less-favoured guest dare become too relaxed in the Queen's company. When Lady Derby asked the Queen if she had read Dizzy's latest book, *Lothair*, and Her Majesty replied that she had been 'the first person' to read it, her ladyship vivaciously went on to inquire if Her Majesty had not found Theodora to be 'a *divine* character'. At this, says Dizzy, the Queen looked 'both perplexed and grave'.[5]

If Disraeli thought Windsor chilly, he found Osborne, in bad weather, even worse. Not only was he obliged to face the crossing of the invariably choppy Solent, but there was endless to-ing and fro-ing between the royal yachts. He was forever having to balance on some tilting, wind-lashed deck.

Unless it were actually raining – and sometimes even then – the Queen would have her large écru parasol-tent, fringed and lined in green, pitched on the lawns below the house. Here, surrounded by assorted dogs, liveried footmen, Highland attendants and black-clad ladies-in-waiting, the Queen would eat her breakfast and then deal with her dispatch boxes. Here, too, she would receive Disraeli. Although, he once reported, 'Our Sovereign Lady' tried to make his stay as agreeable as possible, 'I was very ill and could scarcely get through it.'

The Queen was indeed very concerned about Disraeli's health. She would chide him if he visited her when he had a cold and once, when they both had colds, he claimed that 'the kingdom was never governed with such an amount of catarrh and sneezing'.[6] For fear of him catching cold, she once scribbled hurriedly to him, she would excuse him from wearing the obligatory pantaloons that evening. She was forever urging him to see her doctor, Sir William Gull, and if he were ill, she would bombard him with telegrams. Yet she was very amused by a letter to Ponsonby in which Dizzy claimed to have recovered his youth by doing exactly what the doctors had for years been warning him against: drinking very good wine. 'The Queen quite agrees,' wrote Victoria.

It did not take Disraeli long to convert the relaxed and cheerful atmosphere between the two of them into something more intimate. During his first premiership, the Queen had sent him flowers. Now, to symbolize their increasingly close relationship, he chose flowers. Not, as one might expect, something exotic like lilies or orchids, but simple spring flowers: snowdrops and primroses. He assured her that 'of all flowers, the one that retains its beauty longest, is sweet primrose...', and that he liked primroses 'so much better for being wild'.

The Queen, charmed by such simplicity (as he knew she would be), was quick to enter into the spirit of the thing. Each time she sent him another offering of these artless flowers, she was rewarded with one of his lyrical letters. He would have imagined himself like Proserpine in Hades, he wrote, 'had the gift of primroses from Osborne not reminded him that there might yet be spring and tho' Prosperpine be absent there is happily for him a Queen to whom he is devoted at Windsor.'

And he was ready to wax more lyrical still. Before long, his ardent imagination had converted the dowdy and dumpy Queen Victoria into something altogether more exotic. He pretended to believe that, like Edmund Spenser's Elizabeth I, she was a Faery Queen. Her flowers now became like 'an offering from the fauns and dryads of the woods of Osborne; and camellias, blooming in the natural air, become your Majesty's Faery Isle.' Primroses meant that 'your Majesty's sceptre has touched the enchanted isle'.

When she sent him snowdrops he pinned them to his breast to prove to his lavishly beribboned and bemedalled fellow guests at an official banquet that he, too, had been decorated by a gracious Sovereign.

'Then, in the middle of the night,' he told her, 'it occurred to him that it might all be enchantment, and that, perhaps, it was a Faery gift and came from another monarch: Queen Titania, gathering flowers, with her Court, in a soft and sea-girt isle, and sending magic blossoms, which, they say, turn the heads of those who receive them.'

Can one wonder that it was the Queen's head that was turned?

★

But those who saw the association between Victoria and Disraeli purely in terms of a wily and accomplished old seducer toadying to a plain and susceptible widow were somewhat wide of the mark. In both appearance and manner Disraeli was an amalgam of all those men to whom she was always attracted. He combined the urbanity of Lord Melbourne, the gentleness of Prince Albert, the flamboyance of Napoleon III, even the unorthodoxy of John Brown. He was part mentor, part lover.

An added attraction was the fact that Disraeli had also lost his life's partner. 'The Queen,' Victoria had written on the death of Mary Anne Disraeli, 'knows also *what* Mr Disraeli has lost and what he must suffer.' And Dizzy confessed to Lady Bradford that 'It is strange that I always used to think that the Queen, persisting in these emblems of woe, indulged in morbid sentiment, and yet it has become my lot, and seemingly an irresistible one.'[7] Neither of them, of course, felt quite as much grief as they showed, but their respective losses brought them even closer, and that was comforting.

With a lifetime's experience of women behind him, Disraeli knew exactly how to handle the Queen. Employing a shade more courtesy and a shade more deference, he treated her as he had treated all his women: gently, gallantly and, above all, romantically. He had long ago realized that the Queen would respond to a personal approach: that he must cut through the splendour of her position and the stiffness of her bearing. In short, he must treat her as a human being. More even than most monarchs, Queen Victoria needed someone with whom she could be herself, and Dizzy had been quick to sense this. He knew that dour expression and that imperious manner masked a shy, warm, indeed ardent temperament; that if she were treated with tact and affection, her reserve would melt.

And so, skilfully and consciously, Dizzy set out to woo her – just as surely as he had wooed any of that long procession of wives and widows and dowagers. It may have been the most discreet, respectful and innocent of courtships, but it was a courtship none the less.

Conscious as all this might have been on Dizzy's part, it was not entirely calculated and certainly not unscrupulous. This was the way he had always behaved. A natural gallant, he quite easily embarked on his decorous flirtation with the Queen; it would not have occurred to him to approach her in any other fashion. With him, dalliance was second nature. The death of Mary Anne, which undoubtedly left a void in his life, none the less allowed him to carry his flirtation further, perhaps, than he might have otherwise.

An encouragement to his carrying it further still was the fact that his love affair with Selina, Countess of Bradford, was dying a death. She had never really returned his love, and within a year or two of his assumption of the premiership Dizzy was beginning to realize that Lady Bradford felt very little for him. Faced with her indifference, Disraeli came to depend more and more on the one person of whose admiration, solicitude and devotion he could be quite certain. After all, Queen Victoria still perfectly epitomized the indulgent and adoring mother-figure of his life-long search. Indeed, there were times when he even imagined himself in love with the Queen.

He certainly never minded fostering the impression that the Queen was a little in love with him. Any suggestion that she might be jealous of his attentions to other women, he would pass on with great delight. When the Empress Augusta, wife of Kaiser Wilhelm I, spent a few days at Windsor in the spring of 1876, Disraeli was in his element. The old German Empress, with her brightly painted face, her skittish clothes, her vivacious manner and her intellectual pretensions, could hardly have been in greater contrast to the English Queen.

'The two Empresses sate next to each other at dinner . . .', he reported in inimitable style and spelling to a friend. 'Carnarvon sate next to the Empress of Germany, and I sate next to the Empress of India. The conversation of the *partie carrée* was good: animated and natural – but whenever Augoosta had got involved in some metaphysical speculations with Carnarvon, the Faery took refuge in confidential whispers in which she indulged in the freest remarks . . . After dinner I was attached to Augoosta who threw out all her resources, philosophical, poetic, political – till the Faery was a little jeal, for she had originally told Lady Ely that some one "was not to make his pretty speeches to Augoosta, who only wanted to *draw him to her*"!!!! However, all went off very well, and the Faery made a happy dart and had the last word.'[8]

Was Queen Victoria in love with Disraeli? Not, one imagines, in the generally accepted sense of the term. But the particular form taken by her love is not important. What is important is its effect on her personality. Disraeli made the Queen feel, for the first time in many years, like a desirable woman; a woman who was worth flirting with, and joking with, and flattering. Her ego, as she basked in the apparently whole-hearted attention of this fascinating man, was given a tremendous boost.

Disraeli provided the Queen with those elements of glamour, colour and fantasy which always struck a chord in her passionate nature. More than any man she had ever known, Disraeli had the ability to kindle her imagination. Never before had Queen Victoria's innate romanticism been brought to such full flower. The make-believe of the Faery Queen, the gifts of primroses and snowdrops and violets, the entire magical, serio-comic plane on which the two of them moved, aroused an undercurrent of excitement in the normally sensible Queen. If it was not exactly love, it was something very like it.

In February each year, Victoria and Disraeli exchanged valentines. Here was yet another opportunity for some deliciously titillating flirtation. 'He wishes he could repose on a sunny bank, like young Valentine in the pretty picture that fell from a rosy cloud this morn,' wrote Dizzy on receiving the Queen's latest card, 'but the reverie of the happy youth would be rather different from his. Valentine would dream of the future, and youthful loves, and all under the inspiration of a beautiful clime! Lord Beaconsfield, no longer in the sunset, but the twilight of his existence, must encounter a life of anxiety and toil; but this, too, has its romance, when he remembers that he labours for the most gracious of beings!'

Years later, when Queen Victoria was a very old lady, she told Lord Rosebery that Disraeli had once sent her, without any inscription, a little box; 'on one side was a heart transfixed by an arrow, and on the other the word *Fideliter*'. Had that not been, asked Her Majesty, 'touching?'[9]

Queen Victoria's passion for Disraeli in no way lessened her passion for John Brown. In fact, she was in the enviable position of having the best of both worlds: one man to supply the romance, the other the security. Together, Disraeli and Brown gave the Queen all the support and attention she craved. What one lacked, the other supplied. Where Brown made her feel like a helpless 'wumman', relying on him for protection, Dizzy made her feel like some desirable and almost mythical creature – an undoubted Queen. In the presence of either of them she felt cherished.

No wonder Queen Victoria found this period so gratifying. It was like a more extended version of that other extremely exciting time, when she could flirt with the fascinating Napoleon III while remaining Prince Albert's '*Fräuchen*'.

Between them, Dizzy and Brown coaxed Queen Victoria out of her long period of mourning. Her renaissance dates from this time when both men, in their very different ways, were paying her court. If she did not actually forget Prince Albert, she certainly spent less time thinking about him. Gradually, in the reassuring company of these two friends, her health improved, her interest was reawakened, her vitality revived. No one seeing the Queen dancing with Brown at a gillies' ball at Balmoral or bantering with Disraeli in her tent at Osborne could reconcile her with the grief-stricken Queen of popular imagination. In any case, to some her unremitting stream of complaints had long since become suspect. Henry Ponsonby, in describing Disraeli's handling of her, claimed that 'his sympathy is expressed while his tongue is in his cheek – but are not her woes told in the same manner?'[10]

How did Disraeli and John Brown – these two rivals for the Queen's attention and affection – regard each other? Not, in fact, as rivals at all. Disraeli was too worldly a man to resent the gillie's influence with the Queen. More than any other man in her circle, Disraeli would have appreciated the nature of her relationship with the Highlander. He would have appreciated, too, the fact that she was able to divide her affections between Brown and himself; that each appealed to different facets of her complex nature. Dizzy understood Brown's role and was grateful to him for his part in enticing the Queen out of her morbid obsession with the late Prince Consort. In many ways Brown had eased Disraeli's task: if Disraeli had heightened Queen Victoria's interest in life, it was Brown who had first re-awakened it.

There were even times when Disraeli was able to reach the Queen through Brown. On once being asked why he did not propose a certain measure to the Queen, Disraeli answered that he must first make sure that it had the approval of 'the two J.B.s – John Bull and John Brown'.[11]

For his part, John Brown approved of Disraeli. The astute Dizzy, unlike others surrounding the Queen, had always taken care to treat Brown with the utmost friendliness and respect. And Brown, who was so touchy, so suspicious and so surly, was quick to respond to Dizzy's overtures. Those little messages to Brown with which Disraeli so often ended his letters to the Queen were greatly appreciated. Moreover, John Brown – who had the Queen's interests sincerely at heart – could only be grateful for the way in which the Prime Minister was contributing to the Queen's 'comfort'.

And, of course, the more Disraeli played up to Brown, the better he pleased the Queen. With Brown causing so much friction in the royal household, it was a relief for her to know that there was someone whom this rough-tongued gillie did not rub up the wrong way. Dizzy's tactful treatment of Brown could only increase the Queen's affection for her Prime Minister.

★

However flirtatious or entertaining Disraeli's behaviour towards Victoria might be, he never forgot that she was the Queen of England. In truth, that remained her chief attraction. Cynical in so much else, Disraeli, like Lord Melbourne before him, remained positively sentimental in his attitude towards the throne. He revered the monarchy. The fact that his monarch was a queen rather than a king enhanced all this royalist reverence. A queen on the throne fired his imagination as no king ever could have. Parchment-skinned and stiff-kneed he might be but Dizzy none the less saw himself as a knight, a liegeman, a loyal servant of his royal mistress. He liked to inform the House that he stood there 'by favour of the Queen'. He liked to pretend that he might lose his head at her command. He made a dull debate, says Philip Guedalla, 'sound like a tournament reported to the Queen of Beauty by her Unknown Knight'.[12]

It was, claims one of Disraeli's biographers, 'after the romantic fashion of Raleigh's service to Queen Elizabeth that Disraeli conceived of his own service to Queen Victoria'. Once, thanking her for a gift of pink may from Windsor, Dizzy wrote, 'It was a gift worthy of Queen Elizabeth, and of an age when great affairs and romance were not incompatible.'

In Disraeli's imagination this plump, homely, middle-aged constitutional monarch was transformed into a second Queen Elizabeth, a second Catherine the Great. In his eyes, and hers, she became the embodiment of Great Britain. Not only was he reviving her interest in the business of monarchy, but he was making her more conscious of the importance of her position. He saw her, and encouraged her to think of herself, in her historical perspective: not merely as the ceremonial head of a self-governing nation, but as the latest in a glorious line of British monarchs; as the heir to King Alfred, William the Conqueror, the Plantagenets, the Tudors and the Stuarts.

From being a withdrawn, doleful, insecure, self-obsessed, self-pitying and hypochondriacal creature, clinging to the late Prince Consort's set of precepts and constantly bewailing the fact that she was being pushed beyond her limits, Queen Victoria – under Disraeli's tactful direction – was developing into a remarkable figure. Her confidence in her own judgement increased; her zest became little short of miraculous.

But Disraeli's influence was not all beneficial. With his encouragement, she began to think of him – as she would of future prime ministers – as the servant of the Crown rather than of the people. It could almost be said that she was coming to regard the government of the country as a partnership between the Sovereign and her Prime Minister, a partnership to which they each brought their vast store of knowledge and experience. Not only did Disraeli keep the Queen fully informed of what was going on, but he was forever asking her opinion and advice. Never before had she felt so involved in the day-to-day workings of the government; never before had she considered herself to be so indispensable, so important, so powerful.

All this intimacy between Sovereign and Prime Minister might have been overlooked, had there not been a strong whiff of something unconstitutional about it all. Not only did they spend hours closeted together, they even wrote directly to each other, without using the customary third person and without the knowledge of the Queen's private secretary. 'She is always at him', grumbled Ponsonby, 'about something that we know nothing of.'[13]

Was the Queen bringing too much influence to bear on Disraeli; or he too much to bear on her? Were they working too closely together? Was he encouraging her to be something more than a constitutional monarch? Surely all his flowery talk about her being the 'Directress' and 'Arbitress' of Europe was not only foolish, but dangerous? 'Is there not just a risk', asked one of Disraeli's ministers, 'of encouraging her in too large ideas of her personal power, and too great indifference to what the public expects?'[14]

There was certainly a risk, but Disraeli was prepared to take it. Provided, that is, the Queen was in accord with his ideas. He never hesitated to encourage her authoritarianism, nor to use her name to further his schemes. In the Queen's mind, Disraeli's policy became 'our' policy; and 'our' policy became, in turn, the 'imperial policy of England'. Any criticism of Disraeli's actions was to her a criticism of the Crown. For a constitutional monarch, this was a perilous path to be treading.

In fact, Queen Victoria's concept of the role of a constitutional monarch was undergoing a change. The suspicion that Disraeli was giving the Queen too inflated an opinion of her position was to some extent justified. She was by now determined not to become a mere cipher, a mere puppet-like signer of bills and opener of parliaments. She developed a somewhat exaggerated idea of her royal prerogative; she certainly dug in her heels at any sign of it being whittled away. 'I do think Dizzy has worked the idea of personal government to its logical conclusion...', complained Mary Ponsonby, wife of the Queen's private secretary. 'If there comes a real collision between the Queen and the House of Commons, it is quite possible that she would turn restive, *dorlotée* as she has been by Dizzy's high-sounding platitudes . . .'.[15]

What Disraeli was re-creating for Queen Victoria, or what he had led her to believe he was re-creating, was what he called 'a real Throne'.

'One Whose Dear Memory Will Ever Live in her Heart'

DISRAELI HAD not only presented Queen Victoria with an imperial crown; he had opened her eyes to the glories of imperialism itself. During the early years of the Queen's reign, the imperial idea was in its infancy; imperialism, was still a vague and suspect doctrine. The British Empire was a haphazard affair, a collection of widely scattered, widely varying and only loosely connected possessions, which a great many politicians were only too ready to scrap. The Queen's previous political mentors – first Lord Melbourne, and then Prince Albert – had not been especially interested in imperial or colonial affairs: Melbourne because they tended to bring nothing but trouble, Albert because he was so passionately concerned with things nearer home. Only in India had the Prince Consort shown any particular interest. Like the Queen, he wanted India administered in a spirit of 'generosity, tolerance and religious toleration'.[1]

But Disraeli, by his expansionist policies and his bold gestures, made Queen Victoria conscious of her position as the Sovereign of this great jumble of peoples and territories. He encouraged her to think of herself as an imperial mother-figure, as the Great White Queen, as the Queen-Empress of the mightiest Empire that the world had ever known. From the time of Disraeli's second premiership and for the following two decades, Queen Victoria came to symbolize the strident, swaggering, and in so many ways glorious, ideal that was the British Empire.

Having had her eyes opened to the glory of imperialism, the Queen tended to champion it rather more fervently than Disraeli may always have wished. Happy enough with the concept of a powerful and kaleidoscopic Empire, Disraeli was still far more interested in maintaining British supremacy in Europe. He particularly wanted to avoid the sort of costly and often unsuccessful colonial ventures that might weaken Britain's standing on the Continent.

In this he came up against the Queen. She was by now determined to uphold British prestige wherever it be threatened: in the deserts and jungles of Africa or the plains and mountains of Asia no less than in the chancelleries and embassies of Europe. And it was on this question of imperial prestige that, in the year 1879, the Queen and her Prime Minister all but fell out.

The scene of the national disaster which led to this personal disagreement was that graveyard of so many Victorian military reputations – South Africa. Sir Bartle Frere, the newly appointed Governor of the Cape Colony and High Commissioner for South Africa, was one of those 'prancing proconsuls' who firmly believed in an expansionist imperialist policy. Determined to extend Britain's power in South Africa, Frere let the British government know that he was contemplating a war against the powerful Zulu nation in Natal. Disraeli wanted none of it. Frere was told that he must do his utmost to avoid any such war.

The Governor refused to listen. In January 1879 Frere sent a British army, commanded by Lord Chelmsford, into Zululand. On 22 January, on the slopes of a dramatic-looking mountain named Isandhlwana, this British invading force was all but annihilated.

Disraeli was both appalled and angry. Not only had Frere disobeyed orders, but Chelmsford had failed disastrously. Reinforcements had to be rushed out to Natal and Disraeli found himself with a full-scale war on his hands.

Queen Victoria was no less appalled by Isandhlwana, but rather less angry with Frere and Chelmsford. They had merely been, she thought, unfortunate. So when the incensed Disraeli appointed Sir Garnet Wolseley effectively to supersede both Frere and Chelmsford, the Queen balked at the proposal. She had never liked Wolseley; she considered him too cocksure by half. Moreover, she considered it quite wrong for Lord Chelmsford to be superseded in the middle of what she felt sure was a difficult campaign. In this she was right. Disraeli should have either dismissed both Frere and Chelmsford outright, or else given them his support.

In spite of the Queen's protestations, Disraeli stuck by his decision to appoint Wolseley. The disgruntled Queen was obliged to give way. She would sanction Wolseley's appointment, she told Disraeli, but she would not '*approve*' it.

And in case there might be any lack of martial spirit on the part of the government, or any attempt to conclude a hasty peace, the Queen reminded her Prime Minister that 'if *we are to maintain* our position as a *first-rate* Power – and that no one can doubt, we must with our Indian Empire and large Colonies, be *Prepared for attacks and wars, somewhere or other,* CONTINUALLY, and the true economy will be to be *always ready.* Lord Beaconsfield can do his country the greatest service by repeating that again and again, and by *seeing it carried out.'*

This already difficult situation was further complicated by the fact that among the reinforcing troops dispatched to South Africa was the young Prince Imperial of France. Since the death of his father the Emperor Napoleon III in 1873, the Prince Imperial – who lived with the Empress Eugénie in Kent – had been the Bonapartist pretender to the French throne. Particularly fond of the Empress, Queen Victoria had also developed a strong affection for the twenty-three-year-old Prince. The young man had something of his late father's exotic air and charm of manner; to this was added a frankness and a vivacity inherited from his mother. In short, the Prince Imperial was the sort of swashbuckling young man to whom the Queen was always drawn.

Disraeli could not share his Sovereign's enthusiasm for the Prince Imperial. Pretenders to foreign thrones were always something of an embarrassment to a government. Disraeli had no quarrel with the French Republic and, as far as he was concerned, the less fuss made about the Prince Imperial, the better.

So when the Prince, who had done his military training at Woolwich, expressed a wish to join the reinforcements going out to Natal, Disraeli would not hear of it. The venture would be fraught with risks. The government, already reeling under the blow of Isandhlwana, did not want the death of a French pretender on their hands.

But the Prince, anxious to see active service and to draw French attention to himself, was determined to go. Both he and the Empress applied directly to the Commander-in-Chief of the British Army – the Queen's cousin, the Duke of Cambridge. The Duke passed the Prince's application on to the Queen. She was charmed. Nothing, she thought, could be more natural than that the dear young Prince Imperial should wish to repay her hospitality by fighting with her troops.

In the face of this combined onslaught, from the sympathetic Queen and the partisan Empress, Disraeli was obliged to give way. The government agreed to let the Prince go. 'Well,' Disraeli was afterwards to say, 'my conscience is clear. I did all I could to stop his going. But what can you do when you have to deal with two obstinate women?'

On one thing, though, Disraeli insisted. In letters to Frere and Chelmsford, the cabinet made it abundantly clear that the Prince was going to Natal in the capacity of a spectator only. Under no circumstances was he to be allowed to take part in any fighting.

Disraeli was reckoning without the Prince's sense of adventure; the young man lost no opportunity of joining in whatever action was going on. On 1 June 1879, while on a reconnaissance mission, he was killed in a surprise Zulu attack. If that were not bad enough, it was later learned that he had been deserted by his companions and left, quite alone, to face the Zulu assegais.

The Queen, when John Brown broke the news to her, was horrified. She took the unprecedented step of cutting short her Balmoral holiday to hurry south to comfort the bereaved Empress. To make amends for the loss of the Prince Imperial's life and the cowardice of his companions, she was determined that he be given as magnificent a funeral as possible. It was Disraeli's turn to be horrified. Fearing the effect of such an insult to the French Republic, who less than a decade before had rejected the Bonapartes, he wanted the whole unfortunate affair played down. The Prince Imperial's death was certainly no fault of the British government: Disraeli's cabinet saw no reason why they should be associated with any manifestation of national self-reproach. A state or semi-state funeral would only draw attention to the ineptitude with which Britain was conducting the campaign in Zululand.

Queen Victoria held firm. When she announced her intention of placing the Order of the Bath on the Prince's coffin with her own hands, it needed all Disraeli's celebrated persuasiveness to talk her out of it. When the cabinet decided against attending the funeral at all, she flew into one of her towering rages. So outspoken was her indignation that the cabinet was forced to relent. It was agreed that two ministers – the War Minister and the Colonial Minister – should go in full dress.

Poor Disraeli, whom the Queen had been bombarding with telegrams for days, was finally obliged to journey down to Windsor in person. He went in considerable trepidation, expecting, as he put it, 'a distressing scene'. His apprehensions were more than justified. The Queen kept him for an hour and a half and held forth, he complained to a friend, 'only on one subject'.

The funeral, on 12 July 1879, was as impressive as the Queen had intended it to be. Arriving back at Windsor when it was over, she at once sent a telegram to Disraeli, expressing her entire satisfaction with the day's ceremonial.

'I hope', wrote Disraeli to Lady Chesterfield, 'the French Government will be as joyful. In my mind, nothing could be more injudicious than the whole affair.'[2]

The matter of the Prince Imperial's funeral was not the last of the differences between Victoria and Disraeli to arise from the ill-fated Zulu War.

Lord Chelmsford, on learning that Sir Garnet Wolseley had been sent out to supersede him, was galvanized into action. He advanced rapidly into Zululand and, by winning a great victory at Ulundi, brought the campaign to a successful end. Queen Victoria was delighted. Judging that the victory at Ulundi had cancelled out the disaster at Isandhlwana, she was all for giving Lord Chelmsford a hero's welcome. Disraeli was not. When the Queen asked him to invite Chelmsford to Hughenden, his country home, Disraeli refused. In a very strong letter, Disraeli gave the Queen his reasons for this refusal. The Queen's answer was equally strong. But Disraeli remained firm. So, while the Queen received Chelmsford at Balmoral, Disraeli made a point of *not* receiving him at Hughenden.

These misunderstandings – and they were not much more than that – upset both Queen Victoria and Disraeli considerably. It was he who made the first move towards a reconciliation. He wrote to Lady Ely, one of the Queen's ladies-in-waiting, knowing that she would show the letter to her royal mistress.

'My nature demands perfect solitude, or perfect sympathy . . .', he wrote. 'I am grieved, and greatly, that anything I should say, or do, should be displeasing to Her Majesty. I love the Queen – perhaps the only person in this world left to me that I do love; and therefore you can understand how much it worries and disquiets me, when there is a cloud between us.'

In the face of these mellifluous phrases, the cloud was dispersed. When next the two of them met, the sun was shining as warmly and as brilliantly as ever.

Astute in so many things, Disraeli was especially astute in his dealings with Queen Victoria's family. He treated the princes and princesses with just the right shade of deference. He knew exactly how far he could go in defending them against their mother's often unjustified complaints, and how to give the impression that he found their talents and opinions more remarkable than was, in fact, the case. 'When I left the dining-room after sitting next to Mr Gladstone, I thought he was the cleverest man in England,' runs a story told by one of the princesses.

'But after sitting next to Mr Disraeli, I thought I was the cleverest woman in England.'[3]

The Prime Minister could be relied upon to rescue the Queen's sons from diplomatic gaffes or social scandals, and at one stage he arranged for her youngest son, the haemophilic Prince Leopold, to be usefully employed in acting as part personal assistant and part confidential secretary to the Queen. Prince Leopold, Disraeli assured the gratified Queen, was a prince 'whose intelligence I have from the first recognised'.[4] What Prince Leopold felt about having to work so closely with his intimidating and exacting mother is another matter.

While he was attending the Congress of Berlin, Disraeli had reported to the Queen from Potsdam on the cleverness and vivacity of her eldest daughter Vicky, the German Crown Princess. She and Crown Prince Frederick had 'showered kindnesses' on him. What rendered these kindnesses even more delightful, he took care to add, was the fact that they were 'owing to the inspiration of one to whom he owes everything'. They were indeed. Dizzy was touched to discover that the Queen had given her daughter strict instructions about the care of his health while he was in Berlin. The Crown Princess was to see that he had a fire in every room and that he was not to walk, much less stand, on cold marble floors.

But it was in his dealings with the Queen's eldest son Bertie, the Prince of Wales, that Disraeli was at his most adroit. Indeed, it was in no small measure due to the Prime Minister's tactful championing of the Prince that the relationship between mother and son was beginning to improve.

Where the Prince Consort had always considered Bertie to be entirely feckless and foolish, Disraeli had a high opinion – or professed to have a high opinion – of the Prince's abilities. He made a show of consulting him, he kept him informed on certain issues, he tried to involve him in the business of monarchy. Although the two men were not really compatible – the Prince was too bluff and philistine for Disraeli's taste, and Disraeli too flamboyant and enigmatic for the Prince's – the Prime Minister was quick to appreciate that the Prince's special qualities – his verve, his love of display, even his boisterous behaviour – could be of as much value to the monarchy as the Queen's very different virtues. Young Hal, as he perceptively called him, could certainly be relied upon to endow the monarchy with that show of splendour which the Queen, despite Disraeli's promptings, felt herself unable to provide. Not for a moment did Disraeli make the mistake of either ignoring or underestimating Victoria's heir.

This, in turn, made the Queen look at her son with new eyes. If dear, clever Lord Beaconsfield was prepared to take Bertie seriously, then perhaps there was more to him than she had hitherto imagined. And although Queen Victoria could never quite overcome her reservations about her heir's political abilities, she did come to a gradual appreciation of his other good points.

However, Disraeli took good care to avoid any appearance of conniving with the Prince behind his mother's back. He realized that he had only to pay a few visits to Marlborough House – particularly if the Queen were on her by now annual Continental holiday – for there to be speculation about the exact nature of these meetings. It would never do for the Queen to suspect him of being in political collusion with her heir. Their contact had to be purely social.

Even on a social level, Disraeli had to tread carefully. The Queen might be prepared to admit that Bertie was not entirely without good qualities, but nothing would reconcile her to his frenetic social life. So it would not be advisable for Disraeli to be seen too often at Marlborough House or Sandringham. 'This morning a telegram in cypher', he once reported to Lady Bradford, 'disapproving of my going to Sandringham as I shall catch cold. A little jealous on that subject.'[5] And on another occasion he announced that the Queen was 'delighted' that he was not going to Sandringham after all.

Once, when Bertie suggested that he should spend a night, *en garçon*, at Hughenden, Disraeli took fright. He was apprehensive, both of the Prince's notorious restlessness and of the Queen's possible disapproval. But it all went beautifully. The Prince was kept busy with drives, walks, whist, gargantuan meals and the antics of his carefully chosen fellow guests. The Prime Minister was greatly relieved. He was even more relieved by the Queen's reaction. 'I heard today from the Faery, who highly approves of the visit,' he reported to a friend. 'I thought, on the contrary, we should have our ears boxed.'[6]

What the Prince of Wales thought of his mother's close association with Disraeli is uncertain. But on ascending the throne as Edward VII the King asked Lord Rothschild, the trustee of Disraeli's estate, to return all the letters which Queen Victoria had written to her Prime Minister. These letters have been described as '*very* Private'.[7] King Edward VII had all the more intimate letters destroyed. Only those dealing with political subjects were returned to Lord Rothschild.

What the '*very* Private' contents of these letters between Victoria and Disraeli were, one will never know.

★

On 5 February 1880, for the fourth time during Disraeli's term of office, the Queen opened Parliament in person. She did so, moreover, in such a way as to ensure that the occasion would be more spectacular than ever. Although she still did not actually enjoy the duty, the Queen no longer shirked it. She was by now prepared to comply with Disraeli's request that 'the procession should be as splendid as might be convenient to your Majesty'. There was nothing, the Prime Minister went on to assure her, 'which the great body of the people more appreciate than this spectacle ... because the splendour of royalty delights the people'.

So the Queen, wearing a small diamond and sapphire coronet atop her diamond-edged cap with its floating tulle veil, drove to Parliament in a new state coach which sported so much glass that she could be seen more clearly than ever before. Within the House of Lords the scene was one of exceptional brilliance; 'a great sea of colour, beautifully variegated and harmonized'.[8] One thing only spoiled the pageantry of this particular occasion: Disraeli felt too weak to carry the heavy Sword of State in the procession.

But if he could not carry it literally, he was confident of carrying it figuratively. The Tories won two by-elections early that year and the Queen was able to follow up her customary valentine to her beloved Prime Minister with a triumphant telegram: 'I am greatly rejoiced at the great victory ...' she wired, in happy disregard of her constitutional position. 'It shows what the feeling in the country is.'

Disraeli agreed. He agreed so strongly, in fact, that he decided on an early general election. The Queen, who had no doubt that the Tories would be returned 'stronger than ever', set off for Darmstadt to attend the confirmation of two of her granddaughters.

While the Queen and her Prime Minister prepared themselves for a Tory victory, Gladstone was laying the foundations for a Tory defeat. With an energy that was astonishing in someone over seventy, the Grand Old Man addressed meeting after meeting, denouncing, in his thunderous voice, the immorality of Disraeli's administration. Not only did he infuriate the Queen by lashing out against the 'theatrical bombast and folly' of her new imperial title but, with what she must have regarded as unbelievable effrontery, he directed his call to 'the nation itself.'

The call was successful. The election was spread over two weeks and by the beginning of April 1880 it was clear that Gladstone's Liberals would win.

Queen Victoria was at Baden–Baden when she received the telegram from Disraeli preparing her for his defeat. Its effect was overwhelming. 'This is a terrible telegram,' she exclaimed. So bitter, so indignant, so desolate was her reaction to the news that the long-suffering Sir Henry Ponsonby (he had been knighted the year before) considered it was well that she was alone with her household at the time: some of the language used, he claimed, would hardly have been suitable for other ears.

Worse even than the prospect of having to work with the hated Gladstone was that of losing her adored Disraeli. His letter to her almost broke her heart. 'His separation from Your Majesty is almost overwhelming,' he wrote. 'His relations with Your Majesty were his chief, he might say his only, happiness and interest in this world. They came to him when he was alone, and they have inspired and sustained him in his isolation.'

On her return to England, the Queen sent at once for Disraeli. Unpalatable as it might be, she had to face the question of his successor. Although the names of several prominent Liberals were mentioned, there was really no choice. The Queen braced herself to do what she had at one stage sworn she would rather abdicate than do: she sent for Gladstone. Without hesitation, he accepted the responsibility of forming a government.

On 27 April 1880, Disraeli travelled to Windsor to take formal leave of the Queen. For them both, it was a poignant occasion. The Queen's desolation was somewhat tempered by her conviction that the new Liberal administration would never last. In the meantime, Lord Beaconsfield was to promise her that he would allow no 'lowering of Great Britain's proud position!'

'My audience was very long,' wrote Disraeli of this last official visit to Queen Victoria, 'and everything was said that could be said ...'.[9] The Queen presented him with a bronze statuette of herself and made him promise that he would come and see her.

'Today,' Disraeli had once written to Queen Victoria on the occasion of her birthday, 'which has given to my country a Sovereign whose reign, it is my hope and ambition, may rank with that of Elizabeth, has also given to me, her humble, but chosen servant, a Mistress, whom to serve is to love ...'.

Well, if he could no longer serve her, he could still love her.

In a way, he was able to do both. During the year of life that was left to him, the seventy-five-year-old Disraeli kept in close touch with the Queen. They wrote to each other ('Ever your affectionate and grateful friend V.R.I.' was how the Queen ended her letters), and on several occasions Disraeli was Victoria's guest at Windsor. In general, Disraeli kept off political topics. The Queen might assure him that 'I *never* write except on *official* matters' to Gladstone, and that 'I look always to *you* for ultimate help' but, in the main, Disraeli did not encourage her in this attitude. When the Queen appealed to him for political advice, he did his best to keep it as impartial as possible.

Yet even these exchanges had to be kept dark. The Queen would refer to some of her letters as '*very secret*', and knowing that Henry Ponsonby disapproved of the correspondence, she advised Disraeli not to write to her through her secretary. He could use her son Prince Leopold, or a groom-in-waiting, or a woman of the bedchamber: they were 'all QUITE SAFE', she assured him.

But Disraeli's attitude was not always constitutionally impeccable. At the opening of the parliamentary session of 1881 he gave her the most dangerously misleading piece of advice. In her Speech from the Throne (written, of course, by her ministers) was an announcement to the effect that British troops would be withdrawn from Kandahar in Afghanistan. This the Queen refused to sanction. With such cowardly, retrogressive, 'little England' policies she wanted no truck. At the end of an extremely stormy cabinet meeting at Osborne, with the Queen's exasperated ministers threatening resignation, Sir William Harcourt, the Home Secretary, pointed out that 'the Speech of the Sovereign' was merely 'the Speech of the Ministers'. What he was saying, in effect, was that she was obliged to make it whether she approved of its contents or not.

Harcourt's assertion seems to have astonished the Queen. She appealed to Disraeli. His reply was devasting in its sophistry. Sir William Harcourt's principle, he declared unblinkingly, 'is a principle not known to the British Constitution. It is only a piece of Parliamentary gossip.' At a stroke, Disraeli was brushing aside the entire concept of ministerial responsibility. Can one wonder that Queen Victoria developed a somewhat exaggerated idea of her constitutional position?

But it was, as always, as much for personal as for political reasons that the Queen valued her continuing contact with Disraeli. The old wizard could still weave his magic spells; he could still enchant the Queen with his romantic imagery. From Hughenden, at which he spent that first summer out of office, he wrote to her of the splendours of the countryside: of 'the mysterious and sultry' call of the cuckoo, of the cooing of the wood-pigeons, of the sweetness of the may blossom. From Windsor she replied to say that 'I often think of you – indeed constantly – and rejoice to see you looking down from the *wall* after dinner.'

And if Disraeli looked down from the wall on the Queen at Windsor, she – in her Angeli portrait – looked down at him in the drawing-room at Hughenden. He ate his Christmas dinner alone that year, but the Queen had not forgotten him. 'Oh Madam and most beloved Sovereign,' he wrote on Christmas Day, 'what language can express my feelings when I beheld this morning the graceful and gracious gifts upon my table. Such incidents make life delightful and inspire even age with the glow and energy of youth.'

But this glow and energy of youth were illusory. By the time the Queen was sending her customary gifts of early primroses Disraeli, by now back in his London home, was failing. On 1 March 1881 the couple dined together at Windsor Castle; it was their last meeting.

Less than a month later, the Queen received her last letter from Disraeli. He had been ill for a week with bronchitis and, in pencil, he had scrawled an answer to her anxious inquiry. 'I am prostrate but devoted', he told her. His message did nothing to reassure the Queen. Knowing that he was in the care of the celebrated homoeopath Dr Joseph Kidd, she was anxious that there be a second, more orthodox medical opinion. Her wish, treated as a command, overcame the reluctance of a specialist in chest diseases to associate himself with a homoeopath, and he agreed to examine the patient. By now, though, Disraeli was beyond medical help, be it conventional or not.

Every day the Queen wired from Windsor for news. She wrote him letters; she sent him boxes of primroses and violets. 'I sent some Osborne primroses and I meant to pay you a little visit this week, but I thought it better you should be quiet and not speak,' she wrote on one occasion. 'And I beg you will be very good and obey the doctors and commit no imprudence.'

When he became too weak to read her letters himself he insisted, with that blend of reverence and irony which never deserted him, that his Sovereign's letter be read to him by a Privy Councillor. It was, and the voice of the Privy Councillor was heard intoning the royal, if intimate, phrases: 'I send you some of your favourite spring flowers ...'.

And in the end, not even his beloved Sovereign herself could escape his mordant wit. When it was suggested that she come and visit him, he decided against it. 'No, it is better not,' he said. 'She would only ask me to take a message to Albert.'[10]

★

Disraeli died on 19 April 1881, at the age of seventy-six. It was, as always, John Brown who was entrusted with breaking the news to the Queen. She was desolate. In her own hand Victoria composed the announcement of Disraeli's death for the Court Circular and, with tears blurring her eyes, wrote a letter of condolence to Disraeli's devoted secretary, Montagu Corry. She had never lost a friend, she assured Corry, 'whose loss will be more keenly felt'. Her dearest wish was to see Corry in order to hear about his master's last days. Corry duly hurried down to Osborne where, he afterwards said, he spent hours telling the Queen 'all she wished to know of her loved Friend. And she did love him'.[11]

To Lord Salisbury the Queen admitted that she was '*quite* overwhelmed with this dreadful loss, irreparable to the country and Europe, to his many friends, and above all to herself! His devotion, unselfishness, and kindness she can *never, never* forget; her gratitude is everlasting as well as her regret to have lost *one* whose dear memory will ever live in her heart . . .'.

The Queen, with her penchant for funerals, was quite prepared for Disraeli to go to his grave in the most grandiose manner possible. Even Gladstone, assuming that his rival would have liked to go out with a flourish, decided that a state funeral in Westminster Abbey was called for. But when Disraeli's will was read it was discovered he had left instructions that he should be buried, quietly, beside his wife Mary Anne at Hughenden church. Gladstone was astonished. He could not bring himself to believe that Disraeli's wish for a simple funeral was anything other than a final piece of charlatanism; the 'artful dodger's' crowning affectation.

But Victoria was touched. She considered the choice of a humble village church entire typical of him. Dear Lord Beaconsfield had always 'hated display', she announced emphatically.

She was not, though, prepared to deny him *all* display. Although tradition prevented a sovereign from attending the funeral of a subject, the Queen saw to it that three of her sons – the Prince of Wales, the Duke of Connaught and Prince Leopold – were present. She herself sent two wreaths of primroses. On her card she wrote: 'His favourite flowers from Osborne, a tribute of affection from Queen Victoria.'

The revelation that primroses were Disraeli's favourite flower was met with considerable scepticism. Was the choice of this unassuming spring flower – like his choice of Hughenden church rather than Westminster Abbey – merely another example of his insincerity? Gladstone certainly thought so. The flamboyant lily, declared Gladstone to a friend, would have been more to Disraeli's taste.

But the Queen knew better. Primroses were part of the make-believe, magical, midsummer's night dream of a world in which the two of them had moved; the world in which she had been transformed into the Faery Queen and he into her devoted liegeman. To others the choice might seem paradoxical; but then, what couple other than the Queen and her Prime Minister could afford to choose so artless and unostentatious a flower to symbolize their romantic association?

Victoria's tribute did not end with those wreaths of primroses. Above Disraeli's seat in the chancel in Hughenden church she had a huge marble tablet erected in his memory. Beneath the marble profile was cut a frank inscription: 'This memorial is placed by his grateful Sovereign and Friend, Victoria R.I.'

Four days after Disraeli's funeral, the Queen travelled to Hughenden to visit his grave. It was a showery, blustery April day. The little church was filled with flowers and more flowers were heaped on the coffin which lay in the specially opened vault. To these tributes, the Queen added a china wreath. From the church, she went on to the house. In the company of Montagu Corry, she trailed sadly through the rooms. Every piece of furniture, every ornament, every picture, was a heartbreaking reminder of him. 'I seemed to hear his voice, and the impassioned eager way he described everything,' wrote the Queen.[12]

If one thing could have comforted Queen Victoria in her grief, as she drove back through the slanting rain to Windsor, it would have been Corry's assurance that in Disraeli's coffin 'there lies, and will ever lie, close to that faithful heart, the photograph of the Queen *he* loved...'.[13]

Part Six

THE MUNSHI

18

'If the Queen Thinks a Person Good Enough . . .'

IF, WITH the death of Disraeli, some of the brilliance had gone out of Queen Victoria's life, there remained the more sterling qualities of John Brown. In her day-to-day existence, he was by now the supreme arranger and arbiter.

No one could equal Brown when it came to ensuring the Queen's privacy and comfort. Once, when there was an acrimonious discussion about how many of her courtiers should share Her Majesty's pew at Crathie church, Brown cut it short by declaring, 'She had better have a place all to herself and have done with this hombogging.' On another occasion as the Queen, on a visit to Coburg, was setting out for a drive, he silenced the furiously drumming German guard of honour by marching up to the officer and shouting, 'Nix boom boom'. Even Gladstone was not safe from Brown's rough tongue. When the gillie decided that the Queen had been subjected to her Prime Minister's notorious verbosity for far too long, Brown ended the audience with an abrupt 'You've said enough.'[1]

She would never reprimand him. On the contrary, the Queen often allowed herself to be reprimanded, and corrected, by Brown. One day the Queen and Ponsonby were in disagreement about something. Her Majesty, certain that Brown would back her up, had him summoned. Brown agreed with the secretary. As meekly as a lamb, the Queen admitted that she had been wrong.

'He was the only person who could fight and make the Queen do what she did not wish,' claimed Ponsonby. 'He did not always succeed nor was his advice always the best. But I believe he was honest and with all his want of education – his roughness – his prejudices and other faults he was undoubtedly a most excellent servant to her.'[2]

But not for much longer. On 17 March 1883, as the Queen was

coming downstairs for her afternoon drive at Windsor, she fell and twisted her knee. Instead of cancelling the drive, she insisted on being helped into her carriage by Brown. On her return, her knee was found to be so badly swollen that she had to be carried upstairs by Brown and one of the footmen.

The next morning she heard that Lady Florence Dixie – a celebrated advocate of what the Queen would have considered such outlandish causes as sex equality, 'rational' dress and the abolition of blood sports – who lived near Windsor Castle, had been assaulted while out walking. Her assailants had been, claimed her ladyship, a couple of men dressed in women's clothing. As the rationality of Lady Florence's dressing did not, apparently, preclude the wearing of steel-stayed corsets, she had survived what she described as a vicious knife attack. Only when her dog Hubert came bounding onto the scene did the two men pick up their skirts and run. The attackers had been, it was generally assumed, Fenians – Irish terrorists.

The Queen, who lived in dread of a Fenian attack, was extremely upset by the thought of this outrage taking place so close to Windsor Castle. She immediately sent Brown to investigate the matter. In spite of the bitter March weather, Brown drove to Lady Florence's home in an open dog-cart, dressed only in his usual kilt and thin, broadcloth jacket. Having heard her ladyship's account of the attack, Brown shook his head and said, 'What a thing to be happening to a lassie. Have ye got a picture of the dog, for I'd like one for mysel'. If ye canna spare one, I'll be willing to pay forre it.'[3] Lady Florence promised to send him one.

His inspection of the site of the alleged attack tended to temper Brown's sympathy somewhat. He could detect no signs of a struggle on the soft, damp ground. His scepticism was echoed, both by eye-witnesses on the day and by the police in their official enquiry. It was widely assumed that Lady Florence Dixie had been, as always, in search of publicity.

For Queen Victoria the affair was to have more serious consequences. Brown returned home thoroughly chilled, but because the Queen was still suffering – her fall had started a series of painful rheumatic attacks – he refused to go to bed. She needed him too badly. By 24 March she was feeling slightly better and, despite the fact that he was feeling slightly worse, Brown carried her downstairs and put her into her little pony chair. She had not used it since 1865; since, in fact, Brown had first been summoned from Balmoral to attend to her after Prince Albert's death.

By the next day Brown was worse still. And so was the Queen. 'Had not a good night,' she complained in her Journal. 'Vexed that Brown could not attend me, not being at all well, with a swollen face, which it is feared is erysipelas.' It was indeed erysipelas, an affliction from which Brown had suffered for many years. Often, in the past, his skin had become blotchy and his limbs inflamed and swollen; it was a condition made worse by the chronic alcoholism of his later years. By the evening of 26 March he was suffering from delirium tremens and on the night of Tuesday 29 March 1883, at the age of fifty-six, he died.

The news was broken to the Queen by Prince Leopold. Victoria, on her own admission, was 'utterly crushed'. Her life, she admitted to Henry Ponsonby, 'has again sustained one of those shocks like in '61' when, on the death of the Prince Consort, 'every link has been shaken and torn.' As on that occasion, the Queen temporarily lost the use of her legs. Even though the swelling in her knee had subsided, she was unable to stand, much less walk. 'Weep with me for we all have lost the best, truest heart that ever beat ...' she wrote to John Brown's relatives, for it was to them that she turned in her sorrow. Her grief, she cried out, was 'unbounded, dreadful, and I know not how to bear it, or how to believe it possible'.[4]

For six days John Brown's body lay in state in the Clarence Tower at Windsor. On 3 April, accompanied by the faithful Princess Beatrice, the Queen attended the brief funeral ceremony. From the castle windows she watched as the coffin, in a glass-sided hearse, went trundling out of the gates on its way to the railway station, from where it would begin its long journey to Scotland. On top of the coffin lay the Queen's wreath of myrtle and white flowers; on the card was written, in her own hand, 'A tribute of loving, grateful, and everlasting friendship and affection from his truest, best and most faithful friend, Victoria R and I.'

When, two days later, John Brown was finally laid to rest in Crathie cemetery, the pall covering his coffin was the tartan plaid which had always accompanied the Queen and her gillie on their many outings at Balmoral.

And Lady Florence Dixie? Stung by accusations that John Brown's inspection of the scene of the alleged attack had led directly to his death, she did what she imagined to be the most gracious thing: the photograph of her dog Hubert, originally promised to John Brown, she sent to the Queen instead.

★

Just as Queen Victoria had previously directed her energies to the immortalization of Prince Albert, so she now set about perpetuating the memory of John Brown. Not even the deaths of two of her children – Princess Alice, Grand Duchess of Hesse in 1878 and the haemophilic Prince Leopold in 1884 – brought forth such an orgy of commemoration.

The room in which Brown had died, in the Clarence Tower at Windsor, was sealed. Instructions were sent for a wreath to be laid on the bed of his room at Balmoral. A tribute, composed by the Queen, filled half a column in the Court Circular. This 'imperial eulogy', as *The Daily Telegraph* described it, was five times as long as that given to the Queen's other 'most valued and devoted friend', Disraeli. Letters of condolence were scrutinized and judged. Gladstone's, with its insensitive references to 'Mr J. Brown' as a 'domestic', and its hope that Her Majesty would be able to 'select a good and efficient successor', passed no tests. But even this far from felicitous offering was pasted into a special scrap-book.

Tennyson was consulted, and produced some of his less memorable lines. Yet they were inscribed on the headstone of Aberdeen granite with which Brown's grave was marked. Above them was lettered the Queen's more affecting inscription, in which John Brown was referred to as 'the beloved friend of Queen Victoria'. A granite seat was erected in his honour at Osborne. The royal household was deluged with memorabilia, ranging from plaster busts to gold tie-pins. Boehm was commissioned to create a life-sized bronze statue of the gillie. It was set up outside the Queen's little private lodge at Balmoral so that, in death as in life, John Brown could keep guard over his mistress as she sat in the open air, working at her papers. At the base of this bareheaded, kilted and supremely self-confident-looking statue was inscribed one of Tennyson's many tributes.

> Friend more than servant, loyal, truthful, brave;
> Self less than duty, even to the grave.

How much more friend than servant was soon to be made abundantly clear to certain members of the Queen's circle. In February 1884, just under a year after Brown's death, Queen Victoria published a second instalment of her account of life at Balmoral: *More Leaves from a Journal of a Life in the Highlands*. As before, these artless memoirs found great favour with the general public and caused considerable embarrassment to the Queen's family. The Prince of Wales resented the fact that he was not mentioned. His name appeared, countered his mother, five times. Vicky, the German Crown Princess, doubted the wisdom of such an exposure of the Sovereign's private life. Having reigned forty-five years, answered the Sovereign firmly, she knew what her people wanted and what it was good for them to know.

But perhaps most embarrassing of all, as far as the royal family was concerned, was the frequency with which Brown's name cropped up. Not only did it appear on almost every page and in a specially added 'Conclusion', but the book was dedicated, in the most effusive terms, to his memory.

All this was as nothing compared with the Queen's next proposal for the honouring of John Brown's memory. She planned to write a biography – or, as she put it, a 'little memoir' – of her faithful gillie. In it, she hoped to prove that he had been 'a great deal more' than just a devoted servant.

She first approached Sir Theodore Martin, the Prince Consort's biographer, for professional help. Deciding that the Queen's wish to record the achievements of her remarkable husband had been a very different proposition from her wish to eulogize the attributes of her controversial gillie, Sir Theodore declined the honour. The delicate state of his wife's health, he explained, demanded all his time and attention.

The Queen then turned to a Miss MacGregor. Entertaining, pre-sumably, none of his reservations, Miss MacGregor was able, although not a writer of Sir Theodore Martin's calibre, to employ such editing skills as the 'striking out of all unnecessary repetitions.' What the good Miss MacGregor thought of the contents of the memoir one does not know.

In February 1884 the Queen sent the manuscript – free, one assumes, of all repetition – to Sir Henry Ponsonby. Her Majesty was anxious to know what Sir Henry thought of it. Sir Henry was appalled. Neatly side-stepping the issue, he suggested that Her Majesty approach the Bishop of Ripon and Dr Cameron Lees of St Giles, Edinburgh. Both these eminent men knew, he said, about 'authorship'. They did indeed, and as they were no less appalled than Ponsonby, they wanted nothing to do with the project.

Ponsonby then wrote a long and diplomatically worded letter to the Queen. He doubted, he said, the wisdom of Her Majesty making public such 'innermost and most sacred feelings'. They could so easily be misunderstood by less sensitive readers. In a tart reply, in which she pointed out that the 'very full' account was intended for *private* circulation only, the Queen asked Ponsonby to return the manuscript. She wished to send it to the late Lord Beaconsfield's private secretary, Montagu Corry, now Lord Rowton. He was showing, she assured Ponsonby icily, a great interest in the idea.

He was indeed. Rowton found the manuscript so interesting – and so calamitous – that he decided it must never be allowed to see the light of day. He suggested to Ponsonby a strategic delay. The manuscript should be set and printed by one trustworthy, and painfully slow, printer. This would take at least six months, by which time it was to be hoped Her Majesty would have come to an appreciation of the inadvisability of publication.

Clearly Rowton's advice was not acted upon, because the battle was now taken up by Randall Davidson, the new Dean of Windsor. Bravely, he wrote directly to the Queen on the matter. While thanking her for his gift copy of *More Leaves from a Journal* he suggested, in Elizabeth Longford's happy phrase, 'that yet more leaves would be a mistake'.[5] But it was the Dean himself, decided the Queen, who was making the mistake. Resenting his presumption, she let him know that she intended to proceed with publication, regardless of his opinion.

Even more bravely, the Dean wrote a second time. So strongly did he feel about the inadvisability of publication, he argued, that he felt duty bound to do his utmost to dissuade her. The Queen was furious. Through Lady Ely, she asked Davidson to withdraw his remarks and to apologize for the pain he had caused her. He apologized for the pain, but refused to withdraw his remarks. Instead, he offered to resign his post as Dean of Windsor.

For a fortnight he waited. There was no word from the Queen. The sermon was preached, that Sunday, by another clergyman. When next Davidson was summoned into the Royal Presence, the bewildered man found the Queen to be as friendly as ever towards him. No mention was made of the memoir. Her Majesty, Davidson now realized, never bore grudges. In fact, 'she liked and trusted best those who occasionally incurred her wrath'.[6]

As for the memoir, its publication was first postponed and then, according to Sir Henry Ponsonby's son Arthur, it was itself destroyed. Obstinate Queen Victoria may have been, but she would never have been so foolish as to ignore the advice of half a dozen sensible men who had nothing but her interests, and the interests of the monarchy, at heart.

If ever evidence were needed of the innocence of Queen Victoria's relationship with John Brown, it is provided by the eagerness with which she was prepared to tell the world about it.

The death of John Brown having left a void, not only in the Queen's heart but in her day-to-day existence, she came to rely more and more on her youngest, unmarried daughter, Princess Beatrice. Of all the Queen's children Beatrice was the only one still at home, and if she could not take Brown's place in most things, she could at least take it in some. Shy, subservient and somewhat wooden-faced, the Princess now became the Queen's constant companion, her 'Benjamima'. It was Beatrice who read aloud, fetched the shawl, pulled the bell-rope, walked a step or two behind her mother on official occasions, and accompanied her on those daily drives in all weathers, not even sleet or snow being regarded as sufficient reason for cancellation. Quite clearly, Princess Beatrice was destined to become the spinster, stay-at-home daughter. The Queen made no secret of her intention to keep her daughter permanently by her side.

This was why the Queen was so appalled when, in the spring of 1884, the Princess told her mother that she wished to marry Prince Henry of Battenberg.

It was not that Queen Victoria objected to her daughter's choice. On the contrary, she heartily approved of the Battenberg family. In fact, so ardent was the Queen's championship of the four handsome and swashbuckling Battenberg princes that it was known as 'Court Battenbergism'.

The Battenberg dynasty had come into being as recently as 1851 when Prince Alexander, the third son of the Grand Duke of Hesse, shocked royal circles by marrying a commoner – a lady-in-waiting to the Empress of Russia. The children of this marriage, which could only be morganatic, were excluded from the Hessian line of succession and addressed only as *serene*, as opposed to *royal*, highnesses. They were given the surname of Battenberg.

Gradually, and in the face of considerable opposition on the part of the stuffier members of the continental royal families, the Battenbergs were accepted into the golden stockade of royalty. They began the climb which eventually took them to some of the highest pinnacles in the world, including the British throne. They became, to the late nineteenth century, what that other relatively humble dynasty – the Coburgs – had been to the early part of the century.

That the Battenbergs were able to achieve this eminence was thanks in considerable measure, to the exceptional qualities of the four sons,

Louis, Alexander, Henry and Franz Josef. Not only were they extremely handsome young men, but they were all talented, high-spirited and intelligent.

To an even greater extent, though, did they owe their advancement to the championship of Queen Victoria. Far more broad-minded than most of her royal contemporaries, the Queen accepted quite philosophically the fact that the mother of these princes had been a commoner; she was equally tolerant of the resulting morganatic 'taint' in their blood. Indeed, the determination of Prince Alexander of Hesse to marry the woman he loved must have appealed to that strong streak of romanticism in the Queen's nature.

And then, with her appreciation of masculine good looks, the Queen was enchanted by the sons of this romantic union. The Battenberg princes, all in their twenties in 1884, were the sort of dashing young men to whom she was always attracted. Not only did she sanction the marriage of the eldest son, Louis, to one of her granddaughters ('Of course,' wrote the Queen to Vicky, the German Crown Princess, 'those who care only for great matches will not like it, but great matches do not make happiness'), but she encouraged a romance between the second son, Alexander, and yet another of her granddaughters.

It may have been the Queen's absorption in these two Battenberg romances which prevented her from noticing a third blossoming under her very nose. It was during a house party at Darmstadt to celebrate the marriage of Prince Louis of Battenberg to the Queen's granddaughter Princess Victoria of Hesse that Prince Henry of Battenberg (known as 'Liko') began paying court to the twenty-seven-year-old Princess Beatrice. Generally regarded as the most handsome son of 'the most handsome family' in Europe, Liko can hardly have been bowled over by Beatrice's beauty or vivacity, for she had very little of either; but in dynastic terms, he could hardly have done better. Marriage to the Queen of England's shy but sympathetic daughter would be a considerable achievement.

Back home at Windsor, Princess Beatrice's revelation to her unsuspecting mother that she wished to marry Prince Henry of Battenberg was followed by a very curious episode.

Queen Victoria not only refused to discuss the question of Beatrice's marriage to Liko, she refused to speak to her at all. For months she addressed not one word to her daughter; if she needed to communicate with her, it was done through an intermediary or by way of a note pushed across the breakfast-table. Yet she did not actually forbid the marriage.

What were the reasons for Queen Victoria's apparently inexplicable behaviour? One of the strongest, of course, was that she did not want to lose Beatrice. Another was that she was envious. Envious, not only because Beatrice's proposed husband was the sort of man that the Queen liked, but because Beatrice would be getting a husband. 'You have your husband – your support,' the Queen had written enviously to John Brown's sister-in-law the year before, 'but I have no strong arm now.'[7]

And finally – because Queen Victoria was a shrewd as well as a self-obsessed woman – she realized that her refusal to discuss the proposed match strengthened her position. She would have to be persuaded into accepting it. This, in turn, meant that she could set the conditions for her acceptance. The chief one was simple. Prince Henry and Princess Beatrice would have to make their home with her. In this way she would be assured of a strong and sympathetic male presence in the house. She would, quite literally, be gaining a son instead of losing a daughter.

To this condition the couple were obliged to agree. Once they had done so, the Queen was all amiability. Mother and daughter resumed normal conversation and no more notes were pushed between the toast-racks and jam-pots. Prince Henry came to Osborne for Christmas and on 30 December 1884 the engagement was announced. There was, the Queen was pleased to report, 'no kissing etc (which Beatrice dislikes)' and, all in all, she confessed herself to be delighted with the outcome.

The German imperial family was considerably less delighted. This third proposed alliance between Queen Victoria's family and the Battenbergs infuriated the Hohenzollerns. Both the Kaiserin Augusta and Crown Prince Frederick wrote to Queen Victoria expressing their reservations. Victoria was outraged. How *dare* they refer to Prince Henry as not being '*geblüt*' – pure bred — as though he were an animal? And did the Empress Augusta forget that her own daughter, the Duchess of Baden, had married the grandson of 'a very bad woman'? It would never do to inquire too deeply into the history of the royal families of Europe; they would discover many 'black spots'.

'If the Queen of England thinks a person good enough for her daughter,' she quoted Lord Granville as commenting, 'what have other people got to say?'

What, indeed? On 23 July 1885 the Queen presided over the wedding in Whippingham church on the Isle of Wight. She allowed Princess Beatrice to wear the Honiton lace veil which she had worn at her own wedding, forty-five years before, and she insisted that Prince Henry wear the striking all-white uniform of the Prussian *Gardes du Corps*. 'A happier-looking couple could seldom be seen kneeling at the altar together,' she declared. 'It was very touching.' Be that as it may, the Queen allowed them a two-day honeymoon only, and that in nearby Ryde.

Queen Victoria's obsession with the Battenberg princes (in the end the third Battenberg suitor, Alexander, did not marry her grand-daughter; and the fourth Battenberg, Franz Josef, married a daughter of the King of Montenegro) did have one unforeseen consequence. A grandson of Prince Louis of Battenberg (who had married Princess Victoria of Hesse), Prince Philip of Greece in the best Battenberg tradition, married Queen Victoria's great-great-granddaughter, who became Queen Elizabeth II.

The Hohenzollerns have long since lost their throne and disappeared from public life, but the great-grandson of Prince Louis of Battenberg will one day ascend the British throne as King Charles III.

Queen Victoria's scheme for keeping Prince and Princess Henry of Battenberg – Liko and Beatrice – permanently by her side was only partly successful. She remained conscious of a lack in her life. Nothing – not the willingness to please on the part of Princess Beatrice, the amiability of Prince Henry, or, in time, the liveliness of their four children – could fill the void in the Queen's heart. Quite naturally, the young couple's first loyalty was to each other. She could never hope to command from them the sort of undivided support, attention and devotion without which she felt so agonizingly adrift. She still missed that 'strong arm'.

But then, in the summer of 1887, the sixty-eight-year-old Queen Victoria found what she was looking for in the person of a twenty-four-year-old Indian by the name of Abdul Karim.

19

'A High-Minded and Excellent
Young Man'

THAT QUEEN VICTORIA'S new favourite should have been an Indian, and that he should have come into her life in 1887, was entirely appropriate. The year 1887 was the year of her Golden Jubilee: the fiftieth anniversary of her accession to the throne. Although the occasion did not have the stridently imperialistic atmosphere of her Diamond Jubilee celebrated ten years later, it was not without evidences of the great empire over which she reigned. The most kaleidoscopic of these colonial possessions, the great sub-continent of India, was especially well represented. Queen Victoria had by now been Empress of India for a decade. So it was fitting that as she drove through the acclaiming London crowds on 21 June 1887 her open landau should have been preceded by the bobbing turbans and fluttering pennants of a detachment of Indian cavalry.

Even more colourful was the great reception for the Indian princes held in the Green Drawing-room at Buckingham Palace. With her penchant for dark, exotic-looking men, the Queen had been almost overwhelmed by the splendour of the jewels and the costumes of the assembled princes. 'The handsome Rao of Kutch, most beautifully dressed,' she enthused; 'really he and his brother were like a dream . . .'.

To capture in tangible form something of the elusive glamour of her Indian empire, Queen Victoria acquired, a couple of days after her Golden Jubilee, two Indian servants. The one was named Mahomet Baksh; the other Abdul Karim. The first, noted the Queen, was 'very dark, with a smiling expression'; the second who was, she believed, the son of a doctor, was 'much lighter, tall and with a fine, serious countenance.' Both, she said, 'kissed my feet on arrival'. The two men were Muhammadans and *khidmutgars* – male waiters – who, in their

Indian dress, would strike a suitably imperial note as they waited at the royal table.

As always, the Queen knew her own mind exactly when it came to matters of their dress, duties and position in the household. In a long letter to Dr James Reid, who had joined her service in the summer of 1881, and into whose care she entrusted the two Indians, she gave detailed instructions. They were *always* to wear their turbans. During the day – whether serving breakfast or luncheon, in or out of doors – they were to wear their '*new* dark blue dress'; at dinner they were to sport their red dress, with a gold or white turban. As the weather grew colder, they must *gradually* put on thicker underclothes and, when off duty, they could wear tweed, provided the garments were styled in the Indian fashion.

Their duties were not to be confined to waiting at table. They were to accompany her on drives, serve her afternoon tea, and carry her letters and boxes. There was no need for them to hurry away to their rooms after meals: the two of them were to remain within sound of her handbell. They were to be accommodated in the *Upper Servants'* quarters and not in some distant part of the Queen's residences, among the lesser servants. They must have 'every comfort so that they are warm *at night*.'

Astonishingly free of racial prejudice herself, the Queen wanted to make sure that her Indian servants were not treated as inferiors by the rest of the household. She hoped, she told Dr Reid, that a certain Highland attendant would have no hand in these arrangements: 'for he is very prejudiced and was not inclined to be kind.' She engaged tutors to teach the two men English (there was some grumbling at the fact that the pupils were servants) and distributed Hindu phrase books among the senior members of her entourage. She herself began to learn Hindustani. 'It is a great interest for me for both the language and the people,' she noted in her Journal. 'I have naturally never come into real contact with it before.'

Before long, the slim, honey-skinned Abdul Karim, the more handsome and more astute of the two men, began to eclipse Mahomet Baksh. Like John Brown before him, he was soon relieved of all menial duties, such as waiting at table, and was promoted to an altogether more important position. He became known as the Queen's Munshi – her teacher. In this capacity he not only gave the Queen lessons in Hindustani but instructed her in 'the social and religious customs' of his country.

His advancement did not end there. There was a rapid increase in the number of Indian servants (they were becoming almost as numerous as Highlanders), and the Queen made it clear that Abdul Karim was to be treated as the chief among them. Munshi Hafiz Abdul Karim was, she declared in a somewhat muddled memorandum to Dr Reid, 'the *first*, and from the position his family have always held, and his superior education hold a position *now*, and this he was *from the first* entitled to, which is equal to that of Clerk in her Privy Purse and with this addition that Karim is *Personal Indian Clerk to the Queen*'. He was in charge of all the other Indians in her employ; on no account was Dr Reid to listen to, or encourage, any complaints about the Munshi. Such complaints were 'extremely wrong'.

From Indian Clerk, Abdul Karim graduated to Indian Secretary. He was given an office and a staff of clerks. From merely looking after the Queen's letters and papers, he moved on to commenting on those that concerned India and in helping to compose answers. If petitions from India required nothing more than a formal refusal, the Queen would hand them to him. The Munshi's position, she assured the increasingly worried Ponsonby, was 'confidential'.

In short, and to the consternation of the household, another John Brown situation seemed to be developing. Dr Jenner was surprised to hear, in 1889, that Abdul Karim had been given John Brown's old room at Balmoral. And in that same year the Queen took Abdul Karim to stay overnight at Glassalt Shiel, the little lodge on Loch Muick, in which she had sworn she would never again sleep, after the death of John Brown.

Did these moves into John Brown's quarters mean that the Munshi had moved into John Brown's place in the Queen's heart as well?

In many ways, Queen Victoria's last great emotional attachment was her blindest. As far as she was concerned, the Munshi could do no wrong. She believed everything he told her. His father, he assured her, was Dr Mohammed Wazirudin, a surgeon-general in the Indian Army in Agra. His highly respectable family all occupied important positions in government service; at home in Agra, before coming to England to join the Queen's staff, he had been a well-paid clerk. The Queen found the young man's conversation 'instructive', his Hindustani lessons rewarding (he was 'a very strict master') and his almost continuous presence a great comfort. Munshi Abdul Karim was, she claimed, 'a *perfect* gentleman.'

When, in 1890, the Munshi returned to India on leave, the Queen missed him greatly. But ever mindful of his welfare, she wrote to Lord

Lansdowne, the Viceroy of India, asking him to obtain a grant of land for the Munshi in Agra, as well as a place for him and his father at the forthcoming Durbar. The Viceroy, in the face of considerable jealousy on the part of other Indians, was able to arrange the land grant and to find room for him at the Durbar. He could not, though, accommodate the Munshi's father. The father's low earnings, explained Lord Lansdowne, automatically excluded him from attending the Durbar.

Blithely ignoring this clear evidence that Dr Wazirudin's status might not be quite as elevated as his son claimed, the Queen continued to believe the Munshi's version. To the consternation of Dr Reid, she sanctioned Abdul Karim's request for a vast quantity of drugs to be sent to his father (including enough poison to kill between 12,000 and 15,000 adults, exclaimed Reid) and when the doctor refused to accept the responsibility, the Queen agreed that the drugs be ordered through a British chemist in India but that the bill be sent to her. 'The Queen says the Munshi must not in any way be annoyed or put about on the subject,' reported the exasperated Reid. When, in 1892, the Munshi's father visited Britain, the Queen saw to it that he was treated with every consideration.

The Munshi's father was not the only one of his relations to benefit from the Queen's patronage. At an earlier stage, in India, Abdul Karim had acquired a wife and now she, along with various female relations, was brought over to Britain. They were accommodated in the three homes which the Queen had allotted to the Munshi: Frogmore Cottage at Windsor, Arthur Cottage at Osborne and the specially built Karim Cottage at Balmoral. The Munshi's wife and mother-in-law, explained the Queen to her daughter Vicky, were 'the first Mohammaden purdah ladies who ever came over and kept and keep their custom of complete seclusion and of being entirely covered when they go out, except for holes for their eyes.' The Queen was fascinated by their appearance. The Munshi's wife, who wore a ring through her nose, was always 'beautifully dressed with green and red and blue gauzes spangled with gold', while her mother wore tight-fitting silk and satin trousers, topped by a knee-length tunic which made her look 'like a man'.

These two women, together with the others of their extended family, lived quietly, in purdah, playing very little part in the Munshi's increasingly important life. Dr Reid maintained that whenever he was called to attend Mrs Abdul Karim, a different tongue was put out for him to examine. Life within these self-contained compounds was lived along strict Muhammadan lines; animals were slaughtered according to religious rites. 'This privilege much complicated the Queen's journeys when she moved with the Munshi in her train . . .', reports one of the Queen's Continental granddaughters; 'a habitation had to be found within the boundaries of which the Munshi could observe the rituals imposed upon him by his faith.'[1]

The existence of the Munshi's exotic ménage, a stone's-throw from the Queen's own residences, struck visitors as extremely curious. 'I have just been to see the Munshi's wife,' reported one of the Queen's ladies-in-waiting, young Marie Mallet, from Balmoral in the mid-1890s. 'She is fat and not uncomely, a delicate shade of chocolate and gorgeously attired, rings on her fingers, rings in her nose, a pocket mirror set in turquoises on her thumb and every feasible part of her person hung with chains and bracelets and ear-rings, a rose-pink veil on her head bordered with heavy gold and splendid silk and satin swathings round her person. She speaks English in a limited manner and declared she likes the cold. But the house surrounded by a twenty-foot palisade, the white figure emerging silently from a near chamber, all seemed so un-English, so essentially Oriental . . .'.[2]

Hardly less gorgeous by now was the Munshi himself. He very quickly ran to fat and with his coffee-coloured skin, his face-framing beard, his sensuous lips, his gleaming satin tunics and his towering gold or white turbans, he struck a distinctly *outré* note as he moved self-importantly at the elbow of the diminutive, black-clad Queen. As had been the case with all her favourites she had his portrait painted, but in this instance decreed that he be pictured against a sumptuous gold background. At Osborne she gave him not only the room previously occupied by one of her doctors, but also the large sitting-room leading off it, the use of which she had previously denied the doctor. All early photographs, in which Abdul Karim was shown waiting at table, were destroyed.

His name began to appear, not only in the Court Circular, but in newspapers and magazines. 'Previous to coming to England,' read one press report, '[the Munshi] was for several years in the service of the Nawab of Jawara. He has held his present secretarial post since 1888, and is said to have found his position as an instructor of royalty a particularly pleasant one, while the Queen is enthusiastic over his merits as a teacher.'[3]

Any attempt on the part of her household to belittle the Munshi — by fobbing him off with a hired carriage, by seating him among the dressers at theatrical performances, by refusing him entry to the billiard room — was hotly resented by the Queen. 'I am much pained and hurt', she wrote to Dr Reid during the course of some squabble between the Indian servants, 'at your always speaking against *him* and thinking ill of a person *whom I know* so thoroughly and who is in every way such a high-minded and excellent young man.'

In these frequent rows among the Indian servants – for they were all jealous of the Munshi's privileged position – the Queen always took his side. No matter how painstakingly the facts of the matter might be set out to prove that Abdul Karim was at fault, Her Majesty would not hear of it. 'I hope you will not again think the Munshi is to blame,' she wrote to one member of her household, 'when I *tell* you I *know* it is a fact *not* to be so.' Any Indian who quarrelled with the Munshi was invariably 'packed off home' within the week.

When, in 1890, the Munshi was suffering from a carbuncle on his neck, the Queen was extremely worried. He was, she told Dr Reid, 'so excellent, so superior in every sense of the word that she feels *particularly* troubled about anything being the matter with him.' She would visit Karim's sick-room several times a day where she would examine his neck, smooth his pillows and 'stroke his hand'. She would even have her boxes brought in so as to allow her to spend more time in his company. Suspecting that Reid was not doing enough for this 'dear good young man', the Queen suggested that he get a second opinion. The capable Reid had no need of a second opinion and once the abscess had been opened, the Munshi quickly recovered.

The Queen, sighed the long-suffering Dr Reid, was 'quite off her head' about Abdul Karim.

The antagonism of the royal household towards the Munshi very soon outstripped even its previous antagonism towards John Brown. But how justified was this antipathy?

There can be no doubt that racism and snobbery both played a part in this almost general aversion to the Queen's latest favourite. Only if an Indian were a prince would the ladies and gentlemen of Queen Victoria's court consider treating him as an equal; even liberals like Sir Henry Ponsonby referred disparagingly to 'the Black Brigade'. The Queen had been obliged to give instructions that the Indians in her employ were not to be referred to as 'black men', and even Lord Salisbury, who became Conservative Prime Minister in 1886, had to apologize for using the term.

The Queen's third son, Prince Arthur, Duke of Connaught, was so incensed at seeing the Munshi's turban among the hats of the gentry at some gathering that he complained of his presence to Ponsonby. The Queen's secretary, by now an expert in the handling of these delicate matters, blandly suggested that Prince Arthur complain directly to the Queen. 'This entirely shut him up,' reported Ponsonby.[4]

The household was forever exchanging information about the 'lowness' of the Munshi's origins. Sir John Tyler, fresh from India, brought news of the favourite's former 'obscure position'; he was not the sort of person, protested Sir John, with whom he would normally have had any sort of 'social intercourse'. The Munshi's wife and female relations, now living in lady-like purdah on the various royal estates, had enjoyed no such status in their native India; 'as they were never shut up there from public gaze, belonging as they do to quite a low class.'[5]

Any such speculation on the origins of the 'poor good Munshi' infuriated the Queen. To make out, she once objected, 'that he is so *low* is really *outrageous* and in a country like England quite out of place ... She has known two Archbishops who were the sons respectively of a Butcher and a Grocer, a Chancellor whose father was a poor sort of Scotch Minister, Sir D. Stewart and Lord Mount Stephen who ran about barefoot as children ... Abdul's father saw good and honourable service as a doctor and he [Abdul] feels cut to the heart to be thus spoken of.'[6]

Racist and snobbish as the attitudes of the members of the royal household may have been, their antipathy towards the Munshi is understandable. One description of him, as 'bland, smiling, furtive and scheming', seems to have been entirely accurate.[7] He certainly misled the Queen about his origins. He would never have been employed – as it was claimed in one press report – in a secretarial capacity by the Nawab of Jawara. And far from his father being a surgeon-general in the Indian Army, or indeed a doctor of any description, 'Dr' Wazirudin was a hospital assistant, with no medical diploma or qualification that would have secured him a place on a British medical register.

Refusing to believe this, the Queen instructed Sir Henry Ponsonby's son Fritz, at that stage on the Viceroy's staff but soon to become one of Her Majesty's equerries, to investigate the matter. Fritz Ponsonby duly visited 'Dr' Wazirudin and, on reporting to the Queen later that year, explained that Wazirudin was not a surgeon-general but merely 'an apothecary at the jail'. The Queen flatly rejected young Ponsonby's story. He must have seen the wrong person, she said. Assuming the matter to be at an end, Fritz Ponsonby was astonished to find that the Queen was extremely angry with him. For a full year, and in spite of his being an equerry, he was not invited to dine at the Queen's table.

The Munshi was untrustworthy in other ways as well. One afternoon at Balmoral, the Queen missed a brooch that should have been pinned on her shawl by her dresser. On complaining to the dresser, the Queen was assured that the brooch had been pinned on. A search was made but the brooch could not be found. A few weeks later, the dresser heard that the Munshi's brother-in-law had sold a brooch to Wagland, a jeweller in Windsor. She promptly wrote from Balmoral to Wagland, who returned the brooch, together with a letter explaining that it had been sold to him by an Indian in the Queen's employ. The dresser took both brooch and letter to Her Majesty. The Queen was extremely annoyed – not with the Munshi's brother-in-law, but with the dresser and Wagland. How *could* they insinuate that the Indian had stolen the brooch? 'That is what you English call justice!' shouted the overwrought Queen of England.

After a talk to the Munshi, Her Majesty summoned her dresser. Not a word of this matter was to be mentioned to 'a single soul', she instructed. The Munshi's brother-in-law was 'a model of honesty and uprightness and would never dream of stealing anything.' The Munshi himself had picked up the brooch at the 'policeman's box' and as it was 'an Indian custom to keep anything one found and say nothing about it . . . he was only acting up to the customs of his country.'[8]

What the Queen's entourage resented more than his race or his class or his dishonesty was the Munshi's bumptiousness. His growing self-importance was becoming insufferable. Whereas John Brown, even at his most insolent, never regarded himself as anything other than a privileged servant, the Munshi insisted on being treated as an equal of the gentlemen of the household. In this, he was backed up by the Queen. When, in the course of a visit to Germany, the Munshi expressed a desire to see the new house of the Queen's daughter Vicky, by now the widowed Empress Frederick, Queen Victoria made certain that he was treated with due respect. The Empress must 'kindly remember that [the Munshi] is my Indian Secretary and considered as a gentleman in my suite,' ran her instructions. He could eat no meat and 'only a little milk and fruit could be offered him'.

During Queen Victoria's annual spring holidays, on the Continent, when tension within the household tended to mount, the Munshi's behaviour caused particular resentment. It seems to have been especially offensive during the Queen's stay in Florence in the spring of 1894.

Not only did the Munshi complain bitterly to the Queen about the distance of his railway carriage from hers in the royal train to Italy, but he refused to allow any other, less important, Indians to set foot in it and insisted that the bathroom and lavatory be reserved for his own use. Arrived in Florence, he persuaded the Queen to issue instructions that he was to drive out in the same carriage as the other gentlemen of the household. He arranged for a display of photographs in a shop window in which his likeness appeared in pride of place, surrounded by nine photographs of the Queen. The display could only confirm the Florentine conviction that the Munshi was an Indian prince 'with whom the Queen is in love'.[9]

Egged on by the favourite, the Queen gave orders that his name was to appear more frequently in the newspapers. Suspecting that these orders might not be carried out, the Munshi prepared a press release of his own which, together with a photograph of himself (in which he was, he instructed, to be made 'thinner and less dark'), he sent to the *Florence Gazette*.

'The Munshi Mohammed Abdul Karim,' read his barely literate press release 'son of Haji Dr Mohammed Waziruddin an inhabitant of Agra the Cheef City of NWP who left his office in India, and came to England in the service of the Queen Victoria Empress of India in the year 1887.

'He was appointed first for some time as Her Majestys Munshi and Indian Clerk. From 1892 he was appointed as her M's Indian Secretary. He is belonging to a good and highly respectful Famiely. All is Famiely has been in Govt. Service with high position. His father is still in the service of the Govn. 36 years ago. One brother of his is a city Collector. All the Indian attendants of the Queen are under him and he also wholes different duties to perfirm in Her Majesty's Service.'

The Munshi's publicity was not confined to the Italian papers. The French press referred to him as Le Munchy – a man of '*grandes capacités et beaucoup d'intégrité*' who drove out '*dans un riche landau*'. And when a newspaper in Nice, on the occasion of the Queen's visit to the south of France in March 1895, gave the impression that he had helped the Queen from her carriage, the Munshi was highly indignant. His royal mistress lost no time in correcting this misunderstanding.

'By telegraphic error it was made to appear that the Munshi assisted the Queen from her carriage on her arrival at Nice, which is of course not the case, as Her Majesty is always assisted by an Indian servant,' reported *The Galignani Messenger* dutifully. 'The Munshi, as a learned man and the Queen's Indian Secretary and preceptor in Hindustani, is one of the most important personages "*auprès de la Reine*" having several men under him, and being often privileged to dine with his Royal Mistress and pupil.'

★

No less than by the household was the Munshi resented by Queen Victoria's three surviving sons – the Prince of Wales, the Duke of Edinburgh and the Duke of Connaught. John Brown's rudeness had been bad enough; the Munshi's pomposity was almost beyond bearing. This family antipathy manifested itself, in a particularly dramatic fashion, in the spring of 1894.

The Queen had travelled to Coburg for the wedding of two of her grandchildren: Grand Duke Ernest Ludwig of Hesse to Princess Victoria Melita of Saxe-Coburg and Gotha. The bride's father was the Queen's second son, Prince Alfred, formerly Duke of Edinburgh but by now the Duke of Saxe-Coburg and Gotha. In the Queen's train was, of course, the Munshi.

Prince Alfred, in his bluff fashion, told Sir Henry Ponsonby that under no circumstances would he allow the Munshi into the church for the wedding ceremony. The Queen was indignant. Refusing to discuss the matter with her son, she devoted 'most of the day preceding the wedding till very late, and the next forenoon' in consultation – verbal and written – on the subject with Ponsonby. The Munshi, she insisted, must be allowed to attend the ceremony. But with Prince Alfred remaining no less insistent, a compromise was reached. The Munshi would be personally conducted into the gallery of the chapel by the son of one of the Prince's equerries, provided – and on this the Queen was very firm – there were no other *servants* in the gallery.

However, on being conducted into the gallery, the Munshi spotted a couple of grooms. So incensed was he at being seated among servants that he stormed out of the chapel before the ceremony had started. There and then he wrote an outraged letter to the Queen. Only after the bridal couple had left was it handed to her. 'She was greatly distressed,' reports Dr Reid, 'and cried a great deal.'

Having dried her tears, the Queen returned to the fight. She sent for Prince Alfred's private secretary. She informed him that, for the duration of her stay in Coburg, she was taking the matter of the Munshi's 'position' out of the hands of Sir Henry Ponsonby and placing it in his. Queen Victoria knew that she could strike more fear into the heart of her son's secretary then ever she could into the heart of her own. And she was right. From then on the Munshi was invited to all functions and was driven about, in splendid isolation, in a royal carriage with a liveried footman on the box.

One can only marvel at Queen Victoria's tenacity and at Sir Henry Ponsonby's patience. The chief joy of his holiday that year, admitted Ponsonby to Reid, was that he was able 'to forget the Munshi entirely.'

But he was not to be plagued by the favourite much longer. In January 1895 Ponsonby suffered a stroke, and in November that year he died. Yet even to the grave Ponsonby was pursued by the Queen's obsession with the Munshi.

'There is one person who feels your beloved Father's loss more than anyone,' wrote the Queen to Sir Henry's daughter Magdalen, 'and whose *gratitude* to him is *very deep*, and that is my good Munshi Abdul Karim. Your dear father was kinder to him than anyone, always befriending him, and the loss to him is, as he says, that of "a *second* Father". He could not well go to the funeral tomorrow to his regret, but sends a wreath, and I enclose what he wrote on it as I fear in the multitude of similar wreaths this tribute of gratitude might be overlooked.'

But neither wreath nor card had been the Munshi's doing. The wreath, Reid assured Ponsonby's daughter, had been made at Her Majesty's special command, and she herself had 'dictated to the Munshi what he was to write on it'.

A more engaging but no less accurate picture of Queen Victoria, in relation to the Munshi, is given by yet another of the Queen's many granddaughters. This was Prince Alfred's eldest daughter, Marie – known as 'Missy' – who became that most theatrical of twentieth-century queens, Queen Marie of Romania.

In the summer of 1892 the sixteen-year-old Princess Marie, having become engaged to Crown Prince Ferdinand of Romania, accompanied him to Windsor for Queen Victoria's inspection. 'None of her granddaughters,' explained Marie, 'married without her approval.' She had come to Windsor in some trepidation, knowing that her British relations did not really approve of her engagement to a foreign prince, when there were eligible British princes available.

Princess Marie need not have been apprehensive. Grandmamma Queen, as she called her, proved extremely sympathetic. Marie tells us of the occasion when she, Prince Ferdinand and other members of the family stood waiting for their first meeting with the Queen in the Great Corridor at Windsor. A distant tap, tap of a stick and the rustle of stiff silk preceded the Queen's arrival. She rounded the corner, looking astonishingly small. The Queen would have been leaning on the arm of one of her, by now, obligatory Indian attendants (not, of course, the Munshi; he was far too grand for such menial duties), and beside this tall, toweringly turbaned creature she would have looked smaller still. The Queen's shyness, to those who did not know her well, always came as a surprise; her smile, 'with teeth small like those of a mouse', was sweet but diffident.

The Queen now paused in front of Crown Prince Ferdinand (who was even more shy than she), and, in her beautifully modulated voice, asked, in German, after his parents. Ferdinand's mother was a Portuguese Infanta – a daughter of Queen Maria da Gloria of Portugal whose husband had been a Coburg prince: the very Prince Ferdinand of Coburg who, over half a century before, had set Queen Victoria's heart so pleasurably aflutter. The Queen now told the blushing Crown Prince Ferdinand that she always kept a picture of his half-Coburg mother in her private rooms.

'*Sie war so wunderschön,*' said the Queen.

Her comments on Princess Marie were equally generous. 'Missy looked very pretty, and seemed very happy about her engagement,' she afterwards wrote.

The following morning, the Queen sent for her granddaughter. 'My dear Missy,' she explained, 'the Munshi would like to make Ferdinand's acquaintance.' As the Munshi's slightest wish was by now Queen Victoria's command, it was arranged that the young couple would come to the Queen's private sitting-room that very afternoon.

They arrived to find Queen Victoria sitting at her writing-table. All about her the air was sweet with the scent of orange flowers. On an easel beside her was Winterhalter's portrait of Ferdinand's mother. With her shy, captivating smile, the Queen drew the young man's attention to the painting.

'*Wunderschön,*' she said.

'*Wunderschön,*' repeated the tongue-tied Ferdinand.

The silence that followed this far-from-animated exchange was broken by the click of a door-handle. A second later the Munshi stood framed in the doorway. He was dressed in gold, with a white turban. Without moving from the doorway, he greeted the young couple by putting one honey-coloured hand to his heart, his lips and his forehead. He neither moved into the room nor spoke.

Nor did anyone else. No one seemed to know what to do. The Queen sat smiling and hunching her shoulders, Prince Ferdinand simply stared at the golden figure in the doorway. Missy stood in an agony of indecision. The Munshi, for all his self-importance, knew better than to take the initiative. He manifested, says Marie, 'no emotion at all, simply waiting in Eastern dignity for those things that were to come to pass.'

The impasse was finally broken by Marie. Fractionally less shy than her grandmother and her fiancé, she moved towards the Munshi and shook him by the hand. Ferdinand followed her example. 'Grand-mamma, feeling that she had satisfied the favourite's whim by allowing him a glimpse of the royal bridegroom, was only too glad to pronounce the ceremony at an end and to be relieved of the presence of the tongue-tied fiancés, who themselves were only too pleased to escape.'[10]

'The Shamefully Persecuted Munshi'

BY THE YEAR 1895 Queen Victoria's household was beginning to suspect that the Munshi was more than just a pompous and self-seeking charlatan; his activities, they decided, were positively sinister. The Munshi had a close friend, an astute fellow-Muhammadan by the name of Rafiuddin Ahmed. As any friend of the Munshi was automatically a friend of the Queen, it was not long before Queen Victoria was interesting herself in Rafiuddin Ahmed's affairs. As early as 1892 she had ordered Sir Henry Ponsonby to introduce the Munshi to the Lord Chancellor, with a view to helping his friend Ahmed in a career at the bar.

With Ahmed being involved in the Muslim Patriotic League, the household suspected that he was getting hold of secret information – either shown by the Queen to the Munshi or else extracted by the Munshi from Her Majesty's boxes – which he then passed on to various interested parties in India and Afghanistan. Even the Queen's ministers, both Liberal and Conservative, considered it best to be circumspect in writing to her on Indian affairs; they assumed that she showed their letters to the Munshi and that he, in turn, divulged their contents to the more politically informed Ahmed.

In the autumn of 1895 the Queen approached the Prime Minister, Lord Salisbury, with a novel idea. Why not attach a Muslim to the embassy at Constantinople? Who better than a Muslim to win Muslim approval in India or to curb the Muslim Turks who were once again shocking Europe by the harshness of their regime? Her Majesty had the very candidate to hand: the Munshi's friend, Rafiuddin Ahmed.

Lord Salisbury's response to this revolutionary idea was muted. He did not much fancy the idea of a Muslim in the diplomatic service, and he did not fancy the idea of Ahmed at all. Mr Ahmed was undoubtedly able, he told the Queen, but would he be suitable? The answer to that, suggested Her Majesty sensibly, would be for the Prime Minister to interview Ahmed. The interview took place, Salisbury careful to keep the discussion on such bland topics as the desirability of religious toleration. Ahmed was not appointed. But the Queen refused to be fobbed off. In the end, the Prime Minister had to admit that whereas *he* would gladly employ Ahmed, the prejudice in the diplomatic service against 'races of different origins' would never allow for the appointment of a Muslim.

If Lord Salisbury imagined that this was to be the last of Ahmed, he was mistaken. The whole affair of Queen Victoria, Ahmed and the Munshi came to a climax in 1897, the year of the Queen's Diamond Jubilee. For poor Dr Reid, who had to bear the brunt of the upheaval, the year 1897 was not so much Jubilee year, as 'the year of the Munshi'.

The closing years of the nineteenth century saw the town of Cimiez, above Nice, as the place upon which Queen Victoria had finally settled for her annual spring holiday. She would take over the entire Hotel Excelsior – to which the gratified management had added the word 'Regina' – for several weeks and there lead a life which approximated, as closely as possible, to her life at home. 'Our existence', complained one lady-in-waiting, 'is just the same as if we were at Windsor or Balmoral with the exception of taking our meals in a Dining Room so hot that all appetite fades away!' Also distressing to the Queen's ladies-in-waiting, dressed in their dowdy half-mourning, was the extreme elegance of the women on the Côte d'Azur; the French-women's everyday clothes, sighed Marie Mallet, would 'put any Marlborough House Garden Party in the shade'.[1]

This was an aspect of life in the south of France which did not, of course, bother Queen Victoria. Dressed in her usual black and with a sun-hat tied firmly under her chin, she would drive out in the brilliant sunshine to go sightseeing or pay calls. Among those whom she visited regularly was the Empress Eugénie, widow of Napoleon III, who had her own villa at nearby Cap Martin. But not all the Queen's excursions were so predictable. She once visited a private zoo belonging to a retired cocotte, the Comtesse de la Grange. Highly gratified by the Queen's visit, the notorious Comtesse presented her with an ostrich egg on which she had scrawled her own name. Exactly, declared the startled Queen, 'as if she had laid it herself'.[2]

It was at Cimiez, in the spring of 1897, that the long rumbling Munshi affair finally erupted. The person most immediately caught up in the convulsion was Dr James Reid. By now Sir James Reid (the Queen, being at Balmoral at the time, had knighted him with a claymore), the forty-seven-year-old doctor was the sort of honest, plain-spoken man whom the Queen always admired. As he was, at the same time, a person of great ability and discretion, Reid had gradually established himself as an invaluable member of the Queen's circle. He was able to provide that 'strong arm' which the Munshi – in spite of his apparent attractions – could not. Reid became the link between the Queen and the rest of the household; 'Ask Sir James' became Her Majesty's invariable rejoinder to most queries. It was because the Queen trusted Sir James Reid so implicitly that she had put him in charge of the Indians; and it was because he was in charge of the Indians that Reid was now obliged to play a leading part in the painful scenes at Cimiez that spring.

During the months preceding this Cimiez holiday, Reid had been treating the Munshi for a venereal infection. The Queen knew about this; in fact, Reid had had what he calls 'an interesting talk' with Her Majesty on the subject. No venereal infection, though, was going to prevent Queen Victoria from taking the Munshi to Cimiez. On this she was resolved. Equally resolute – on the question of the Munshi not being taken to Cimiez – was the household. It was not that they knew anything about his gonorrhoea (Reid was too honourable a doctor to have told them that); what they objected to was the fact that, in the relatively limited accommodation of the Hotel Excelsior Regina, they would be expected to take their meals with him.

Appalled at the prospect, the gentlemen of the household banded together and deputed Harriet Phipps, the Queen's personal secretary, to tell Her Majesty that she must choose between the Munshi and the household. If the Munshi was to accompany the Queen to Cimiez, the gentlemen of the household would not be prepared to associate with him.

Flying into one of her rages, the Queen swept everything off her writing table onto the floor. Magnificent in its way, the gesture did nothing to resolve the matter. The impasse remained. Either the Queen must lose face – and the Munshi's beloved presence – by giving in to her household, or she must set off for the south of France without her gentlemen. It needed no less a personage than the Prime Minister to settle the matter. Astute as ever, Lord Salisbury persuaded the Queen that the French, being such an 'odd' people, would not understand the Munshi's position; they might well be insulting towards him if he again accompanied her. Her Majesty gave in, but with very bad grace.

And Randall Davidson (who, as Dean of Windsor, had had to speak out against the Queen's determination to publish a memoir of John Brown) echoed Reid's opinion: 'Her Majesty is off her head on this point.'

Although the Munshi did not accompany the Queen's enormous entourage as it made its stately progress down to the Côte d'Azur, he apparently turned up soon afterwards. And so did his friend Rafiuddin Ahmed. Having apparently failed to become a lawyer, Ahmed was now a journalist. The arrival of this politically suspect figure jolted the household into immediate action. So violently did they object to the presence of Ahmed that the Queen was obliged to ask him to leave. In doing so, she clearly hoped to safeguard the Munshi.

But the Queen was reckoning without the resolve of her gentlemen. They were determined to topple, or at least humble, the favourite. Convinced that he had all along been lying about his origins and suspecting that he was engaged in some political skulduggery, they telegraphed the Viceroy in India for full information about the Munshi's background.

In the meantime, the gentlemen had gained two powerful royal allies. One was the Prince of Wales. In nearby Cannes for his annual spring holiday, the Prince sent for Sir James Reid. His Royal Highness was extremely worried, not only about the mounting crisis in the Queen's household, but also about the harm which his mother's obsession with her Indian servant was doing to the monarchy. More than most would the Prince of Wales have been alive to the sexual implications of the affair. The Prince assured Reid that he was prepared to support the gentlemen in any action they might take and, if necessary, to intervene personally. Quite apart from 'all the consequences to the Queen, it affects *himself* most vitally', noted Reid, '... Because it affects the throne.'

The second royal ally was Prince Louis of Battenberg, husband of one of the Queen's Hesse granddaughters. Imagining that Prince Louis, as a member of her family, would take her side, the Queen sent him with an order for her gentlemen to 'associate more' with the Munshi. Not unnaturally, Her Majesty's extraordinary command merely stiffened the opposition: the gentlemen threatened to resign *en masse* if the Queen insisted. There followed a flurry of heated meetings, involving the Queen, Prince Louis, Sir James Reid and all the gentlemen of the household. In the course of all this to-ing and fro-ing Prince Louis became convinced of the validity of the household's case. Like Randall

Davidson, he came to realize that the Queen was 'quite mad on this point'.

Prince Louis's conviction was backed up by two communications which arrived during the week-long crisis. One was a long telegram, in cipher, from the Viceroy. It confirmed that the Munshi's father was merely a 'Hospital Assistant', that the Munshi himself had been a clerk at the Agra gaol, that his brother had also worked at the gaol and that his sisters had all married men in the gaol department. The status of the family was 'humble'. The second communication was a letter from the Chief of Police for London, warning of the Munshi's 'complicity in Muslim Patriotic League affairs'.

The most significant of all the week's meetings were those between the Queen and Dr Reid. In his admirably frank fashion, the doctor set out the household's case against the Munshi. Sometimes his arguments reduced her to tears; at others, to violent rage. Her Majesty, he explained to her in the course of the most dramatic of these audiences (he describes it as 'a very excited interview'), was solely concerned with the Munshi's feelings and quite oblivious of the gravity of her own position. People 'in high places' were saying that the only 'charitable explanation' of the Queen's extraordinary obsession with the Munshi was that she was no longer sane. The time would come, he warned her, when – for the sake of her 'memory and reputation' – it would be necessary for him, as her doctor, to announce that she had indeed gone mad.

That Sir James Reid was able to say such things to Queen Victoria is some measure of the esteem in which she held him.

Having dealt with the Queen, Reid sent for the Munshi. In no uncertain terms, he accused him of being a charlatan. He had lied about his origins and education; he had a 'double face' – a subservient one for the Queen and an arrogant one for the rest of the world; he was dishonest, not least for having assured the Queen that in India no receipts were ever given for money and that therefore he need give none; he had certain of the Queen's letters in his possession which he was refusing to return to Her Majesty. Because the Queen was anxious to retain the Munshi's services, explained Reid, he would not reveal to her the full extent of his duplicity. But the doctor would not hesitate to do so if the Munshi did not immediately stop his double-dealing and curb his pretensions.

If the Munshi had been sobered by the gravity of Dr Reid's warnings, Queen Victoria had not. On the very day after that 'very excited' interview between the Queen and Sir James, the two of them conducted a more excited one still. The doctor reports 'a very painful interview in the morning with the Queen, who got into a most violent passion.' The household had all behaved disgracefully, she thundered. Far from breaking with the Munshi, or even from telling him to behave less insolently, she issued a memorandum in which she made it clear that the Munshi was to be treated with all due respect. Furthermore, her gentlemen 'should not go talking about this painful subject either amongst themselves, or with outsiders, and not *combine* with the Household against the person.'

It was no use, sighed Fritz Ponsonby, who was also at Cimiez. The court had done its best but 'the Queen says that it is "race prejudice" and that we are all jealous of the poor Munshi.'[3]

Whatever the Munshi's faults, there seems to have been no substance in the suspicion that he was a political menace, or even meddler. The Secretary of State, Lord George Hamilton, writing to the Viceroy about the upheaval at Cimiez, said that he had no intention of instigating an inquiry into the Munshi's political activities, for the very good reason that he indulged in none. He assured the Viceroy that it would be quite safe for him to write to the Queen on general matters. As far as he knew, nothing of a political nature was ever communicated to the Munshi by the Queen.

The Queen herself confirmed this. In a letter to Lord Salisbury, written in July 1897, she assured the Prime Minister that '*no* political papers, of any kind, are ever in the Munshi's hands, *even* in her presence'. He only helped her read words which her failing eyesight made difficult for her to decipher and, in any case, the Munshi did not read English fluently enough to be able to understand anything important.

Of the innocence of that more politically controversial figure, the Munshi's great friend Rafiuddin Ahmed, Her Majesty was equally convinced. The fact that she had been forced by her household to expel Ahmed from Cimiez still rankled. She would refer to it as that 'disgraceful affair'. That summer she asked Lord Salisbury to express the government's official regret at Ahmed's expulsion. The Prime Minister was to explain that it had been in his capacity as a journalist, and that alone, that Ahmed had been asked to leave. He had done nothing to displease or offend Her Majesty. As far as she was concerned, he was not a 'security risk'.

Once again, she began badgering Lord Salisbury to give Ahmed a position. If the Prime Minister was not prepared to attach him to the embassy at Constantinople, perhaps he would consider employing him in a less formal capacity. Might Ahmed not, as a Muslim, prove useful in supplying the government with information about his fellow-Muslims? When Lord Salisbury rejected this particular method of recognizing Ahmed's capabilities, the Queen tried another. Could he not be given a Jubilee medal? Thousands received them, argued Her Majesty, including 'clergymen, *actors*, artists'. Lord Salisbury, with commendable forbearance, advised Her Majesty to wait.

If the Munshi and his friend Ahmed *were* guilty of any political activity, then it was activity of an indirect, incidental nature. They biased the Queen in favour of Muslims. During a period of violent Hindu–Muslim antagonism, frequently manifesting itself in bloody riots, such one-sidedness on the part of the Empress of India was deeply regrettable.[4]

Queen Victoria's Diamond Jubilee of 1897 confirmed her position as the most celebrated, most instantly recognizable person in the world. In that small, dignified figure seemed concentrated all the glory, all the power, all the wonder of majesty. She was by now an almost mythical creature: the Doyenne of Sovereigns, the Great White Queen, the *Shah-in-Shah Padshah*, the Grandmama of Europe, *Victoria Regina et Imperatrix*, a monarch who ruled over the greatest empire that the world had ever known.

It was all the more extraordinary, then, that this near-deified figure should have been in thrall to a lowly-born, semi-literate, singularly unappealing impostor; a member of what was generally regarded as a subject race, still in his thirties. It was no less astonishing that this ageing sovereign should have found the time, in the midst of her myriad obligations – political, constitutional, social and matriarchal – to devote her energies to the Munshi's welfare and advancement.

During Diamond Jubilee year, she battled to have him made an MVO – Member of the Royal Victorian Order. Already, in the face of considerable opposition, she had made him a CIE – Companion of the Order of the Indian Empire. Now she met with more determined opposition still. The Queen professed herself 'crushed and annoyed' at the pain caused to 'the poor Munshi' by official reluctance to grant him the order. The long-suffering Sir James Reid was ordered to tackle the no less long-suffering Lord Salisbury on the subject. Reid cornered the Prime Minister at a Buckingham Palace garden party where, together with Lord Rosebery and Disraeli's one-time secretary, Lord Rowton, the matter was discussed at length; all three of their lordships, reported Reid, 'depreciating Her Majesty's proposal'. With his customary blend of tact and craftiness, Lord Salisbury advised Her Majesty against the award of the order: any such honouring of the Munshi would look like favouritism towards her Muhammadan subjects and so rouse the jealousy of the Hindus. By this reasoning the Queen, apparently, was convinced.

Every other day seemed to bring a fresh crisis in the Munshi's affairs. One day the Queen is complaining that his name has been left off the Court Circular; on another she is defending him against the accusation that he is the cause of a certain footman not being promoted. Sometimes the Queen is in tears about the household's treatment of 'the shamefully persecuted Munshi'; at others she is railing against the '*completely false*' stories being made up about her poor, kind friend, whose only interest is in helping others in trouble. Now she is championing the Munshi in a fourteen-page letter to Reid; now she is excusing him in a sixteen-page one.

Nothing – not the threatened resignation of her equerries, not stormy scenes with the always outspoken Reid, not irrefutable proof that the Munshi was at fault – would persuade the Queen that he was anything other than totally honest and altruistic. Not even when the exasperated Reid went so far as to say to her that 'there is a very general belief, not only in Your Majesty's family and household, but also among all the servants, that Your Majesty is entirely under the influence of the Munshi, and that he knows it', would Queen Victoria repudiate her favourite. When at one stage the Munshi threatened to leave, the Queen announced that she could understand his feelings perfectly (his humiliation 'has *always been present* in my mind,' she declared) but she could not possibly let him go.

Another major climax was reached at Balmoral in October 1897. *The Graphic* of 16 October featured a large photograph captioned 'The Queen's Life in the Highlands: Her Majesty receiving a lesson in Hindustani from the Munshi Hafiz Abdul Karim C.I.E.' In it the Queen, in white cape and riotously beribboned hat, is shown sitting at a table, signing documents. At her feet lies one of her dogs. But it is to the Munshi that the eye is drawn. Plump and imperious, staring insolently at the camera, he towers above his diminutive mistress. Of the important position he held in the Queen's esteem and entourage, there could be no doubt.

The publication of the photograph infuriated the household. They were more infuriated still when it was discovered that it was the Munshi who had ordered Milne, the photographer, to have the picture published in *The Graphic*. But their fury was as nothing compared to that of the Munshi himself. He bitterly resented the fact that Sir James Reid had discussed the matter with Milne ('you should not have done it *without* telling me,' chided Her Majesty) and the favourite took his resentment out on the Queen. In interview after interview with Reid, and in one of those inordinately long letters, the Queen poured out her anguish. She blamed herself for allowing the photograph to be published; she felt aggrieved that her gentlemen should have interfered in the matter; she was afraid of the incident leading to a public scandal; and, most of all, she dreaded any further harangues from the Munshi. 'I am feeling dreadfully nervous,' she admitted.

There can be no doubt that, by now, the Munshi's domination of the Queen was almost total. Although even she was beginning to realize that his behaviour was not always as blameless as she claimed, the Queen dared not speak out. For one thing, she did not want to lose face in front of her household; for another, she was clearly afraid of the Munshi. It was an impossible situation. The more she favoured and protected him, the more advantage he took. His insolence and bullying simply increased. One day, in February 1898, the Queen's dresser reported that 'the Munshi had had the most violent row with [the Queen] and had shouted at her. Later she wrote him a long letter.'

This particular row seems to have been about the Munshi's determination to invite his friend Rafiuddin Ahmed to Cimiez the following month. The Queen, anxious to avoid a repetition of the distressing scenes of the previous year, had refused the Munshi's demand. But in the face of his outraged insistence she began to waver. It needed, as always, the weightiness of the Prime Minister's opinion to settle the matter. The malicious French press, Lord Salisbury told Her Majesty, might use Ahmed's presence to ridicule her. So Ahmed stayed home. But the Munshi went and the Queen issued the household with a sternly worded memorandum to the effect that she could not allow any remarks about *her* people to be made by her gentlemen; nor was any report or story or gossip about the Munshi to be listened to or repeated.

The worldly Lord Salisbury expressed another, and rather more valid, opinion at this time. On being told of the Munshi's increasingly tyrannical behaviour towards the Queen, the Prime Minister said he was not unduly perturbed by this. She could, he argued, always get rid of the Munshi, but he believed that 'she really likes the emotional excitement, as being the only form of excitement she can have'.[5]

There was a great deal of truth in this. It would have needed only one word from Queen Victoria for the Munshi to be dismissed. But he fulfilled a very necessary role in her life. Surrounded by so much deference and gentility, the Queen may well have welcomed someone who would speak back to her, even shout her down. This, after all, had been one of John Brown's chief attractions. And although the Munshi may have been a poor reflection of those other male mentors, supporters and protectors in Queen Victoria's life, he, too, treated her as a woman; even if, by the end, it was as a woman who was worth arguing with, rather than one worth playing up to.

In the Munshi Queen Victoria had again found someone whose whole life was devoted – no matter how unsatisfactorily – to her. While they were together, she could command his whole attention. If, in the early days of their relationship, it had been his exotic appearance which attracted her, by now it was his constant presence that gave her satisfaction. He, like John Brown before him, was her companion in a way that the members of her family or household could never be.

This last and most flamboyant of Queen Victoria's male friends remained with her to the end. The final glimpse of the two of them together is in the room at Osborne in which the Queen died on 22 January 1901. Three days after the Queen's death, in accordance with her characteristically detailed instructions drawn up in 1897, Dr Reid had her body transferred from her deathbed to her coffin. First, into the bottom of the coffin he packed all the souvenirs she had asked for – a cast of the Prince Consort's hand, his dressing-gown, 'rings, chains, bracelets, lockets, photographs, shawls, handkerchiefs'; no one who had played any significant part in her long life was forgotten. Over this collection was placed a quilted cushion and, on top of that, the body of the Queen.

'It was so beautiful,' noted one witness. 'Her face like a lovely marble statue, no sign of illness or age, and she still looked "The Queen", her wedding veil over her face and a few loose flowers ...'.[6]

Then, in a steady stream, the various members of the Queen's family – led by the new King, Edward VII – and the members of the household and the servants, filed through the room to take their leave. The last person to be summoned by King Edward VII was the Munshi. Because the King loathed the Munshi, he had left him to the end; in doing so, Edward VII ensured that the Munshi would be the last person – other than the Queen's closest male relations – to see her before the coffin was closed and the lid screwed down.

At an earlier stage that day, when all the members of the Queen's family were safely out of the room and Sir James Reid was alone with the Queen's three trusted dressers, he had carried out the last of her secret instructions. In her left hand, purposely hidden under a posy of flowers and wrapped in tissue paper, the doctor placed a photograph and a lock of hair. They belonged, not to the Munshi, not even to the Prince Consort, but to John Brown.

King Edward VII lost no time in getting rid of the Munshi. He was packed off, at the earliest convenient date, to his native India. But before he left, the King ordered him to destroy the letters written to him by Queen Victoria. What sentiments these letters contained, one does not know. To ensure that all this correspondence was burned, Queen Alexandra and Princess Beatrice attended the bonfire at Frogmore Cottage, the Munshi's Windsor home.

The Munshi settled in Karim Cottage, Agra, where he died, at the age of forty-six, in 1909. He had outlived his protectress by a mere eight years. On his death, King Edward VII commanded the Viceroy of India to organize a second bout of letter-burning. The Munshi's wife was allowed to retain only a few innocuous examples as souvenirs.

The conflagration of Queen Victoria's private letters did not end there. King Edward VII, who ensured that his own often compromising correspondence was destroyed after his death, was resolute about eliminating all traces of his mother's written indiscretions. He had all her 'very Private' letters to Disraeli burned. Also burned were various of the Queen's letters to Lord Granville, at one time Foreign Secretary, and her letters – presumably to Lord Melbourne – about the Lady Flora Hastings affair.

Some of the Queen's correspondence with John Brown may well be under lock and key in the Royal Archives at Windsor, but one may be sure that Edward VII had the bulk of it destroyed, including those 'most compromising' letters with which George Profeit, son of the factor at Balmoral, had tried to blackmail the King. It was the substance of these letters which Dr Reid copied into a notebook: a notebook which was, in its turn, burned at his death. Queen Victoria's proposed *Life of John Brown*, which included extracts from his diary, was likewise destroyed.

Edward VII, normally the most tolerant and forgiving of men, was particularly determined in his efforts to wipe out all evidence of his mother's obsession with her gillie. One of his first commands on ascending the throne was for the destruction of all those busts, cairns and plaques which the Queen had erected in memory of her Highland favourite. Boehm's famous statue of John Brown was moved and re-sited in a remote spot, far from public view, behind the house which the Queen had built for Brown.

The King's sister, Princess Beatrice, was equally energetic in obli-terating all traces of their mother's more intimate revelations. In accordance with Queen Victoria's commands, Princess Beatrice set about editing her mother's famous Journal. It was editing of the most brutal variety. Using her own very questionable discretion, the Princess transcribed pages of that invaluable historical and personal record into a series of copybooks, burning the original as she went along. In this way a great deal of priceless material was lost to posterity, for the Princess not only left out and destroyed substantial parts of her mother's Journal, but often altered such material as she did copy out. One may be quite certain that all reference to what the Princess would have regarded as Queen Victoria's imprudent romantic and emotional attachments were excised.

But it is highly unlikely that anything amoral or reprehensible would have been revealed by the reading of these intimate passages. It would have been their highly emotional tone and not their erotic content that would have been shocking to the likes of Princess Beatrice. Queen Victoria had nothing to hide. It was simply that in her affections, as in everything else, she was honest, outspoken, passionate. The Queen had a heart, as Disraeli once said of his own, that would not grow old.

Acknowledgements

I AM GRATEFUL to Her Majesty The Queen by whose gracious permission material from the Royal Archives, which is subject to copyright, is here republished. I am also grateful for Her Majesty's permission to quote from the Melbourne Papers which are held in the Royal Archives. For arranging this I must thank the Queen's Librarian, Mr Oliver Everett and the Registrar, Lady de Bellaigue. I am also indebted to Miss Frances Dimond of the Royal Photographic Collection and Mr Marcus Bishop, Registrar of the Royal Collection, for their help with illustrations.

I must thank the National Trust, Hughenden Manor for permission to study and quote from the Disraeli Papers. I am indebted to the Department of Manuscripts and Printed Books at the Fitzwilliam Museum, Cambridge, for allowing me to study the Secret Diary of Wilfrid Scawen Blunt. I am grateful to Lady Reid for permission to quote from the papers of Sir James Reid and to the publishers of her book (*Ask Sir James* by Michaela Reid), Hodder & Stoughton, for permission to republish this material.

My chief thanks, as always, are to Mr Brian Roberts for his unfailing interest and expert advice throughout the writing of this book. I must also thank, in alphabetical order, those people who, to a greater or lesser extent, and over a period of many years of research and writing, have given me help. They are: Miss E. H. Berridge, M. Pierre Blanchard, Mr Mervyn Clingan, Mr Anthony Dennison, Mlle Louise Duval, Mr David Griffiths, the Countess of Longford, Mrs Barbara North, Ms Odette Rogers, Mr L. A. Short.

I am grateful for all the help I have received from the British Library, London; the Bibliothèque Nationale, Paris; the Bristol Reference Library; the Bath Reference Library; and from Mrs S. Bane and the staff of the Frome Library, who are always so efficient, so cheerful and, in the matter of finding me books, so helpful. To all previous biographers, not only of Queen Victoria, but of the various personalities with whom this book deals, I am especially indebted.

Bibliography

All books were published in London unless otherwise specified.

Albert, Prince Consort, *Letters of the Prince Consort 1831–1861* (ed. Kurt Jagow), 1938

—— *The Prince Consort and his brother: two hundred new letters* (ed. Hector Bolitho), 1933

Airlie, Mabell Countess of, *Thatched with Gold*, 1962

Alice, Grand Duchess of Hesse, *Letters to Her Majesty the Queen*, 1885

Alice, Princess, Countess of Athlone, *For My Grandchildren*, 1966

Antrim, Louisa Countess of, *Recollections*, 1937

Aubry, Octave, *Eugénie, Empress of the French*, 1939

Anon, *The Notebooks of a Spinster Lady*, 1919

Baily, F. E., *Lady Beaconsfield and her Times*, 1935

Bell, G. K. A., *Randall Davidson*, 1938

Bennett, Daphne, *King without a Crown*, 1977

Benson, E. F., *Queen Victoria*, 1935

Blake, Robert, *Disraeli*, 1966

Bolitho, Hector, *The Reign of Queen Victoria*, 1949

Bradford, Sarah, *Disraeli*, 1982

Burghclere, Lady (ed.), *A Great Lady's Friendship; Letters to Mary, Marchioness of Salisbury*, 1898

Cambridge, George Duke of, *A Memoir of his Private Life* (ed. Revd E. Sheppard), 2 vols., 1907

Cecil, Algernon, *Queen Victoria and Her Prime Ministers*, 1952

Cecil, David, *Melbourne*, 1955

Cope, V. Z., *A Versatile Victorian*, 1915

Cowley, Baron Henry, *The Paris Embassy during the Second Empire*, 1928

Crawford, Emily, *Victoria, Queen and Ruler*, 1903

Creevy, Thomas, *The Creevy Papers* (ed. Sir H. Maxwell), 1904

Croker, John Wilson, *Correspondence and Diaries*, 3 vols., 1885

Cullen, Tom, *The Empress Brown*, 1969

Cust, Sir Lionel, *Edward VII and His Court*, 1930

Disraeli, Benjamin, *Home Letters 1830–1831*, 1885

—— *Lord Beaconsfield's Correspondence with his Sister, 1832–1852,* 1886
—— *Lord Beaconsfield's Letters,* 1887
—— *Letters from Benjamin Disraeli to Frances Anne, Marchioness of Londonderry,* 1938
—— *Henrietta Temple: A Love Story,* 1837
Duff, David, *The Shy Princess,* 1958
—— *Albert and Victoria,* 1972
Esher, Reginald, Viscount, *Journals and Letters,* (ed. M. V. Brett), 2 vols., 1935
Fraser, Sir William, *Disraeli and his Day,* 1891
—— *Napoleon III: My Recollections,* 1895
Froude, J. A., *Lord Beaconsfield,* 1890
Fulford, Roger, *The Prince Consort,* 1966
Gladstone, W. E., *The Gladstone Diaries,* 9 vols., Oxford, 1968–86
Gooch, G. P., *The Second Empire,* 1960
Gorst, H. E., *The Earl of Beaconsfield,* 1900
Gower, Lord Ronald, *My Reminiscences,* 2 vols., 1883
Greville, Charles, *The Greville Memoirs,* 8 vols., 1938
Grey, Charles, *The Early Years of H.R.H. The Prince Consort,* 1867
Guedalla, Philip, *Idylls of the Queen,* 1937
Guest, Ivor, *Napoleon III in England,* 1952
Hardie, Frank, *The Political Influence of Queen Victoria 1861–1901,* Oxford, 1935
—— *The Political Influence of the British Monarchy 1868–1952,* 1970
Hardwick, Mollie, *Mrs Dizzy,* 1972
Huntly, the Marquis of, *Auld Acquaintance,* 1929
James, Robert Rhodes, *Rosebery,* 1963
—— *Albert, Prince Consort,* 1983
Jerman, B. R., *The Young Disraeli,* Oxford, 1960
Jerrold, Blanchard, *The Life of Napoleon III,* 4 vols., 1874–82
John, Katherine, *The Prince Imperial,* 1939
Kebbel, T. E., *Life of Lord Beaconsfield,* 1895
Kennedy, A. L., *'My Dear Duchess',* 1956
Kurtz, Harold, *The Empress Eugénie,* 1964
Lambert, Angela, *Unquiet Souls,* 1985
Lee, Sir Sidney, *King Edward VII,* 2 vols., 1927
Longford, Elizabeth, *Victoria R.I.,* 1964
—— *A Pilgrimage of Passion,* 1979
Lytton, Edith, Countess of, *Lady Lytton's Court Diary 1895–1899,* (ed. Mary Lutyens), 1961
Magnus, Sir Philip, *Gladstone,* 1954

—— *King Edward VII,* 1964

Mallet, Marie, *Life with Queen Victoria,* 1968

Marie Louise, Princess, *My Memories of Six Reigns,* 1956

Marie of Romania, Queen, *The Story of My Life,* 1934

Martin, Sir Theodore, *Life of H.R.H. The Prince Consort,* 5 vols., 1877–80

—— *Queen Victoria as I knew Her,* 1908

Maurois, André, *Disraeli,* 1951

Maxwell, Sir H. (ed.), *Life and Letters of the Fourth Earl of Clarendon,* 1913

McClintock, M. H., *The Queen thanks Sir Howard,* 1945

Melbourne, Lord, *Lord Melbourne's Papers* (ed. Lloyd Sanders), 1889

Menzies, Amy, *Further Indiscretions,* 1918

Meynell, Wilfred, *Benjamin Disraeli: An unconventional biography,* 2 vols., 1903

Millais, John Guille, *Life and Letters of Sir John Everett Millais,* 1905

Monypenny, W. F. and Buckle, G. E., *The Life of Benjamin Disraeli,* 6 vols., 1910–20

Morley, John, *The Life of William Ewart Gladstone,* 2 vols., 1905

Nevill, Lady Dorothy, *Reminiscences,* 1900

North Peat, A. B., *Gossip from Paris during the Second Empire,* 1903

Palmerston, Lady, *Letters,* (ed. Tresham Lever), 1957

Pearson, Hesketh, *Dizzy,* 1951

Ponsonby, Arthur, *Henry Ponsonby: His life from his letters,* 1942

Ponsonby, Sir Frederick, *Recollections of Three Reigns,* 1951

—— *Sidelights on Queen Victoria,* 1930

Ponsonby, Mary, *A Memoir, Some Letters and a Journal,* 1927

Raymond, E. T., *Disraeli: the Alien Patriot,* 1925

Reid, Michaela, *Ask Sir James,* 1987

Roberts, Brian, *Ladies in the Veld,* 1965

Rossetti, W. M., *The Diary of W. M. Rossetti,* (ed. Odette Borncand), Oxford, 1977

Russell, G. W. E., *Collections and Recollections,* 1899

Saunders, Edith, *A Distant Summer,* 1946

Sencourt, Robert, *The Life of the Empress Eugénie,* 1931

—— *Napoleon III: the Modern Emperor,* 1931

Seton-Watson, R. W., *Disraeli, Gladstone and the Eastern Question,* 1935

Somervell, D. C., *Disraeli and Gladstone,* 1932

Stanley, Lady Augusta, *Letters* (ed. Dean of Windsor and H. Bolitho), 1927

Stanley, Edward Henry, Lord, *Journals and Memoirs,* (ed. John Vincent) 1978

Stockmar, Ernst, *Memoirs of Baron Stockmar*, 1879
Strachey, Lytton, *Queen Victoria*, 1924
Sykes, James, *Mary Anne Disraeli*, 1928
Thompson, Dorothy, *Queen Victoria: Gender and Power*, 1990
Thompson, J. M., *Louis Napoleon and the Second Empire*, Oxford, 1954
Tisdall, E. E. P., *Queen Victoria's John Brown*, 1938
Torrens, W. M., *Memoirs of Viscount Melbourne*, 1890
—— *Twenty Years in Parliament*, 1893
Vadgama, Kusoom, *India in Britain*, 1984
Victoria, Queen, *Leaves from the Journal of Our Life in the Highlands,
    1848–1861*, 1868
—— *More Leaves from the Journal of a Life in the Highlands*, 1884
—— *The Letters of Queen Victoria: A Selection of Her Majesty's Cor-
    respondence*. First Series 1837–61 (ed. A. C. Benson and Viscount
    Esher), 3 vols.; Second Series 1862–85 (ed. G. E. Buckle), 3 vols.;
    Third Series 1886–1901 (ed. G. E. Buckle), 3 vols., 1907–32
—— *The Girlhood of Queen Victoria: A Selection from Her Majesty's
    Diaries 1832–1840* (ed. Viscount Esher), 2 vols., 1912
—— *Further Letters*, 1938
—— *Leaves from a Journal* (ed. Nicolas Bentley), 1961
—— *Dearest Child, 1858–1861; Dearest Mama, 1861–1864; Your Dear
    Letter, 1865–1871; Darling Child, 1871–1878; Beloved Mama, 1878–
    1885* (ed. Roger Fulford), 1964–81; *Beloved and Darling Child,
    1886–1901* (ed. Agatha Ramm), Stroud, 1990
Villiers, George, *A Vanished Victorian*, 1938
Vitzthurn von Eckstaeat, C. F., *St Petersburg and London, 1857–64*, 1887
Waddington, Mary, *Letters of a Diplomat's Wife*, 1903
Wake, Jehanne, *Princess Louise*, 1988
Weintraub, Stanley, *Victoria: Biography of a Queen*, 1987
Woodham-Smith, Cecil, *Queen Victoria: Her Life and Times*, 1972
Zetland, Marquis of (ed.), *The Letters of Disraeli to Lady Bradford and
    Lady Chesterfield*, 2 vols., 1929
Ziegler, Philip, *Melbourne*, 1976

Newspapers, Periodicals and Works of Reference:

Burke's *Royal Families of the World, Gazette de Lausanne, Reynold's
News, John O'Groat Journal, The Saturday Review, Tomahawk, Tinsley's
Magazine, The Times, Morning Post, Journal des Débats, Whitehall
Review, Pall Mall Gazette, Illustrated London News, Graphic, Punch,
Annual Register, Dictionary of National Biography*

Notes

UNLESS OTHERWISE indicated, all quotations from Queen Victoria, or from letters written to Queen Victoria, are taken from the Queen's letters and journals. These quotations are from three sources: *The Letters of Queen Victoria*, 9 vols. (John Murray, 1907–30); *Victoria R.I.* by Elizabeth Longford (Weidenfeld and Nicolson, 1964); and *Queen Victoria, Her Life and Times* by Cecil Woodham-Smith (Hamish Hamilton, 1972). All correspondence between the Queen and her eldest daughter Victoria (Vicky) is from the five volumes of letters edited by Roger Fulford (Evans Brothers, 1964–81) and from a sixth volume, edited by Agatha Ramm (Alan Sutton, Stroud, 1990). Quotations concerning the Queen's relationship with Napoleon III are from *Leaves from a Journal* by Queen Victoria (André Deutsch, 1961) and *Napoleon III in England* by Ivor Guest (British Technical and General Press, 1952).

Similarly, unless otherwise indicated, all quotations from Benjamin Disraeli are from the Hughenden Papers; *The Life of Benjamin Disraeli* by W. F. Monypenny and G. E. Buckle, 6 vols. (John Murray, 1910–20); and *Disraeli* by Robert Blake (Eyre and Spottiswoode, 1966).

Quotations from the Ponsonby Papers are from *Victoria R.I.* by Elizabeth Longford and *The Empress Brown* by Tom Cullen (Bodley Head, 1969); and all quoted material from Dr James Reid is from *Ask Sir James* by Michaela Reid (Hodder & Stoughton, 1987).

CHAPTER ONE

1 Longford, *Victoria*
2 Greville, *Memoirs*, Vol. III
3 Croker, *Papers*, Vol. II
4 Woodham-Smith, *Queen Victoria*
5 Greville, *Memoirs*, Vol. III

CHAPTER TWO

1 Victoria, *Girlhood*, Vol. I
2 Ziegler, *Melbourne*
3 Cecil, *Melbourne*
4 *Ibid.*
5 Greville, *Memoirs*, Vol. IV
6 *Ibid.*
7 *Ibid.*
8 Creevy, *Papers*, Vol. II
9 Greville, *Memoirs*, Vol. IV
10 *Ibid.*
11 Cecil, *Melbourne*

CHAPTER THREE

1 Greville, *Memoirs*, Vol. IV
2 Longford, *Victoria*
3 Disraeli, *Lord Beaconsfield's Letters*
4 Longford, *Victoria*
5 Ziegler, *Melbourne*
6 Greville, *Memoirs*, Vol. IV

CHAPTER FOUR

1 Greville, *Memoirs*, Vol. IV
2 *Ibid.*
3 Ziegler, *Melbourne*
4 *Ibid.*
5 Longford, *Victoria*
6 Greville, *Memoirs*, Vol. IV
7 Cecil, *Melbourne*
8 Greville, *Memoirs*, Vol. IV
9 Longford, *Victoria*
10 Cambridge, *Memoir*, Vol. I
11 Airlie, *Thatched with Gold*

CHAPTER FIVE

1 Grey, *Early Years*
2 Bennett, *King*
3 Stratchey, *Victoria*
4 Albert, *Letters*
5 James, *Albert*
6 Ziegler, *Melbourne*
7 Cecil, *Melbourne*
8 Woodham-Smith, *Queen Victoria*
9 Clarendon, *Life*
10 Greville, *Memoirs*, Vol. IV
11 *Ibid.*

CHAPTER SIX

1 Fulford, *Prince Consort*
2 Greville, *Memoirs*, Vol. V
3 Ziegler, *Melbourne*
4 *Ibid.*

5 Greville, *Memoirs*, Vol. V
6 James, *Albert*
7 Greville, *Memoirs*, Vol. IV
8 Woodham-Smith, *Queen Victoria*
9 Bennett, *King*

CHAPTER SEVEN

1 Ziegler, *Melbourne*
2 Cecil, *Melbourne*
3 *Ibid.*
4 Ziegler, *Melbourne*
5 *Ibid.*
6 James, *Albert*
7 Cowley, *Paris Embassy*
8 James, *Albert*
9 *Ibid.*

CHAPTER EIGHT

1 Monypenny, *Disraeli*
2 Torrens, *Melbourne*
3 James, *Albert*
4 Cowley, *Paris Embassy*

CHAPTER NINE

1 Greville, *Memoirs*, Vol. IV
2 Villiers, *Vanished Victorian*
3 Cowley, *Paris Embassy*

CHAPTER TEN

1 Victoria, *Dearest Child*
2 Cowley, *Paris Embassy*

CHAPTER ELEVEN

1 Martin, *Prince Consort*
2 Mary Ponsonby, *A Memoir*
3 *The Times*
4 Victoria, *Leaves*

CHAPTER TWELVE

1 Ponsonby, *Henry Ponsonby*
2 Disraeli, *Londonderry*
3 Vitzthum, *St Petersburg*
4 Stanley, *Letters*
5 Crawford, *Victoria*
6 Huntly, *Auld Acquaintance*
7 Cullen, *Empress Brown*
8 Menzies, *Further Indiscretions*
9 Longford, *Victoria*
10 Cullen, *Empress Brown*

CHAPTER THIRTEEN

1 McClintock, *The Queen thanks*
2 Antrim, *Recollections*
3 Maxwell, *Letters*
4 Benson, *Queen Victoria*
5 Ponsonby, *Henry Ponsonby*

CHAPTER FOURTEEN

1 Ponsonby Papers
2 Stanley, Lady, *Letters*
3 Ponsonby Papers
4 Ponsonby, *Henry Ponsonby*
5 *Ibid.*
6 Stanley, *Journals*
7 *Ibid.*
8 Longford, *Pilgrimage*
9 Ponsonby Papers
10 Blunt, Secret Diary, MS9
11 Ponsonby Papers
12 *Ibid.*
13 *Ibid.*
14 Rossetti, *Diary*
15 Blunt, Secret Diary, MS9
16 Lambert, *Unquiet Souls*
17 Reid, *Ask Sir James*
18 Cullen, *Empress Brown*
19 Ponsonby Papers
20 Reid, *Ask Sir James*

CHAPTER FIFTEEN

1 Magnus, *Gladstone*
2 Zetland, *Letters*
3 Disraeli, *Henrietta Temple*
4 Kebbel, *Lord Beaconsfield*
5 Zetland, *Letters*
6 *Ibid.*
7 *Ibid.*
8 James, *Rosebery*
9 Ponsonby Papers
10 Zetland, *Letters*
11 *Ibid.*
12 Ponsonby, *Henry Ponsonby*
13 Zetland, *Letters*
14 *Ibid.*
15 Longford, *Victoria*

CHAPTER SIXTEEN

1 Torrens, *Twenty Years*
2 Millais, *Life*
3 Zetland, *Letters*
4 *Ibid.*
5 *Ibid.*
6 *Ibid.*
7 *Ibid.*
8 *Ibid.*
9 James, *Rosebery*
10 Ponsonby Papers
11 Anon, *Notebook*
12 Guedalla, *Idylls*
13 Ponsonby, *Henry Ponsonby*
14 Moneypenny, *Disraeli*
15 Mary Ponsonby, *A Memoir*

CHAPTER SEVENTEEN

1 Martin, *Prince Consort*, Vol. IV
2 Zetland, *Letters*
3 Marie Louise, *Memories*
4 Alice, *Grandchildren*
5 Zetland, *Letters*
6 *Ibid.*

7 Esher, *Journals*
8 *The Times*, Feb. 1880
9 Zetland, *Letters*
10 Blake, *Disraeli*
11 Zetland, *Letters*
12 Blake, *Disraeli*
13 *Ibid.*

CHAPTER EIGHTEEN

1 Ponsonby Papers
2 *Ibid.*
3 Roberts, *Ladies*
4 Cullen, *Empress Brown*
5 Longford, *Victoria*
6 Bell, *Davidson*
7 Cullen, *Empress Brown*

CHAPTER NINETEEN

1 Marie of Romania, *Life*, Vol. I

2 Mallet, *Life*
3 Vadgama, *India in Britain*
4 Ponsonby, *Henry Ponsonby*
5 Reid, *Ask Sir James*
6 Ponsonby, *Henry Ponsonby*
7 *Ibid.*
8 Reid, *Ask Sir James*
9 *Ibid.*
10 Marie of Romania, *Life*, Vol. I

CHAPTER TWENTY

1 Mallet, *Life*
2 *Ibid.*
3 Longford, *Victoria R.I.*
4 *Ibid.*
5 Reid, *Ask Sir James*
6 *Ibid.*

Index